Innovative Social Practice and Community-Based Approach to the Ocean

Michael C. Huang • Jih-Gau Juang • Hongshi Jin
Editors

Innovative Social Practice and Community-Based Approach to the Ocean

Implications for Blue Impact Finance

Springer

Editors
Michael C. Huang
Ocean Policy Research Institute
Sasakawa Peace Foundation
Tokyo, Japan

Jih-Gau Juang
National Taiwan Ocean University
Keelung, Taiwan

Hongshi Jin
Faculty of Policy Science
Ryukoku University
Kyoto, Japan

ISBN 978-981-96-9103-6 ISBN 978-981-96-9104-3 (eBook)
https://doi.org/10.1007/978-981-96-9104-3

This Springer imprint is published by the registered company Springer Nature Singapore Pte Ltd.
The registered company address is: 152 Beach Road, #21-01/04 Gateway East, Singapore 189721, Singapore

Foreword: Revitalizing Oceans, Empowering Communities

Oceans span more than two-thirds of our planet's surface, supporting an astonishing array of life and serving as an indispensable source of protein for communities worldwide. They also play a pivotal part in regulating our climate and global water cycles. Preserving these functions is paramount, and a marine-based economy that integrates ecologically responsible growth is crucial to securing benefits for current and future generations. Such an approach protects biodiversity and ecosystem adaptability while spurring pioneering solutions, including clean technologies, renewable energy, and circular material flows. Yet, as ocean industries expand, unchecked practices threaten to erode the foundations of ocean health—leading to environmental, regulatory, and reputational consequences that urge financial institutions and policymakers to act with foresight and accountability.

It is more important than ever before to reevaluate and push up the necessity of international collaborations and corporations to develop and activate international projects addressing the beyond-border agenda humankind is now facing. In response to these concerns, a UN-convened global coalition has introduced a guiding structure for financing ocean-related enterprises, rooted in the Sustainable Blue Economy Finance Principles. This roadmap enables alignment of investments, underwriting, and lending with the UN Sustainable Development Goal 14—Life Below Water. By uniting scientists, policymakers, and industry leaders, the financial sector is emboldened to revitalize ocean prosperity, restore marine biodiversity, and fortify stewardship of our shared waters.

Nevertheless, even the most comprehensive blueprint demands broad partnerships and enduring commitment to achieve tangible results. Effective implementation relies on cooperation across governments, the private sector, academic institutions, and local communities. Centers of higher learning, in particular, are integral to training the next generation of ocean champions and bridging the gap between theoretical knowledge and on-the-ground practice. When these institutions collaborate with think tanks and grassroots movements, they can catalyze transformative breakthroughs with a lasting imprint.

This collective endeavor is especially urgent in an era defined by climate upheaval, demographic shifts, and frequent natural disasters. The 2011 Great East

Japan Earthquake and Tsunami highlighted the vulnerability of coastal regions, which now also wrestle with declining fish stocks and shrinking populations. Through research, entrepreneurship, and adaptive governance, academic institutions working hand in hand with local actors can reenergize these fragile coastal areas—turning adversity into innovative opportunities.

The potential benefits of blue economy in Asia-Pacific regions extend beyond conservation. They also open doors for revitalizing tourism, particularly within Small Island Developing States (SIDS). Through cultural respect and environmental guardianship, tourism can become a regenerative force that safeguards natural resources while upholding the collective heritage of local populations.

During visits to several case study sites presented in this book, I was profoundly inspired by faculty members' passion and the far-reaching effects of their community engagements. This unity of academic insight and grassroots action exemplifies the robustness needed to foster novel blue industries, grounded in shared values and inclusive growth.

Oceans have historically had a special character in international relations. Oceans have been recognized and appreciated as common assets for all nations and all people. I trust that this publication will spark fresh thinking among policymakers, researchers, entrepreneurs, and engaged citizens alike. May its pages encourage the formation of meaningful alliances and guide us toward a renewed, enduring relationship with our oceans. Together, we can champion a future where human advancement and ocean well-being rise in unison—ensuring that the seas remain a beacon of life, innovation, and hope for generations to come.

Former Permanent Representative
The Permanent Mission of Japan to the United Nations
NY, USA

Tsuneo Nishida

Foreword: Universities Driving Blue Impact

Universities play a uniquely influential role in society. Far beyond providing tertiary education, they serve as powerful catalysts for social good by leveraging their facilities, expertise, and human resources to uplift neighboring communities. This tangible community impact reinforces public trust in the altruistic mission of higher education institutions.

Recognizing this transformative potential, the Taiwanese Ministry of Education has advanced the University Social Responsibility (USR) initiative since 2018. Rooted in people-centered approaches, USR directly addresses local needs and has significantly advanced community engagement, industry collaboration, environmental sustainability, food safety, and elderly care. With measurable outcomes and practical impacts, these initiatives strengthen community connections and foster regional development.

From 2020 onward, the emphasis has broadened to incorporate regional revitalization and global partnerships, reflecting Taiwanese strategic pursuit of balanced and inclusive development. This evolution has also aimed to expand Taiwanese universities' global reach through enhanced international collaboration.

Meanwhile, Japan and Taiwan face similar structural challenges—such as aging populations and regional disparities—requiring context-specific solutions. In recent years, universities in both countries have taken diverse approaches to local talent cultivation and regional revitalization. Increasingly, these institutions are emerging as primary implementers, integrating academic research and pedagogy with practice-based methods to strengthen community engagement.

Within this context, the Taiwan-Japan Alliance for Local Revitalization and Social Practice (TJ Alliance) was established in 2021. The Alliance offers a structured platform for public and private universities in Japan and Taiwan, particularly those focused on regional revitalization and social innovation, to collaborate in areas such as research, program design and implementation, curriculum development, faculty engagement, and community network management. All of these efforts are centered on robust regional engagement and social practice.

Importantly, the TJ Alliance explicitly focuses on maritime sustainability and the "Blue Impact," aligning with global initiatives such as the United Nations Sustainable

Development Goals, particularly Goal 14: Life Below Water. By sharing innovative methodologies—such as logic models, Jobs Theory, and the Sustainable Livelihoods Framework—this Alliance supports robust evaluation practices, evidence-based policymaking, and transparent impact reporting. These methodologies not only facilitate improved policy decisions but also incubate new startups and social enterprises dedicated to ocean-linked industries.

We are grateful for the partnership with the Ocean Policy Research Institute (OPRI) of the Sasakawa Peace Foundation, which further strengthens the TJ Alliance's mission. This volume features a wide array of case studies encompassing methodology, ocean education, marine technology clusters, eco-tourism, digital transformation, the blue economy, and ocean conservation. We trust these shared insights will be valuable for faculty, students, practitioners, policymakers, and community leaders seeking practical guidance in fostering sustainable and resilient coastal communities.

Department of Fisheries Technology and Management
National Kaohsiung University of Science and Technology
Kaohsiung, Taiwan

Wen-Hong Liu

Advisory Board of Editorial Committee

Contents

List of Contributors

Shingo Akaike Kochi University, Kouchi, Japan

Weiming Chen National Cheng Kung University, Tainan, Taiwan

Hsueh-wen Chow National Cheng Kung University, Tainan, Taiwan

Masahiro Hashimoto Hosei University, Tokyo, Japan

Li-Yun Hsu International Cooperation and Development Fund, Taipei, Taiwan

Michael C. Huang Ocean Policy Research Institute, Sasakawa Peace Foundation, Tokyo, Japan

Hongshi Jin Ryukoku University, Kyoto, Japan

Jih-Gau Juang National Taiwan Ocean University, Keelung, Taiwan

Hsiao-Chien Lee National Kaohsiung University of Science and Technology, Kaohsiung, Taiwan

Weilin Lee National Cheng Kung University, Tainan, Taiwan

Cheng-Yi Eric Lin National Dong Hwa University, Hualien, Taiwan

Chih-Cheng Lin National Kaohsiung University of Science and Technology, Kaohsiung, Taiwan

Wen-Hong Liu National Kaohsiung University of Science and Technology, Kaohsiung, Taiwan

Jyh-Yeuan Lo LOHAS Ocean Leisure, Tainan, Taiwan

Miko Maekawa The Sasakawa Peace Foundation, Tokyo, Japan

Mitsutaku Makino The Sasakawa Peace Foundation, Ocean Policy Research Institute (OPRI), The University of Tokyo, Tokyo, Japan

Sachiko Oguma The Sasakawa Peace Foundation, Ocean Policy Research Institute (OPRI), Tokyo, Japan

Kenji Okamura Kochi University, Kochi, Japan

Hideyuki Shiozawa Division of Island Nations, Ocean Policy Research Institute (OPRI), The Sasakawa Peace Foundation, Tokyo, Japan

Shota Tajima Chiba University, Chiba, Japan

Junko Toyoshima Institute for Global Environmental Strategies (IGES), Hayama, Kanagawa, Japan

Sheng-Wen Tseng National Taiwan Ocean University, Keelung, Taiwan

Ching-Ying Tung National Chi Nan University, Puli, Nantou, Taiwan

Hui-Chiao Wang National Taiwan Ocean University, Keelung, Taiwan

Ching-Yu Yang National Kaohsiung University of Science and Technology, Kaohsiung, Taiwan

Ming-Hao Yang National Taiwan Ocean University, Keelung, Taiwan

Chapter 1
Investigating the Assessment and Evaluation of Blue Impact from Community-Based Approach for Ocean Through Think Tank-University Social Responsibility

Michael C. Huang, Jih-Gau Juang, and Hongshi Jin

Abstract Universities play a vital role in bridging research and education to create innovative solution for community as partnership. Both Japan and Taiwan share the similar concern as maritime states and recognize that collaboration emerges as the linchpin for strengthening relationships between faculty, students, and local residents, ensuring sustainability with a positive societal impact. This chapter introduces the book, underscoring the significance of effective assessment within a community-based approach for ocean-related projects under the framework of think tank-university social responsibility. The book's structure encompasses four key sections: (1) Methodology of Problem-Solving Structure for Coastal Region; (2) Challenges and Opportunities of Ocean-link Industries; (3) Innovative Forms of Blue Impact; (4) Evaluating Blue Impact from the Social and Environmental Perspective. These experiences rely on problem identification, assessment, and endeavors driven by shared motivations and the establishment of trust among research institutes, universities, and communities.

Keywords Think Tank-University Social Responsibility · Blue impact · Community-based approach · SDG4 · SDG14 · SDG17

M. C. Huang (✉)
Ocean Policy Research Institute, Sasakawa Peace Foundation, Tokyo, Japan
e-mail: michael-huang@spf.or.jp

J.-G. Juang
National Taiwan Ocean University, Keelung, Taiwan
e-mail: jgjuang@mail.ntou.edu.tw

H. Jin
Faculty of Policy Science, Ryukoku University, Kyoto, Japan
e-mail: jinhongshi@policy.ryukoku.ac.jp

M. C. Huang et al. (eds.), *Innovative Social Practice and Community-Based Approach to the Ocean*, https://doi.org/10.1007/978-981-96-9104-3_1

1.1 Introduction

The Earth's surface is predominantly covered by the ocean, comprising approximately 70% of the planet's area. This vast marine environment plays a pivotal role in our global ecosystem, providing sustenance, regulating climate patterns, supporting livelihoods, and facilitating economic development. However, the realization of these benefits hinges upon the responsible and sustainable utilization of ocean resources. Within this context, the "blue economy" concept, as defined by the World Bank, promotes the idea of harnessing ocean resources for economic growth, improving living standards, and job creation, all while safeguarding the health of marine ecosystems. Achieving these goals presents a significant challenge, necessitating a comprehensive understanding and effective management of various aspects of oceanic sustainability, including sustainable fisheries, ecosystem health, and pollution prevention. Furthermore, it underscores the need for unprecedented cross-border and cross-sector collaboration [1].

Assessing the progress and effectiveness of ocean-related projects is crucial in ensuring that we are on the right course. This involves evaluating the "blue impact," which includes measurable changes in physical, chemical, or biological variables within ocean ecosystems or water-related systems using quantitative indicators [2]. It's important to note that not all aspects of blue impact are easily quantifiable, especially those related to social dimensions, which can manifest in diverse ways in different contexts, such as ocean literacy, fisheries, community relationships, cultural preservation, local revitalization, and the development of ocean-link industry.

The United Nations Environment Programme's (UNEP) Finance Initiative (FI) has put forth 14 principles for financing the blue economy, highlighting the importance of collaboration among different stakeholders. This collaboration is essential to ensure the accuracy, credibility, and sustainability of impact assessments, primarily because of the complexities involved in studying the ocean, which often require significantly higher investments compared to land-based research. Especially for the Asia-Pacific region, surrounded by vast oceans, is home to Small Island Developing States (SIDS), which face significant challenges in accessing the resources required to build capacity for the blue economy.

To address this, the Ocean Policy Research Institute (OPRI) of the Sasakawa Peace Foundation collaborates with the Taiwan-Japan Alliance of Local Revitalization and Social Practice (TJ Alliance) to select thematic case studies that illuminate the methodology of impact assessment and evaluation for ocean-link initiatives within the framework of Think Tank-University Social Responsibility.

As universities are pivotal in providing tertiary education, conducting research, and fostering development, this collaboration aims to strengthen the synergy between central ministries, local governments, private businesses, and scholars to collectively develop solutions for regional social issues and needs. In contrast, think tanks possess the analytical capacity to provide policy recommendations with flexibility and timely advocacy. These "social innovations" are expected to facilitate exchanges between academia and practical implementation, leading to enhanced

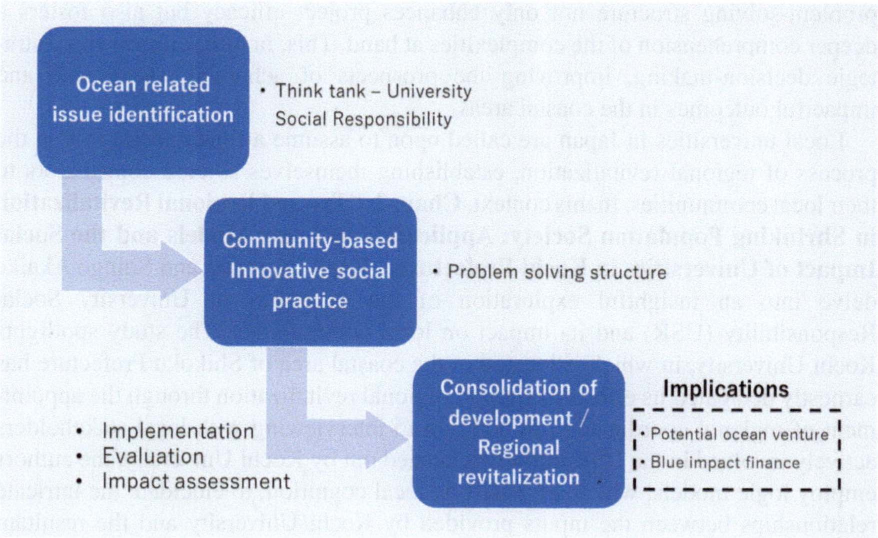

Fig. 1.1 The analytical flow of the book. Source: Authors

policy design, operational experience, curriculum development, faculty community building, and local network management related to local linkages and social practices with the implications for potential ocean venture through the support of blue impact finance (Fig. 1.1).

Japan and Taiwan both belong to maritime states that face similar challenges such as aging society and shrinking population, especially in the fishery village. Nevertheless, by utilizing the university capacity with the shared value, it would be prominent to strengthen the collaboration on blue economy from both scientific and social perspective to cope with difficulties while ensuring the impact assessment as evidence-based policy-making (EBPM) [3].

This book, comprising selected case studies from the TJ Alliance and the OPRI, seeks to propose practical solutions to pressing contemporary social issues. It also provides a detailed guide for implementing and assessing ocean- and community-based approaches, with the aim of promoting the exchange, refinement, and dissemination of relevant research findings and practical experiences. Ultimately, this fosters global collaboration in support of sustainable ocean prosperity. The book is structured into three parts to address the issues in a logical sequence.

1.2 Part I: Methodology of Problem-Solving Structure for the Coastal Region

Identifying the problem-solving structure is a pivotal aspect of developing a successful framework for blue impact finance projects. This process entails dissecting the intricate challenges and intricacies of such initiatives. A well-defined problem-solving structure not only enhances project efficacy but also fosters a deeper comprehension of the complexities at hand. This, in turn, informs more strategic decision-making, improving the prospects of achieving sustainable and impactful outcomes in the coastal areas.

Local universities in Japan are called upon to assume a fundamental role in the process of regional revitalization, establishing themselves as core contributors to their local communities. In this context, **Chap. 2: "Toward Regional Revitalization in Shrinking Population Society: Application of Logic Models and the Social Impact of Universities in Kochi Prefecture,"** Kenji Okamura and Shingo Akaike delve into an insightful exploration of the dynamics of University Social Responsibility (USR) and its impact on local communities. The study spotlights Kochi University, in which is located in the coastal area of Shikoku Prefecture has earnestly dedicated its efforts to support regional revitalization through the appointment of regional coordinators. In addition to interviewing with local stakeholders actively involved in the USR initiatives carried out by Kochi University, the authors employ logic models, which are based on local cognition, to elucidate the intricate relationships between the inputs provided by Kochi University and the resultant local impact. The findings reveal a critical aspect of the interplay between USR inputs and social impacts: these impacts may not be immediately discernible when the projects are initiated, or when one considers individual inputs in isolation. In instances where the USR's inputs and their corresponding social impacts manifest over an extended period, the selective extraction of the university's impact becomes notably challenging. Furthermore, when the impact is distributed thinly across a broad geographic area and not directly perceived by the local population, the university's contributions may not be fully recognized by the community. These findings serve as a pivotal lens through which to comprehend the intricate dynamics of USR initiatives and their effects on local communities, offering insights for local governments, policymakers, and other relevant stakeholders.

In **Chap. 3: "Social Implementation of Mobile Off-grid Architecture aimed at Regional Revitalization: Application of Jobs Theory in Nagara, Japan,"** Shota Tajima embarks on an investigation into the potential applications of mobile off-grid architecture (MOA) for regional revitalization, with a specific focus on the product-market fit of EcoCabin, a prototype conceived by the author. MOA, which has garnered increasing prominence in Japan at the local level, poses questions regarding its relevance and the needs it addresses within local communities. The chapter takes the form of a collaborative effort involving researchers and students from various academic disciplines. This chapter entails interviews with five potential users to gauge the product-market fit of EcoCabin within the local community of Nagara Town, Chiba Prefecture, Japan, encompassing a diverse array of stakeholders, including farmers, resort facilities, farmers' markets, and tourist farms. Through this evaluation process, the study captures the evolving needs and unresolved issues articulated by the interviewees, providing insights into the value proposition of EcoCabin. The outcomes underscore the potential efficacy of MOA in facilitating regional revitalization, particularly by fostering communication among individuals. The study calls for further research to substantiate the compatibility of the product with the market, indicating that its successful application can enhance the prospects of MOA in contributing to sustainable regional development.

1.3 Part II: Challenges and Opportunities of Ocean-link Industries

Enhancing ocean literacy stands as a significant imperative in the endeavor to cultivate greater public awareness and understanding of the marine environment to recognize the risk and potential for the ocean-link industry. In **Chap. 4: "Challenges of Ocean Literacy and Ocean Education in Japan,"** Sachiko Oguma conducts a textual analysis of ocean education content to explore the issues encountered by schools. This analysis involves an examination of practice reports submitted by 988 schools participating in the Pioneer Schools Program for Ocean Education (PSP). The most allocated time for ocean education is within subjects like integrated study, social studies, and science. Text-mining techniques were then employed to discern the defining characteristics of the aims, results, and issues associated with ocean education. The findings suggest that sustaining these efforts necessitates collaboration among teachers within schools, with considerations for teacher transfers and coordination with related organizations. Furthermore, the assessment of universities' contributions to PSP participating schools and communities as part of university social responsibility is deemed essential. To address these challenges, a support network for ocean education is proposed, emphasizing curriculum management in alignment with the Courses of Study.

The leisure industry is regarded as the prominent sector in the blue economy. The burgeoning yacht manufacturing sector in Taiwan serves as a notable asset; however, there is a critical need for enhancing both hardware planning and software management in the leisure yacht industry. Notably, many marinas have undergone transformation from former fishing ports, and yet, they lack international certification, which diminishes their appeal to global consumers in the yacht industry, disregarding the untapped potential of local resources. In **Chap. 5: "Challenges and Opportunities faced in Developing Taiwan's Leisure Yachting Industry,"** Hsueh-wen Chow, Weilin Lee, Weiming Chen, and Jyh-Yeuan Lo underscore this issue by elucidating the insights derived from interviews conducted with local yacht operators. It provides a comprehensive appraisal of the challenges plaguing Taiwan's yacht industry and proceeds to examine the successful models adopted in neighboring nations such as Japan, South Korea, and Singapore. The chapter's objective is to enable Taiwan's marinas to effectively consolidate resources into their operational and management frameworks, adapting them to the local context while aligning them with international standards. The research is poised to furnish valuable guidelines for marina management entities and governmental authorities, thereby contributing to the continued growth and sustenance of Taiwan's yacht service sector and leisure marine activities.

The cluster of ocean-link industries could provide the breed land for startups with a spillover effect. In **Chap. 6: "Creating New Industries by Blue Tech: Challenges of Marine Open Innovation in Japan,"** Masahiro Hashimoto introduces a noteworthy marine open innovation project, with a specific focus on marine biotechnology, which has been actively underway in Shizuoka Prefecture, Japan, since 2019. This ambitious initiative seeks to establish a platform for the utilization of marine genetic resources and other marine-related technologies, culminating in the creation of novel industries. In addition to exploring this project, the chapter introduces the concept of the Blue Tech Cluster, which is being advocated globally, including in the United States. This concept aligns with sustainable technology development and industrialization rooted in scientific principles at the urban and regional levels, spanning industries related to oceans and water. Moreover, it is compatible with the Sustainable Development Goals, especially Goal 14, which pertains to life below water. The chapter serves to elucidate the specifics of the Marine Open Innovation (MaOI) project, which represents a novel form of industrial cluster formation and offers an illustrative example of how innovative solutions can be forged in the pursuit of sustainable development. The project emerges as a valuable beacon in advancing the objectives of the region's sustainable development, grounded in the integration of marine technology and resources. This contribution extends to the broader discourse of sustainability, underscoring the significance of collaborative innovation aimed at fostering sustainable development within the region.

1.4 Part III: Innovative Forms of Blue Impact

Tourism has long been recognized as a promising avenue for economic development, especially in Small Island Developing States (SIDS). In recent years, eco-tourism and nature-based strategies have emerged as viable models for blue impact finance [4]. During the 2010s, however, Palau grappled with over-tourism, which reduced visitor satisfaction and placed significant strain on local infrastructure. In 2015, the Sasakawa Peace Foundation (SPF) responded by launching an environmentally conscious tourism program. While initially tailored to Palau—where rapidly increasing inbound travel had led to both economic growth and social, environmental pressures—this model also offers valuable insights for other SIDS facing economic hardships and the lingering effects of the Covid-19 pandemic. By championing eco-tourism, it is possible to create a form of tourism that benefits and inspires both travelers and local residents.

In **Chap. 7, "People-Centered Approach: Community-Based Eco-Tourism in Palau,"** Li-Yun Hsu and Hideyuki Shiozawa detail methods for managing mass tourism effectively, including the use of carrying capacity surveys and the introduction of community-based eco-tourism. Their approach seeks to balance economic gains at the local level with the sustainable stewardship of Palau's natural and cultural resources. The International Cooperation Development Fund (ICDF) has played a pivotal role in supporting this initiative, offering workshops, training, and other capacity-building activities to develop local talent and raise awareness. Through these efforts, Palau's tourism sector is better positioned to achieve a delicate equilibrium: diversifying its economy while preserving the cultural heritage and environmental integrity that draw visitors from around the world.

Preserving cultural heritage and artifacts can be a formidable challenge, particularly in rural areas and museum settings. In **Chap. 8, "Dynamic Material Culture and Digital Preservation: A case study on Talugan the Bunun Cultural Relics Museum,"** Ching-Ying Tung conducts action research, focusing on the cultural sustainability of Austronesian peoples, who are often numerically small and susceptible to influences from mainstream culture and changing times. Tung employs the Talugan Cultural Relics Museum of the Bunun tribe as a case study, exploring the contextual significance of Talugan cultural relics through the lenses of authenticity and ethnographic research by Chia-ch'in Ch'iu in 1966. In 2021, a total of 146 items and 14 exclusions were listed, and efforts were made to hold physical and small-scale online special exhibitions from September to December 2022. Notably, some items in the collection are believed to originate from the priest class. Given the evolving social structures and beliefs, many items have lost their contextual relevance and are challenging to preserve. As a potential solution, the concept of a digital museum is explored, which has the potential to extend the longevity and accessibility of cultural relics.

1.5 Part IV: Evaluating Blue Impact from Social and Environmental Perspective

In **Chap. 9: "Impact Assessment of Sustainable Livelihoods Framework: Badouzi Fishing Village,"** Hui-Chiao Wang deepdives into the assessment of livelihood changes brought about by the University Social Responsibility Program (USR Program) in Badouzi Fishing Village, drawing from the Sustainable Livelihoods Framework (SLF). Within this context, the livelihood shifts are scrutinized through the dynamic interplay of vulnerability contexts, livelihood resources, transforming structures and processes, livelihood strategies, and livelihood outcomes. This investigation applies SLF to construct a set of evaluative criteria tailored to the sustainable livelihood of fishing villages. These criteria encompass factors such as vulnerability contexts, livelihood assets, and transforming structures and processes.

Additionally, by conducting interviews with key stakeholders, the study reveals that the USR Program, implemented by the National Taiwan Ocean University (NTOU), significantly contributes to increased income, decreased vulnerability, and the sustainable utilization of natural resources within the fishing village. Beyond these economic and ecological gains, the USR Program has proven to be a catalyst for bolstering local fishing and fisheries, as well as fostering the growth of tourism, leisure, and recreational activities. The findings of this research, therefore, offer valuable insights that can guide governmental authorities and city administrators in formulating pragmatic strategies for the development of sustainable fishing communities.

In **Chap. 10: "Advancing Sustainable Fishing Village through University-Community Engagement: Building-up Excellent Neighbor Fishermen,"** Ching-Yu Yang, Wen-Hong Liu, Hsiao-Chien Lee, and Chih-Cheng Lin illuminate the exemplary case of the National Kaohsiung University of Science and Technology (NKUST) in its endeavor to foster sustainable development within the aquaculture industry through community engagement. The study identifies five key outcomes that arise from the performance evaluation of this concerted effort including the implementation of eco-friendly technologies, transformation of fishery by-products into locally-featured products, the establishment of online and offline shops as central components of direct habitat-based selling modes, development of experiential tourism centered on fishing village culture and fish-based dietary education, and the initiation of international collaborations. These findings offer valuable insights for local government officials, policymakers, community stakeholders, and industry experts, enabling them to gain a comprehensive understanding of the vital indicators underpinning sustainable fishing village development.

In **Chap. 11: "Sustainable Financing for Marine Protected Areas (MPAs): Satoumi Activities in Shiretoko,"** Miko Maekawa, Junko Toyoshima, and Mitsutaku Makino center on the examination of the Shiretoko marine protected area (MPA), a component of the Natural World Heritage Site located in Hokkaido, Japan, designated as such in 2005. The focal point of this examination is the financial sustainability of the Shiretoko MPA and the pertinent mechanisms supporting its conservation efforts. In the backdrop of global marine biodiversity loss and renewed commitments to biodiversity conservation under the Kunming-Montreal Global Biodiversity Framework (GBF), the scrutiny of a case marked by relatively successful conservation endeavors becomes particularly relevant. This analysis encompasses the challenges and opportunities associated with sustainable financing and explores innovative funding mechanisms. The insights gleaned from this case study have the potential to furnish valuable lessons applicable to other MPAs and conservation initiatives within Japan and on a global scale.

In **Chap. 12: "Re-imagining of Island through Digital Narrative: Theme-Based Itinerary Planning in Matsu,"** Cheng-Yi Eric Lin and Sheng-Wen Tseng set out to explore the images associated with Matsu Islands, a historically significant military forefront boasting abundant ecological and cultural resources that draw tourists, as perceived by students from a public university in Northern Taiwan. Through the utilization of digital narrative assignments embedded within the liberal arts curriculum, the action research methodology and narrative inquiry approach were employed to structure the course and analyze research data. The analysis meticulously examines six short films created by forty-four research participants as part of Theme-Based Travel Planning. Their results indicate that three iconic images—military posts, beaches, and liquor—serve to represent the historical narrative of Matsu Islands. Moreover, it is notable that the research participants demonstrate proficiency in crafting narrative elements, such as point of view, dramatic questions, and soundtrack selection. However, room for improvement is identified in terms of emotional content and the delivery of narration. These findings serve as a foundation for recommendations aimed at refining the liberal arts curriculum, grounded in the results of this study.

These case studies and methodology presented in this book aim to offer readers a practical guide for executing ocean-link projects with trackable assessment for blue impact finance. These projects involve a collaborative effort between think tanks, universities, and local communities. It plays a crucial role in ensuring that the outcomes and effectiveness of policy decisions are rigorously evaluated and traced over time. This collaboration holds the potential to generate substantial and quantifiable positive impacts in the realm of ocean conservation and sustainability. By employing this approach, it becomes possible to measure the real-world impact of these policies, thereby enhancing accountability and transparency. By delving into the experiences shared within these case studies, readers can gain valuable insights and guidance on how to effectively implement similar initiatives.

Furthermore, we hope that the knowledge and expertise gained from these case studies can extend beyond the immediate context and be applied to other regions facing similar challenges and opportunities for blue impact finance. This transfer of knowledge can foster broader collaboration and innovation, ultimately contributing to the shared global goal of safeguarding our oceans and coastal ecosystems for sustainable development.

References

1. Morgan, P., Huang, M., Voyer, M., Benzaken, D., & Watanabe, A. (2022). *Blue economy and blue finance: Towards sustainable development and ocean governance*. ADBI Press. https://doi.org/10.56506/HDLZ1912
2. International Finance Cooperation (IFC). (2022). *Guidelines: Blue finance*. The World Bank. https://www.ifc.org/content/dam/ifc/doc/mgrt/ifc-guidelines-for-blue-finance.pdf
3. Tanaka, H. (2023). *Definition and evaluation methodology of the blue economy: Focusing on the difference from the Ocean/Marine Economy*. OPRI Perspective No. 26. https://www.spf.org/opri/en/global-data/opri/perspectives/prsp_026_2023_tanaka_en.pdf
4. SYSTEMIQ. (2022). *The Ocean Impact Navigator: A new impact measurement framework for the ocean innovation ecosystem*. SYSTEMIQ.

Part I
Methodology of Problem-Solving Structure for Coastal Region

Chapter 2
Using a Logic Model to Assess the Social Impact of USR: How Universities Contribute to Local Communities

Kenji Okamura and Shingo Akaike

Abstract Universities in Japan are required to play a role in regional revitalization as core members of the local community. This study examines some of the ways in which University Social Responsibility (USR) influences social impact. The primary focus is on the case of Kochi University, which supports regional revitalization through its regional coordinators. Based on interviews with stakeholders in two local communities, a logic model of local cognition was constructed. Using the model made it possible to visualize the connections between the inputs of Kochi University and their local impacts. Such connections were difficult to establish prior to the construction of the model or when looking only at individual inputs. In situations where the social impacts of USR require a significant period before being realized, it is extremely difficult to selectively extract only the impact of the university's contribution. Moreover, for populations that do not directly benefit from the USR or where the impact is spread thin and over a wide area, the local community may not fully recognize the university's contributions.

Keywords University social responsibility · Coordinator · Regional revitalization · Logic model · Social impact · Sustainable cities and communities

2.1 Introduction

In Japan, the University Social Responsibility (USR) of local universities is not limited to providing specialized knowledge based on research seeds or implementing regional education. Rather, the universities are required to establish university-wide systems to promote community-oriented education, research, and social contributions, and to strengthen their functions as core members of their local communities. In 2013, when the Ministry of Education, Culture, Sports, Science and Technology's Program for Promoting Regional Revitalization by Universities as

K. Okamura (✉) · S. Akaike
Kochi University, Kochi, Japan
e-mail: okamurakenji@kochi-u.ac.jp

M. C. Huang et al. (eds.), *Innovative Social Practice and Community-Based Approach to the Ocean*, https://doi.org/10.1007/978-981-96-9104-3_2

Centers of Community (COC Program) was introduced, regional coordinators were assigned to each university and charged with the task of "connecting the region and the university" as part of strengthening the university's functions [1]. In December 2014, the Act for Overcoming Population Decline and Vitalizing Local Economy (the Regional Revitalization Law) was approved by the Cabinet, adding to the external factors impelling universities to become more deeply involved in policy planning by local governments. Recognizing the role of USR in strengthening the relationship between universities and local communities, this research focuses on the social impact of USR activities.

The beneficiaries of USR activities can be broadly divided into two groups: the university conducting the USR activities and the local community in which the USR activities are conducted. There have been numerous studies on changes in universities due to USR activities, such as those by Kondo et al. [2], Suzuki et al. [3], and Kinoshita [4]. However, there are few studies dealing with changes in the regions targeted in these USR efforts. Uchihara and Nakatsuka [5] examined the correspondence between USR and seven impacts using the CPI (Capacity, Performance, Impact) model. Ueda and Koriyama [6] focused on the process of behavioral change in local residents and found that "USR activities can bring change to rigid organizations and closed communities and enable the participation of diverse actors."

To increase our ability to assess changes in the community due to USR, it is necessary to identify the cognition of the local community as beneficiaries, something that existing studies have not fully explored. For the most part, prior studies have limited the discussion to the evaluation of behavior change and the creation of an evaluation framework. In contrast, this research identifies local cognition regarding the process of creating social impact.

This study seeks to clarify the relationship between USR and its social impacts in cases that involve regional cooperation. Using two case studies involving the USR activities of Kochi University, a Japanese national university located in Kochi, Japan, local cognition is visualized as a logic model. The model was developed through a series of interviews clarifying the structures by which USR produced social impacts for the region. Such methods have been applied in other research, primarily in the field of transportation.

Using transportation policy as an example, Kato et al. [7] analyzed the structure of transportation problems by creating a cognitive map via interviews with the relevant parties. The authors [8] then proposed using the logic model based on local cognition to evaluate traffic safety projects by incorporating information technology (IT). In another study [9] that dealt with the functional design of ICT to watch over the elderly utilizing a logic model based on regional cognition, Okamura et al. proposed a method for logically designing IT projects from explicit knowledge, whereas IT projects had previously been designed from a tacit knowledge of the problem. Mawatari et al. [10] constructed a logic model for the social implementation of autonomous driving through interviews with people who had experience in areas where such services have been introduced. Using a logic model, the authors evaluated cases where autonomous driving had already been implemented and attempted to identify future issues.

This research examines the practices of two regional coordinators hired by Kochi University in 2014 to construct a logic model for problem recognition and solution structure that could be used to examine how USR worked to solve problems.

The target areas for this study were Kuroshio Town and Yasuda Town in Kochi Prefecture, Japan, both of which have experienced rapid population decline. According to the Japanese Government, the threat of being struck by a massive tsunami caused by a Nankai Trough earthquake has caused an exodus of residents from Kuroshio Town; as a result, depopulation has become a serious social problem. In response, a regional coordinator from Kochi University joined the Canning Project in Kuroshio Town, which was implemented as a regional revitalization measure. The second area in the study, the Nakayama district of Yasuda Town is located in a mountainous area of Kochi Prefecture and has an economy based on agriculture. This local community's decline has become apparent due to its decreasing population.

2.2 Method

Similar to previous studies using logic models based on local cognition, this research constructed a cognitive map and logic model from interviews. The model was then used to examine the relationship between USR and its social impact. However, whereas previous studies used interviews focused on experiences and awareness from only the most recent few years, the interview questions in this study covered a period of up to 10 years. While this provides both greater uncertainty and completeness in interview results, it also makes it easier to verify the social impact on a region after the fact due to the long-term implementation period of the project being examined.

The interviews in this study were conducted with individuals who were involved in each case. An in-depth interview survey was used in order to understand the subjects' tacit recognition of the issues and causes for the case, their impact on the region, and the role of Kochi University. By having the University's USR regional coordinator act as the interviewer, it was possible to move forward while mutually confirming both the facts and the intentions of the interviewees' remarks.

In the case of the Canning Project in Kuroshio Town, the interviews were conducted in person with four individuals between July and October 2022. The subjects were asked about "the challenges of the Canning Project," "the role of Kochi University in relation to the Canning Project," and "the impacts of the Canning Project on the region." The four interviewees were local government officials in the Kuroshio Town Office who had been or are still involved in the planning and management of the Canning Project. Although a sample size of just four interviewees is small when compared to previous studies focused on the creation of cognitive maps, only these four individuals had been centrally involved in the Canning Project over an extended period.

In the case of the Nakayama district, in-person interviews were conducted with three individuals to create a cognitive map for the purpose of understanding regional issues. The interviews took place in July 2022. The interviewees were members of the Council for Energizing Nakayama. Two of the interviewees were from the Nakayama district; one was a member of the Local Vitalization Cooperator. All three had been members of the Council for Energizing Nakayama for several years. In-depth interviews were conducted with the three subjects, beginning with questions such as "What are the local issues?" and then gradually moving on to questions about the background of these issue and possible influencing factors. The co-authors were present during the interviews to confirm that there were no discrepancies in the interviewees' intentions and the logic model that was created.

The responses individually obtained from the survey participants were then used to create a cognitive map for each individual. The overlapping portions of the individual cognitive maps were then integrated to create a single map. The results of this integrated cognitive map and the interviews, along with their relevance, were then considered, and a series of logic models were constructed to visualize connections between inputs and impacts. Finally, the constructed logic model was used to determine the social impacts of Kochi University's USR activities.

2.3 University Social Responsibility in the Kuroshio Town Canning Project

2.3.1 Overview of the Canning Project and How the University Is Involved

Kuroshio Town is located in the western part of Kochi Prefecture, approximately 100 km from Kochi City, or approximately two hours by car. It has a population of 10,262 (2020 census); 45% of the residents are elderly. In 2012, the Nankai Trough Megathrust Earthquake Damage Forecast announced by the Cabinet Office identified Kuroshio Town as the town most likely to be struck by the largest tsunami ever experienced in Japan. In response, the town has actively promoted the creation of evacuation charts for all residents and the construction of a disaster prevention tower. In addition, the High School Students Summit on World Tsunami Awareness Day was held. The town is now considered an advanced disaster prevention area.

The Kuroshio Town Canning Project was introduced as an industry creation project in Kuroshio Town, with the Kuroshio Town Office establishing the Kuroshio Town Canning Factory Co., Ltd to manufacture and sell canned foods. Because of the dire tsunami forecast, the town developed a strong sense of crisis as the number of people moving away continued to grow. It was in this environment that the decision was made to create a new industry. The canning project has since attracted attention as an initiative begun as a way to take advantage of the forecast of a record-breaking tsunami.

Three years prior to the 2012 forecast, Kuroshio Town and Kochi University had signed a cooperative agreement under which they would jointly engage in activities such as practical training in regional collaborative studies by students and residents, and academic activities related to skipjack tuna. Since 2014, the authors have been stationed in the neighboring area as regional coordinators, and the University's USR was begun.

Regional coordinators receive information on local issues from the community and then work to resolve the issues. In Kuroshio Town, in addition to the Canning Project, the coordinators have dealt with a total of 68 issues over the past 8 years. These include project activities such as the development and support of a government publicity website, a program for expanding donations using the *furusato nouzei* system (hometown tax donation system), and consultation services such as providing advice on policy planning.

With regard to the Canning Project, the regional coordinators have been in charge of project planning, ongoing project management, and disseminating information, as well as conducting research in the field of food science and pursuing joint research on quality control methods.

2.3.2 Creating the Cognitive Map

The results of the interviews on Canning Project issues were first shown as a cognitive map for each of the four interviewees. In these individual maps, the starting points A and end points B represented the causal relationships that the interviewees perceived as "A is the reason for problem B." Next, individual cognitive maps that had the same meaning were integrated to create an integrated cognitive map. The integrated map is shown in Fig. 2.1 According to the integrated cognitive map, the issues that the Canning Project was experiencing can be organized into nine categories.

A portion of the cognitive map can be used to clarify. According to the map in Fig. 2.2, the reasons for "1. Development will take time" are "Don't know direction of development," "No matter how many attempts, it hasn't produced well," and "Can't decide how to label non-use of specified raw materials." Factors such as "Inexperienced with this work" and "Worried about contamination" were also cited.

2.3.3 Logic Model Derivation (from Outcomes to Outputs)

A logic model was derived from this cognitive map, with "Ensure the sustainability of the Canning Project" as the targeted final outcome (or ultimate goal). Possible direct outcomes from the nine issues shown in the cognitive map were set as the outcomes for the model. For example, if issue 1 in the cognitive map is "Development will take time," then the direct goal will be to reduce development time. Therefore,

Fig. 2.1 Locations of Kuroshio Town and Yasuda Town

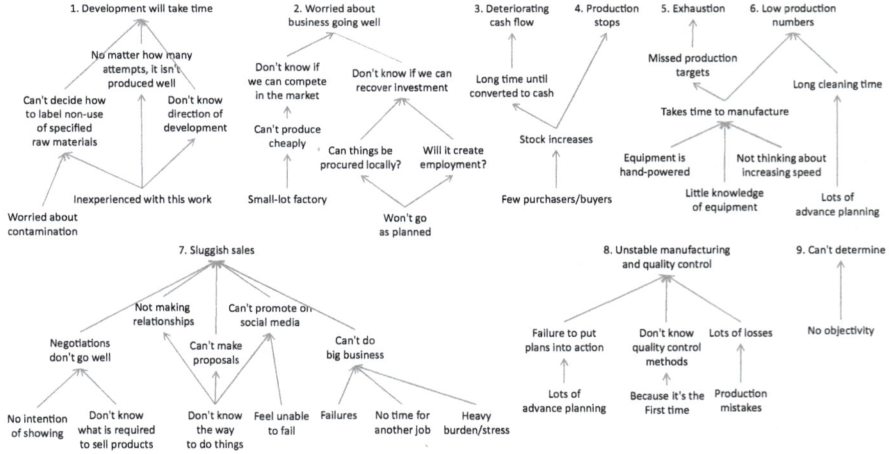

Fig. 2.2 Integrated cognitive map

"reduce development time" was set as the outcome in the logic model. Based on this idea, the factors for the nine issues in the cognitive map were similarly reconfigured to become outcomes and outputs. Notably, factors in the cognitive map that are difficult to control, such as the project environment ("Small-lot factory" and "Can't produce cheaply") and the attributes of those involved in the project ("Inexperienced with this work" and "Failures") are not set as outputs or outcomes in the logic model.

As a result of using these procedures to create a logic model from the cognitive map, 17 outcomes and 22 outputs were derived, as well as the relationships between those outcomes and outputs. Figure 3.2 shows the logic model, from outcome to output. The 17 outcomes include 9 intermediate outcomes (a. to i. in Fig. 2.3) related to the final outcome, "Ensure the sustainability of the Canning Project," and 8 related initial outcomes. For example, intermediate outcome "d. Stable manufacturing" is related to the initial outcome "Improved inventory turnover" and the output "cd1. Buyers/purchasers."

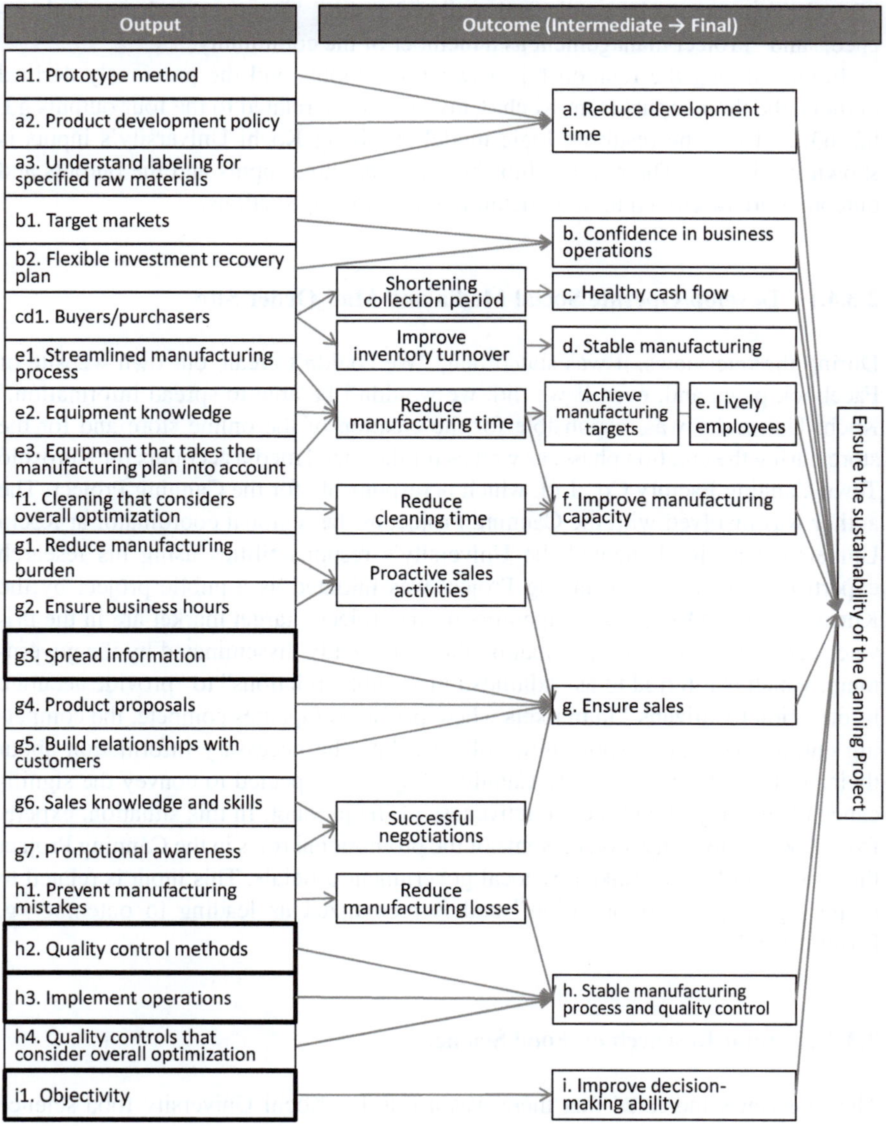

Fig. 2.3 Logic model (outcomes and outputs)

2.3.4 *Logic Model Derivation (from Outputs to Inputs)*

Based on the previously derived outputs and the results of the question about the role of Kochi University in relation to the Canning Project obtained from the interviews, the relationships between the outputs and the inputs from Kochi University were derived. From the responses of the interviewees and from the authors' experience with the project, three inputs were extracted for "Role of Kochi University": "Develop/operate social media and mail-order site," "Joint research on food science," and "Project management as a member of the community."

In considering the relationship between the inputs and the previously derived outputs, the three inputs from Kochi University were related to the four outputs g3, h2, h3, and i1. The resulting logic model involving Kochi University's inputs is shown in Fig. 2.3. The relationships between the three inputs and the outputs and outcomes are discussed in more detail in the following sections.

2.3.4.1 Develop/Operate Social Media and Mail-Order Site

During the interviews, it was stated that, "We couldn't create our own website or Facebook page, and, even if we did, we wouldn't be able to spread information." Kochi University was responsible for the creation of the online store and for the store during the creation phase, as well as for the social media accounts for Kuroshio Town Canning Factory Co., Ltd, which is responsible for the Canning Project. The author was involved with the Canning Project as the regional coordinator at Kochi University and implemented the University's responsibilities using his research expertise. Although the Canning Project was initiated as a public project by the Kuroshio Town Office, its competitors in the project's target market are in the private sector. In contrast to information that is typically disseminated by the government, which is referred to as "administrative public relations" to "provide accurate information to citizens," in markets where private companies compete, the competing entities have the responsibility of providing the necessary information about their products. In this case, the Canning Project is expected to convey the significance of the project and the attractiveness of the product. In this situation, experts from Kochi University took on some of the promotional roles in the Canning Project that could not be undertaken by local government officials. This input is related to output "g3. Spread information," and is recognized as leading to outcome "g. Ensure sales."

2.3.4.2 Joint Research on Food Science

The interviews indicated that there was a role for Kochi University food science researchers in testing for contamination by major food allergens. This was the result of joint research conducted by the Kuroshio Town Office and Kochi University, which tested for the presence of potentially harmful allergens and trained local personnel on inspection methods. The promotional material for the project's canned products states that the products do not contain major food allergens and, therefore, can be eaten even by evacuees who are allergic to such major food allergens. This input is related to output "h2. Quality control methods," and is recognized as leading to outcome "h. Stable manufacturing process and quality control."

2.3.4.3 Project Management as a Member of the Community

The most frequent comments in the interviews regarding the role of Kochi University concerned its role in project management. For example, there were comments that, "In talking about vague ideas, the regional coordinator made them clear, one at a time; we then formed a team," and "The regional coordinator became a common point of contact with outside experts." These comments refer to visualizing the community's thoughts and ideas in the form of proposals or plans, as well as inviting and managing the experts needed to implement those plans. There were also comments about money-related matters such as financial planning and cost accounting, and comments about task management and schedule management for resolving the problems that appeared. The role for this type of project management was taken on by the author, who was stationed in the region as a regional coordinator.

Additionally, comments on Kochi University's role included: "The university as well couldn't afford to fail in the project," "The regional coordinator was fully involved," "We'd prefer to have someone with less expertise and more passion than someone with more expertise and less passion," "The regional coordinator put himself in our position and thought about things empathetically," and "We couldn't make up our minds, but the regional coordinator guided us through the darkness." Although these types of comments cannot be called roles, they are among the results of the interviews and are indispensable in expressing the role of the University; in other words, the University's readiness to be a member of the community. It should be noted that, among the roles of Kochi University that have been described so far, the authors saw their role in project management as members of the community rather than as project managers that are externally sourced, believing that this readiness to be part of the community is the most important aspect of their work. This input is related to output "h3. Implement operations" and "Objectivity," and, respectively, is recognized as leading to outcomes "h. Stable manufacturing process and quality control" and "i. Improve decision-making ability."

2.3.5 Impacts of the Canning Project on the Region

Based on the results of the interviews, a list of the impacts that the Canning Project has had on the region was compiled. Four impacts were identified: "Secure new jobs," "Revitalize businesses in the region," "Improve name recognition for the region," and "Secure new leaders."

"Secure new jobs" refers to jobs that were created by the Canning Project. It was found that Kuroshio Town Canning Factory Co., Ltd, which oversees the Canning Project, employs 17 to 20 people at any given time. "Revitalize businesses in the region" refers to the impact on businesses in neighboring municipalities with which Kuroshio Town Canning Co. does business. It was found that Kuroshio Town Canning Co. annually purchases approximately ¥60 million in raw materials from businesses in nearby municipalities, including Kuroshio Town. "Improve name recognition for the region" means using media coverage of the Canning Project to improve Kuroshio Town's name recognition. Kuroshio Town, which was forecast to be hit by a record tsunami, took advantage of that negative factor to revitalize the town. From the beginning stages of the project's planning until the present day, that point has often been raised in the media, both regionally and nationally. It is clear that this has played a significant role in increasing the town's name recognition. "Secure new leaders" refers to the skills and human resources that have been developed through the Canning Project and its canned food products. By manufacturing canned goods that do not use certain raw materials, the project workers that were seconded from the Kuroshio Town Office were, in particular, required to have knowledge and practical skills in food hygiene. Additionally, while working as employees of the local government, these individuals were seconded to a private company and were able to experience firsthand some of the problems of such companies, as in matters of cash flow. It was found that, even after leaving the project, these individuals used their experience with the company to formulate and implement economic and practical measures against infectious disease during the COVID-19 pandemic. It was also found that the amount of donations to Kuroshio Town through Japan's *furusato nouzei* system (hometown tax donation system) increased measurably. In FY2021, donations to Kuroshio Town through the *furusato nouzei* system totaled ¥1.2 billion. Interestingly, canned goods were included in the gifts that people received for donating to Kuroshio Town through the system. Thus, the acquisition of new abilities by local government officials and acquiring supporters for Kuroshio Town were categorized as "Secure new leaders."

2.3.6 Consideration Using a Logic Model

The relationship between the Canning Project social impact on the region and the inputs of Kochi University was considered using a logic model constructed on the basis of local cognition. Figure 2.3 shows the impacts of the Canning Project and the inputs of Kochi University using this model. While the structure of Kochi University's inputs as they relate to local impacts could be logically established based on local cognition, there are multiple factors with complex connections involved, which made it difficult to intuitively understand the effects that the inputs had on creating the impacts.

From the perspective of the community, Kochi University carried out three main activities in the Canning Project: "Develop/operate social media and a mail-order site," "Joint research on food science," and "Project management as a member of the community." The four outputs from these activities contributed to the overall outcome (or ultimate goal), "Ensure the sustainability of the Canning Project," through the intermediate outcomes "Ensure sales," "Stable manufacturing process and quality control," and "Improve decision making." This, in turn, can be interpreted as having produced social impacts in the region such as "Secure new jobs," "Revitalize businesses in the region," "Improve name recognition for the region," and "Secure new leaders."

The logic model and local cognition made it possible to visualize the social impacts of Kochi University's inputs in the region. The University's involvement in the Canning Project includes both a secondary type of involvement, such as developing the mail-order site and conducting food science research, as well as a more central and substantive involvement, such as "Management as a member of the community." The logic model also suggests that the University is involved in the project's overall decision making insofar as the management structure has objectivity as an output and improving decision making abilities as the outcome.

On the other hand, the inputs and outputs from Kochi University are only part of the whole. As shown in Fig. 2.4, only 4 out of the 22 outputs were directly affected by Kochi University's inputs. Furthermore, the outputs created by Kochi University's inputs were not created solely through the University's efforts. The impacts and inputs are intricately related through the outcomes and outputs and have a structure that makes it difficult to intuitively imagine how Kochi University's role affected the impacts. In the logic model, it could be interpreted that the University oversaw the dissemination of information and that this increased Kuroshio's name recognition; however, the perception is that Kuroshio's name recognition increased due to the attention that was paid to the town's efforts to reverse the negative effects of the tsunami forecast.

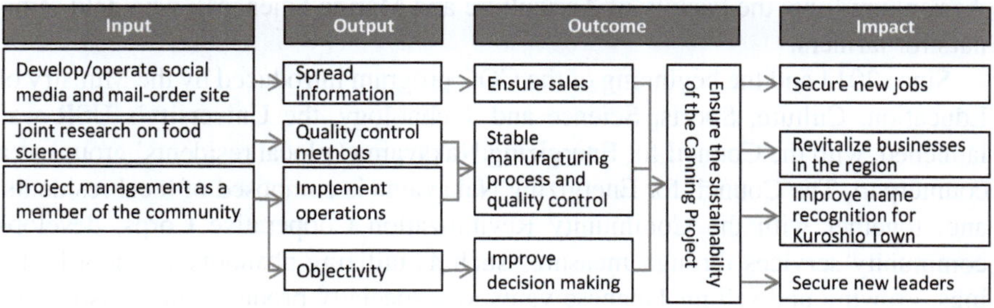

Fig. 2.4 Logic model (inputs from Kochi University to impact)

2.4 University Social Responsibility in the Nakayama District of Yasuda Town

2.4.1 The Nakayama District of Yasuda Town

The Nakayama district in Yasuda Town is located approximately 60 km, or less than two hours by car, from Kochi City, in the center of Kochi Prefecture. It occupies the central and northern part of Aki-gun in Yasuda Town and consists of 12 communities. As of April 2022, the district had a population of 446; 258 (57.8%) of the residents were aged 65 or older. In all, 189 of the total 236 households can be considered elderly. Of these, 97 are single elderly households where an elderly person lives alone. In addition to rice farming, yuzu (a type of citrus fruit) and Japanese yams are cultivated, which are both specialties of the area. Yuzu accounts for the majority of agricultural income, with an annual production value of over 100 million yen in the Nakayama district alone.

2.4.2 Collaboration Between Kochi University and Yasuda Town

Yasuda Town and Kochi University signed the Yasuda Town/Kochi University Collaboration Agreement in March 2013 and have since been working on collaborative projects. When the agreement was signed, at the request of the Yasuda Town Office, Kochi University's involvement was centered around utilization of the specialized knowledge of University researchers. Included were members of the Faculty of Science (now the Faculty of Science and Technology) who conducted research on fossil excavation, Medical School faculty who participated in and provided support for projects promoting health, and members of the Faculty of Agriculture (now the Faculty of Agriculture and Marine Sciences), who held seminars for farmers.

Since 2014 and the beginning of the COC program introduced by the Ministry of Education, Culture, Sports, Science and Technology, the University's USR was launched, with the Council for Energizing Nakayama (a local residents' group) as a counterpart. The Council for Energizing Nakayama is composed of local residents, and, together with the Community Revitalization Cooperative Corps, develops community services through measures such as utilizing abandoned school buildings, growing and selling Japanese yams as a specialty product, and assisting the elderly with hospital visits and shopping.

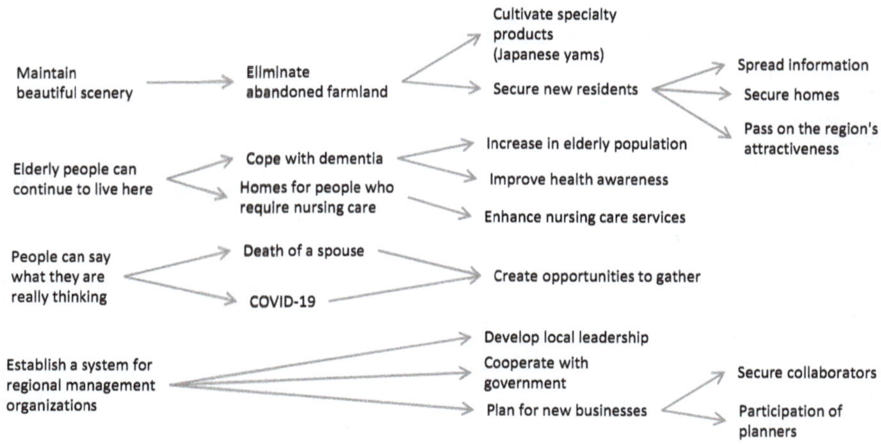

Fig. 2.5 Integrated cognitive map

2.4.3 Creating the Cognitive Map

The results of interviews with three interviewees in the Nakayama district of Yasuda Town were illustrated as a cognitive map for each of the three. Figure 2.5 shows the map. As indicated in the left column of the figure, the regional issues faced by the Council for Energizing Nakayama can be classified into the four categories.

A portion of the cognitive map can be used to illustrate. According to the map, to make it so that "Elderly people can continue to live here," the issues to be dealt with are "Homes for people who require nursing care" and how to "Cope with dementia," and the solutions to these problems are to "Improve health awareness" and "Enhance nursing care services" to handle the "Increase in elderly population."

2.4.4 Logic Model Derivation (from Outputs to Outcomes)

Based on the integrated cognitive map, a logic model showing cause-and-effect relationships was derived (Fig. 2.6), with "A region where people can continue to live" as the ultimate goal (final outcome). For example, looking at the issue of "Maintain beautiful scenery" in the cognitive map, "Eliminate abandoned farmland" is set as an intermediate outcome, with the output for that being set as "Cultivate specialty products" and "Agricultural maintenance work such as mowing." In the cognitive map, factors that are difficult for resident groups or individuals to control, such as "Increase in elderly population," "Death of a spouse," and "COVID-19," were not set as outputs or outcomes of the logic model.

The logic model created from the cognitive map with such a procedure includes 7 outcomes and 12 outputs, together with their relationships.

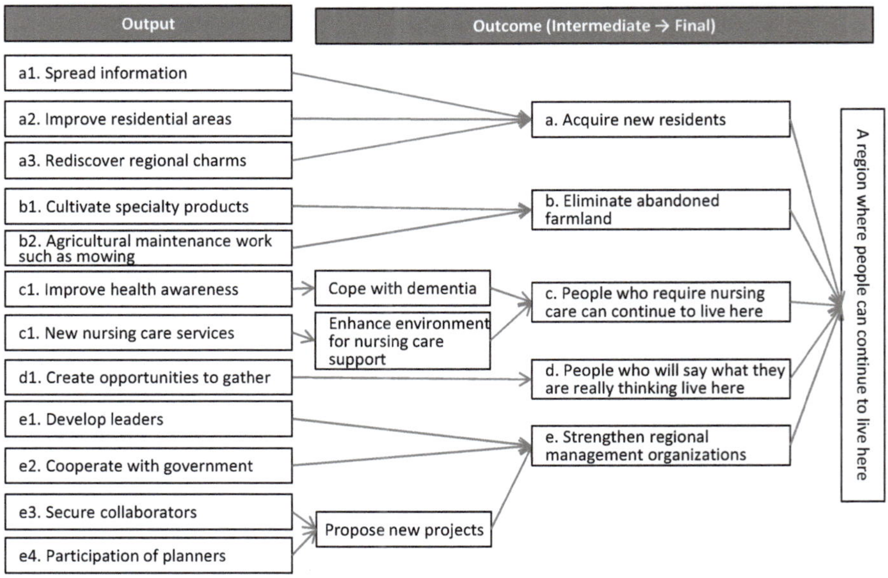

Fig. 2.6 Logic model (from outputs to outcomes)

2.4.5 Logic Model Derivation (from Inputs to Impacts)

Figure 2.7 shows the logic model for social impact after extracting the inputs of USR.

The relationship between outputs and the result "solving local problems and the role of Kochi University" (inputs) was derived. The solid lines indicate relationships with the University's input that were explicitly given as responses in the interviews. The dotted lines represent relationships that, while not included in the direct responses of the interviewees, can be described as inputs of the University based on the experience of the two authors as regional coordinators.

2.4.5.1 Rural Village Service-Learning Training

Since 2014, the Nakayama district in Yasuda Town has welcomed not only Kochi University students, but also students from Indonesia and Malaysia. These students have come to Japan for "Rural village service-learning training," which seeks to understand the current state of living in rural villages in Japan. The students also engage in community activities and education that contribute to resolving issues. Each year, approximately 15 students spend up to 10 days in August in the Nakayama district. The students conduct fieldwork, primarily through interviews with local residents and then report the results to the community in debriefing sessions.

In their interviews, the interviewees recounted their memories of such training with the Indonesian students, observing that "I could talk with students on a daily

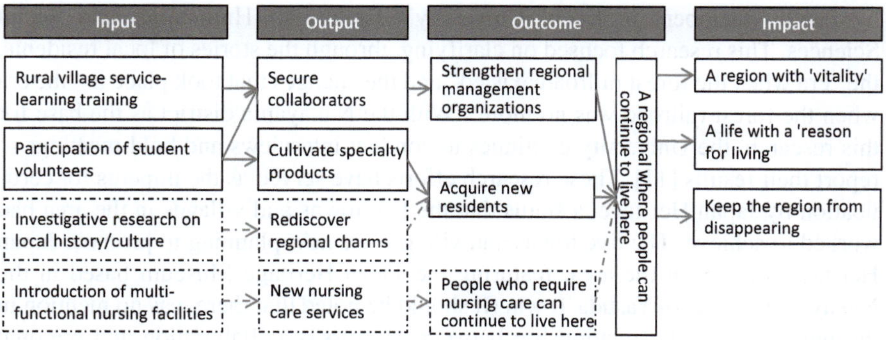

Fig. 2.7 Logic model (from impact to inputs). Note: Solid lines indicate a relationship between the university's inputs and outcomes that was explicitly pointed out in the interviews; dotted lines each indicate a relationship that was not clearly indicated in the interviews

basis" and "I could hear opinions from outside the area." This led to "Secure collaborators" (output) which in turn led to "Propose new projects."

2.4.5.2 Participation of Student Volunteers

In 2014, a Local Vitalization Cooperator and member of the Council for Energizing Nakayama approached Kochi University, stating that "Through interactions with students, we want to break out of the rut of community activities." This began an exchange project with student volunteers. Following discussions with members of the local community, it was decided that the student volunteers would work to eliminate abandoned farmland by cultivating Japanese yams. The students were dispatched to the area three times each year, planting Japanese yams in May, harvesting the yams in early December, and supporting yam sales events in mid-December. In all, more than 400 volunteers (which includes the period from 2020 to 2022, when the program was suspended due to the COVID-19 pandemic) have visited the Nakayama district to implement various exchange projects.

In their interviews, the three interviewees made comments such as "Many of the residents look forward to the arrival of the university students" and "Participation in the events leads to community vitality." Participation in the events by student volunteers directly contributes to "Cultivate specialty products," and is recognized as an output of the regional management organization for "Secure collaborators."

2.4.5.3 Investigative Research on Local History/Culture

Kochi University was consulted on the matter of preserving memories of the Chugei area by the Association for Preserving and Utilizing the Chugei area's Forest and Railway Heritage, a citizens group composed of members from five of the surrounding towns and villages. In response, historical and cultural research was conducted by faculty members in Kochi University's Faculty of Humanities and Social Sciences. This research focused on clarifying, through the stories of local residents, the "era when the forest railroad existed" and the changes that took place in "the era when the forest railroad was no more." With the Nakayama district as the base for this research, the University continues to conduct interviews and hold meetings to report their results [11]. These research efforts have served as the impetus for certification by Japan Heritage, a status that the five towns and villages in the area had worked to achieve. The five towns and villages are now planning to promote Japan Heritage tourism in the area, featuring the Japan Heritage Museum based in the Nakayama district of Yasuda Town. (It should be noted that there was no mention in the interviews of the relationship between University collaboration and regional issues regarding research on history and culture.)

2.4.5.4 Introduction of Multifunctional Nursing Facilities

In April 2022, a small-scale multifunctional home nursing facility based in Yasuda Town's Nakayama district was opened. A former faculty member of the Department of Nursing at Kochi University Medical School runs the NPO that manages the facility.

Since 2015, the Department of Nursing in the University's Medical School has conducted Support Training for Regional Residents in the Nakayama district, with the aim of having students learn about the living environment in rural areas and about the lives of people living with chronic illnesses, as well as develop practical skills as nurses. The training is conducted over 3 days and two nights, immediately after the students receive their initial training at the University. The students travel around the area on their own and make home visits to hear directly from residents with chronic diseases. The students then create activity plans and present them to the local residents and government officials.

The faculty member in charge of the training had retired from the University and founded a non-profit organization in December 2019. In July 2020, the NPO established a home-visit nursing care business based in Yasuda Town. As noted earlier in this section, the NPO later (in April 2022) became the designated manager of the new multifunctional in-home nursing care facility in the Nakayama district. The NPO provides home nursing, home care, day care, and short-stay nursing care services in the surrounding towns and villages, including Yasuda Town. (As in the case above, there was no mention of this university connection in the interviews.)

2.4.6 Consideration of University Social Responsibility by Using a Logic Model

From the regional perspective, Kochi University has been involved in resolving local issues in two ways: the "Rural village service-learning training" and the "Participation of student volunteers." These created the two outputs, "Secure collaborators" and "Cultivate specialty products," and led to the outcomes, "Strengthen regional management organizations" and "Acquire new residents," which are thought to have indirectly contributed to the social impacts that make it possible to have "A region where people can continue to live."

On the other hand, the "Investigative research on local history/culture" and the "Introduction of multifunctional nursing facilities," which were primarily conducted by the university, are directly linked to the results, "Rediscover regional charms" and "New nursing care services," respectively; however, no association in the regional cognitive map was found.

In summary, in the case of Yasuda Town's Nakayama district, there have been two types of University involvement in the community: (A) projects in which students have opportunities to engage with an unspecified number of residents, and (B) projects that are highly specialized and limited to engagement with specific residents. Furthermore, it can be said that the type A projects tend to have stronger recognition among residents [12]. On the other hand, even if the University's professional involvement creates output outcomes, those outcomes may be positioned outside of the residents' cognitive map.

Type A projects appear to be superior to type B projects when considering USR and the regional cognitive map. However, this logic model does not reflect the financial scale of the inputs or the time that elapses between the introduction of the inputs and their social impact. It also does not consider the scope of the social impact. Type B projects, in particular, require a significant passage of time between input and output/outcome creation. Moreover, the scope of their social impact is not limited to the Nakayama district but extends to surrounding municipalities as well. In this case, through the continuous observation of the University's regional coordinator, it was possible to associate the type B USR activities with their social impact.

Should USR in the form of type A and type B projects continue, it will be necessary to discuss the social impact of the University that is not represented in the regional cognitive map in relation to time and financial scale, as well as address the scope of the social impact.

2.5 Conclusion and Discussion

2.5.1 Usefulness of the Evaluation Model

USR involves a variety of relationships with local communities, through education, research, and their social contributions. The use of logic models makes it possible to concretely visualize the way in which USR inputs create social impacts. In contrast to Uchihira at el., who summarized the impact structure of USR activities by comprehensively analyzing 20 cases and using the CPI model, this research uses a logic model for two cases, enabling the authors to show the specific structure of how a university's inputs connect to their impacts. In the case of Kuroshio Town, clear relationships could be found between inputs and outputs; however, non-university factors intricately interwoven within the relationships between inputs, impacts, and outcomes, made it difficult to intuitively understand their relevance. In the case of Yasuda Town, the participation of student volunteers created the output "cultivation of specialty products," which was directly linked to the outcome "attracting new residents." Analyzing USR using a logic model enabled us to recognize connections with social impacts that could not be recognized simply by looking at the individual inputs.

On the other hand, in the analysis of USR, there were no cases in which University inputs alone were directly coupled with social impact, limiting recognition of their effect on impact creation. In the case of Kuroshio Town, it is difficult to selectively extract only the University's involvement from the social impact, as its contributions are intermingled with the contributions of other external factors. Furthermore, if the USR inputs are continuously implemented over time and the time between inputs and impacts is long, then it is more difficult to selectively extract only the University's inputs from the social impact.

2.5.2 Social Impact and Local Cognition of USR

The results of the two-case analyses showed local cognition of the impact of USR to be "Secure new jobs," "Revitalize businesses in the region," "Improve name recognition for the region," "Secure new leaders," "A region with vitality," "A life with a reason for living," and "Keep the region from disappearing." Of these, "Secure new jobs" may be considered synonymous with the impact "employment support" indicated by Uchihira in previous studies. Similarly, "A region with vitality" and "A life with a reason for living" are presented as "Aged Community Support." In addition, Uchihira positions "Improve name recognition for the region" and "Secure new leaders" as capacities in the CPI model. Although positioned differently in the different evaluation models, these impacts are common changes associated with USR. On the other hand, "Revitalize businesses in the region" and "Keep the region from disappearing" are impacts that have not been identified in previous studies.

Table 2.1 shows the University's inputs and the scope of its impacts on the communities in Kuroshio Town and Yasuda Town. In the case of Kuroshio Town, the University's inputs are highly specialized (for example, research seeds) and their sphere of influence is limited to the people involved in the project. In the case of Yasuda Town, the University's inputs include student volunteers in addition to specialized inputs, and the scope of their influence extends to the entire community.

Regarding regional cognition, type A projects that provide many opportunities for student volunteers to engage with a large number of residents are likely to be of high interest to the community and thus widely recognized, while the University's involvement is not nearly so widely recognized in type-B projects that are highly specialized and limited to engagement with specific residents by faculty members and researchers. This suggests the possibility that, in cases where not all the people directly benefit from the USR, or if the impact is thin and widespread, the local

Table 2.1 Inputs and scopes of impact on the region

Inputs	University seeds	Scope of impact on the region
The Case of Kuroshio Town		
Develop/operate social media and mail-order site	Research seeds	Project stakeholders
Joint research on food science	Research seeds	Project stakeholders
Project management as a member of the community	Coordinators' skills	Project stakeholders
The case of Yasuda town		
Rural village service-learning training	Education programs	Local residents
Participation of student volunteers	Students' activities	Local residents
Investigative research on local history/culture	Research seeds	Project stakeholders
Introduction of multifunctional nursing facilities	Research seeds	Project stakeholders

community may not be sufficiently aware that the University's efforts are the primary inputs.

In promoting USR, there is a need to stop, look back at the path taken so far, and mutually confirm future directions by conducting social impact assessments based on the perceptions of both the university and the community.

2.5.3 *Future Work*

Through the use of a logic model, this study was able to show the characteristics of problem-solving structures based on regional cognition and the challenges of evaluating social impacts. The two cases also showed how university inputs contributed to impact creation.

On the other hand, it was found in some cases that despite their contribution to impact, highly specialized inputs are not generally recognized by the community. In the logic model constructed in the Nakayama district case study, local residents were not aware of University inputs such as historical research and nursing services, even though these inputs led to impacts such as a revitalized community. Although details of student activities in the community often appear in the news, the introduction of highly specialized inputs is rarely reported. While highly specialized inputs have been a traditional USR activity, they are particularly important in this era of regional development. It will be necessary not only for universities to promote such USR activities, but that these activities be better represented and reflected in both local and national cognition. In addition, in social impact evaluations via the use of logic models, it is necessary to pay attention to changes in regional cognition and to USR relationships over time.

In the future, when USR activities are being planned, accumulating a variety of examples of USR analysis via the use of logic models will make it possible to design effective projects that will have specific social impacts. In doing so, it will be important to consider not only the university's perspective but perspectives based on regional cognition as well.

References

1. Akaike, S., Osaki, S., Okamura, K., & Kaji, H. (2019). *Chiiki koudineishon no jissen: Kochi daigakuryuu chihousousei heno tyousen (The practice of reginal coordination: Kochi University's approach to regional revitalizaiton)* (pp. 31–54). Koyo Shobo.
2. Kondo, Y., Itagaki, J., & Watanabe, S. (2020). Consideration of the changes reflection effect for the participants through the local cooperation activity. *Bulletin of Japanese Society for the Science of Design, 67*(2), 49–56. https://doi.org/10.11247/jssdj.67.2_49
3. Suzuki, T., Hara, N., Furukawa, N., Nishinari, N., & Yamada, K. (2018). Evaluating the Seto-uchi Regional Vitalization Project. *Journal of Research in Higher Education 2020, 15*, 175–188.
4. Kinoshita, Y. (2020). A consideration on the method of evaluation in University's Community Contribution Program: Focusing on schools that have been selected as Center of Community project (COC project). *University Evaluation Review, 9*, 125–135.
5. Uchihara, T., & Nakatsuka, M. (2016). Internal effects of and framework for the evaluation of coworking local actions with University Students. *Journal of Rural Problems, 52*(4), 211–216. https://doi.org/10.7310/arfe.52.211
6. Ueda, H., & Koriyama, A. (2016). Process of residents' behavior change and the role of outsiders in local development. *Journal of Rural Planning Association, 35*(3), 402. https://doi.org/10.2750/arp.35.398
7. Kato, H., Shiroyama, H., & Nakagawa, Y. (2005). Problem identification and structuring for regional transport planning: Case study of strategic transport plan in The Kanto Region. *Sociotechnica, 3*, 214–230. https://doi.org/10.3392/sociotechnica.3.214
8. Okamura, K., & Nasu, S. A proposition for evaluation process of its by using a logic model. *Journal of Japan Society of Civil Engineers, D3, 68*(55), I_277–I_284. https://doi.org/10.2208/jscejipm.68.I_277
9. Okamura, K., Nasu, S., & Kikuchi, Y. (2011). Proposition of a function design method of regional ICT by using a logic model. *Society for Social Management Systems Internet Journal, 7*. http://hdl.handle.net/10173/808
10. Mawatari, S., Nakanishi, Y., Todoroki, T., & Hyodo, S. (2022). Evaluation method of key considerations for deploying automated driving transportation service in rural area focusing on the recognition of practitioners. *Journal of Japan Society of Civil Engineers, F5, 78*(1), 16–25. https://doi.org/10.2208/jscejppce.78.1_16
11. Akaike, S., & Iwasa, M. (2021). Regional revitalization through the life history interview: From local memories to Japan heritage. *TJA Newsletters*. https://tja.center/zh-TW/newsletter_units/1
12. Hirai, T. (Ed.). (2021). *Post chihousousei: Daigaku to Chiiki ga kunde dokomade dekiruka (Post Regional Revitalization: How much can the university and community work together to achieve?)* (pp. 18–20). Hirosaki University Press.

Chapter 3
Using Jobs Theory to Evaluate the Use of Mobile Off-Grid Architecture (MOA) as a Means of Regional Revitalization

Shota Tajima

Abstract This research investigated the applicability of mobile off-grid architecture (MOA) to regional revitalization by using Jobs Theory to evaluate the product–market fit of EcoCabin, a prototype MOA developed by the author. In recent years, MOA has found increasing applications at the local level in Japan. However, the specific needs that MOA meets remain unclear. To help fill this gap, a research team composed of the author, who is an assistant professor at Chiba University, a researcher, and students from multiple departments of the university was formed to assess the product-market fit for EcoCabin. To make the assessment, members of the research team interviewed five potential EcoCabin users in Nagara Town, Chiba Prefecture. The interviewed group comprised two farmers, a resort facility operator, the farmers' market manager, and a tourist farm owner. In the evaluation process, the needs of the interviewees were ascertained, and remaining issues were identified. The value proposition of EcoCabin was then assessed. The results suggest that using MOA to induce communications among people, especially those living in rural areas, could be an effective contributor to regional revitalization. However, further research will be necessary to verify the product's compatibility with the market.

Keywords Mobile off-grid architecture · Regional revitalization · Jobs theory · SDG7, SDG11

S. Tajima (✉)
Chiba University, Chiba, Japan
e-mail: shota.tajima@chiba-u.jp

M. C. Huang et al. (eds.), *Innovative Social Practice and Community-Based Approach to the Ocean*, https://doi.org/10.1007/978-981-96-9104-3_3

3.1 Introduction

3.1.1 Regional Revitalization by Chiba University

Japan's population has been in decline since peaking in 2008. Rural areas face depopulation due to population outflow to cities, a declining birth rate, and an aging population. In 2015, the Japanese government launched the "Comprehensive Strategy for Vitalizing Towns, People, and Jobs" aimed at tackling the problem of population decline. However, the issue of population overconcentration in Tokyo has not been resolved, and the influx of people into the Greater Tokyo Area continues [1]. To realize regional revitalization, multifaceted cross-cutting measures are needed from the economic, social, and environmental fields, including measures aimed at achieving the United Nation's Sustainable Development Goals. Accordingly, an interdisciplinary approach is needed to realize regional revitalization.

In 2015, Chiba University launched its COC+ program, a project funded by the Ministry of Education, Culture, Sports, Science and Technology (MEXT) to promote regional revitalization (COC stands for "Center of the Community"). The COC project was initially established by MEXT to address problems in urban areas. However, the "+" was subsequently added to signify a special focus on rural area development. Through partnerships with local universities, the COC+ program seeks to develop industries and create jobs in rural areas in Japan. Chiba University has partnered with local governments in areas of Chiba Prefecture that are experiencing declining populations to conduct research related to local issues. One such area is the town of Nagara, the target area of this research (Fig. 3.1).

In 2015, Chiba University and Nagara signed a regional revitalization partnership agreement to create a continuing care retirement community (CCRC). Modeled after communities that provide medical and nursing care for the elderly in the United States, the project aims to build a community in Nagara to which active older adults from urban areas can move and live healthy and active lives [2]. The Nagara CCRC is notable for its utilization of the town's resort facility and its extensive use of the university's expertise. To date, researchers from Chiba University's Graduate School of Global and Transdisciplinary Studies, the Center for Preventive Medicine, the Faculty of Engineering, and the Faculty of Horticulture have participated in the project, contributing to the design of mental and physical health spaces that increase the walkability of community areas. In 2018, the Nagara CCRC was selected for inclusion as part of the university's inter-department Well Active Community (WACo) project, funded by the JST Industry–Academia Co-Creation Platform Joint Research Promotion Program. WACo's mission is to develop an open innovation platform for healthy town development that extends healthy life expectancy by emphasizing people's social connections. Through WACo, the author developed a walking track (Fig. 3.2) that informs visitors of the health benefits of walking [3]. The author moved to Nagara in 2016 and serves as a town advisor, promoting regional revitalization.

Fig. 3.1 An example of the scenery of Nagara, where many residents are involved in agriculture, mainly rice production, as a key industry

Fig. 3.2 Walking track sign in Nagara

3.1.2 Potential for Implementing Mobile Off-Grid Architecture in Rural Areas

Mobile off-grid architecture (MOA) is a movable space with built-in solar panels and storage batteries [4]. Mobile architecture includes vehicles such as camper vans as well as architectural spaces capable of being transported such as mobile homes. In Japan, the Ministry of Land, Infrastructure, Transport and Tourism (MLIT) relaxed regulations on mobile architecture after the Great East Japan Earthquake in 2011, leading to an increase in their popularity. So far, mobile architecture has been used as construction site offices and food trucks. However, in recent years, mobile architecture has also been used as hotels, stores, and markets. The difference between mobile architecture and buildings is that mobile architecture functions as a temporary structure. Mobile architecture has no foundation or anchors to the ground and includes infrastructure such as water, electricity, and gas that is either built into its structure or can be manually installed and removed.

Research on mobile architecture in Japan has included disaster support for the Kumamoto earthquake [5] and surveys conducted after the Eastern Hokkaido earthquake [6]. In addition, there are reports on the possible use of hut constructions from mobility, combinations, and added value [7] as well as case reports on the use of camping trailers for agricultural experiences and as excursion-type accommodation facilities [8].

Recently, due to the spread of COVID-19, interest in relocating to rural areas has increased among the younger generation [9]. There is also growing interest in hut construction, including tiny houses that allow people to relocate easily. However, the study of mobile architecture has not been systematically organized as an academic field in Japan. Utilizing mobile architecture to realize regional revitalization in Japan, particularly in areas facing severe population decline, is a research subject worthy of thorough examination.

3.1.3 Research Method

There is a strong connection between the UN Sustainable Development Goals (SDGs) and regional revitalization. Creating sustainable communities in Japan's rural areas, where the population is declining, would represent a significant contribution to the achievement of global SDGs. Indeed, achievement of the UN's SDGs is positioned as a cross-sectional goal in the Japanese government's Comprehensive Regional Revitalization Strategy. Globally, a growing middle class is increasing consumption and impacting rare resource supply [10]. Today's businesses must find ways to reduce resource consumption while simultaneously meeting increasing consumption needs [11].

This research is conducted from the perspective of Jobs Theory. Jobs Theory is the theory of consumption and needs mechanisms advocated by Clayton M. Christensen [12]. It is also called "jobs-to-be-done" because it "hires (buys)" products or services to get "jobs" done. For instance, carpenters hire (buy) drills to do the job of drilling holes.

Jobs Theory identifies potential early adopters through customer interviews, analyzes customer segments (name, age, gender, attributes) and the mechanism of their needs, and considers the product–market fit. By verifying the feasibility of the social implementation of the product, it is possible not only to develop specific and highly probable products but also to contribute to the realization of sustainable local communities.

3.1.4 Purpose of Research

Mobile architecture has come to function not only as a temporary space but also as a social space. In addition, MOA with various functionalities is being used in a variety of places. Importantly, MOA has the potential to be a tool that contributes to disaster response activities and industrial development in rural areas where infrastructure is especially vulnerable. Accordingly, the author began researching the usefulness of MOA that can contribute to regional revitalization, using a multifaceted and interdisciplinary approach to address increasingly complex regional issues. In the course of his work, the author developed EcoCabin, a prototype MOA, in 2022 (Fig. 3.3).

The primary purpose of this research was to examine the applicability of MOA to regional revitalization by verifying the product–market fit of EcoCabin.

Fig. 3.3 MOA prototype EcoCabin

3.2 Methodology

3.2.1 EcoCabin

EcoCabin was conceived as a prototype MOA that helps to address issues associated with population decline in rural areas. Under the author's supervision, EcoCabin was developed via the industry–government–academia collaboration of an architectural design office, a structural design office, a construction firm, a wood dealer, the government of Nagara, and Chiba University.

EcoCabin is mounted on a chassis that can be towed by a car. It is able to generate and store electricity using solar panels. Excluding the chassis, EcoCabin is 1440 mm wide, 2050 mm long, and 1400 mm high. The internal space is 1238 mm wide, 2000 mm long, and 1190 mm high, providing ample room for people to sit and work (Table 3.1). EcoCabin was given a rounded design that blends in with the various natural landscapes of the region, with the aim of inducing communication among people by making it a familiar design. The left and right sides have hinged doors which unlock to create an open space (Fig. 3.4). The interior is a multifunctional area that can flexibly accommodate a variety of uses.

The curved roof of the EcoCabin features 250-W ultra-lightweight film solar cells, enabling off-grid power generation (Fig. 3.5) of up to 1.2 kWh in sunny weather. The 12-V, 210-Ah lithium-ion storage battery has a capacity of 2.5 kWh. On a sunny day, it is possible to charge a laptop computer or smartphone using only the power generated by the solar battery. The storage battery can power a cooling fan of about 800 W for approximately three hours. In addition, due to the solar cells extending to the rear vertical plane, people are able to visually recognize that EcoCabin uses this space to generate electricity (Fig. 3.5). Moving EcoCabin according to the sun's position can maximize electricity generation.

EcoCabin's easy-to-construct frame is a hybrid structure that combines standard 2 × 4 wood beams and round-shaped steel frames (Fig. 3.6). The frame was manufactured based on the results of structural experiments performed to evaluate its strength and rigidity. Because of its light weight of less than 750 kg, EcoCabin can be towed by ordinary passenger cars without requiring a special license under Japanese law.

Table 3.1 Dimensions of EcoCabin

	Width	Length	Height
Outer dimensions	1440 mm	2050 mm	1400 mm
Internal dimensions	1238 mm	2000 mm	1190 mm
Chassis	1470 mm	3390 mm	590 mm

Fig. 3.4 EcoCabin's rounded design and hinged doors for an open space

Fig. 3.5 EcoCabin's ultra-lightweight film solar cells

Fig. 3.6 EcoCabin's 2 × 4 wood beams and round-shaped steel frames

3.2.2 *Overview of Nagara*

Nagara has an area of 47.11 km^2 and a population of 6480, making it the second smallest town in Chiba Prefecture. It is located on a hilly area in the central part of the Boso Peninsula and is about 70 min from central Tokyo by car (Fig. 3.7). Nagara was established in 1955 through the merger of three villages. The population of Nagara has been in decline since peaking in 1995. This has led to problems such as a decline in public transportation due to decreased patronage.

Nagara's primary industries are manufacturing, medical and welfare services, and construction. It is also home to Japan's largest contract beverage manufacturing company as well as a resort facility. The town produces a variety of crops throughout the year, including rice, bamboo shoots, figs, and wild yams. Taking advantage of its proximity to Tokyo, Nagara focuses on immigration and settlement. A vacant house bank system was launched in 2015 and has been used by 72 migrants from 51 households as of 2020. Chiba University promotes the town's revitalization in multiple ways, including designing a promotional image for the bus wrap of an express bus, creating a guidebook for immigration and settlement, and developing unique area products. In recent years, disaster preparation has also become an issue. The 2019 Boso Peninsula Typhoon caused power outages throughout the town. In the same year, the Ichinomiya River, which runs through the town, overflowed due to the torrential rain from the East Japan Typhoon, causing extensive damage.

Fig. 3.7 Location of Nagara, Chiba

3.2.3 Verification of the Social Implementation of MOA by Jobs Theory

Jobs Theory was used to examine the possible social implementation of MOA as a contributor to regional revitalization. The research team conducted online and face-to-face interviews with five residents of Nagara in Chiba Prefecture, Japan, from July to September 2022 (Table 3.2). The contents of the interviews used for analysis are summarized in Table 3.3.

Jobs Theory is typically implemented according to the process described in Fig. 3.8. In this study, we asked each interviewee about issues they were facing and things they are dissatisfied with (i.e., jobs-to-be-done) in order to elucidate the mechanism of their needs after explaining the purpose of the interview. We asked what measures they took to solve the problem and what issues remained. Then, we explained the functions and features of EcoCabin and evaluated the product–market fit by asking the interviewees whether they would use EcoCabin to resolve their unmet needs. Based on this series of conversations, we determined whether

Table 3.2 Interviewee information

Interviewee	Age	Gender	Position
1. Full-time farmer	60 s	Male	Self-employed
2. Part-time farmer	20 s	Male	Municipality staff and self-employed
3. Worker at a resort facility	20 s	Female	Employee
4. Person in charge of a farmers' market	60 s	Male	Board member
5. Owner of a tourist farm	50 s	Female	Self-employed

Table 3.3 Interview items used for analysis

Attribute	Name
	Age
	Gender
	Characteristic conditions (occupation, hobby, place of residence, etc.)
Needs mechanism	Jobs (what he/she wants to do)
	Background/reason of his/her jobs
	Dissatisfaction and challenges (How he/she currently resolve his/her frustrations and challenges)
	Remaining challenges
Product-market fit	Presence or absence of product-market fit as a product/service
	Proof
	Presence or absence of product-market fit for price
	Contents when different from hypothesis
Judgment	Early adopter or not
	Characteristic conditions of early adopter (if he/she is early adopter)
	Characteristic conditions of non-early adopter (if he/she is not early adopter)
Other	Other things that we noticed

the interviewee was a potential early adopter and summarized their characteristics accordingly. Finally, based on our understanding of them as potential users, we considered the value provided by MOA in terms of promoting regional revitalization.

3.2.4 Consideration Using Socio-Relation Map (SRMap)

Based on the Jobs Theory results, a socio-relation map (SRMap) was constructed. An SRMap is a diagram providing a quantitative evaluation of locally oriented sustainable products in visual form. Such a map helps to numerically understand stakeholders and their relationships by visualizing the connections among the stakeholders involved in building these relations. The map consists of "nodes" (stakeholders) and "edges" (relations) [13]. MOA was considered a locally oriented sustainable product due to its potential to contribute to the social sustainability of a region.

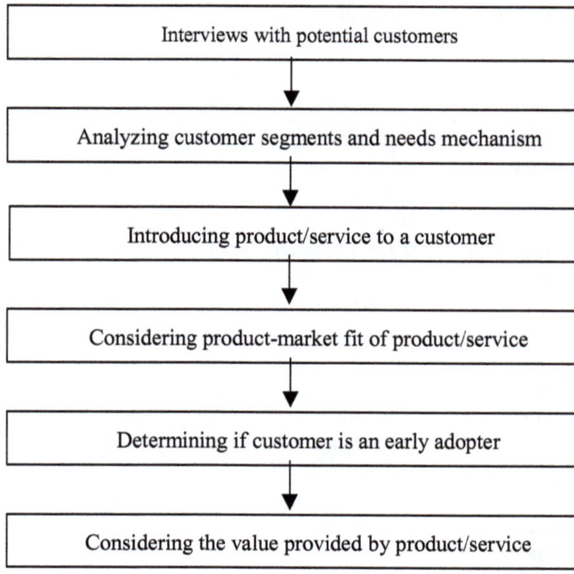

Fig. 3.8 Process of jobs theory

3.3 Results

Table 3.4 summarizes the interview results, including the needs mechanism of the interviewees, the resulting product-market fit and the reason for it, and, finally, the value proposition that was derived from the results.

The first interviewee was a full-time farmer who was seeking ways to help aging farmers throughout the region continue farming. We proposed EcoCabin as a resting space for farmers. However, the product–market fit was not good, as full-time farmers do not take breaks that interrupt their work, and even if they do take long breaks, there is no need for a mobile space, because their homes are close to their farms. Following the interview, we proposed EcoCabin as a shelter that could be mounted on a light truck and deployed by a regional agricultural association when needed.

The second interviewee was a municipal worker who farms part-time, mostly in the early morning and on weekends. He said he wanted to change clothes and use a refrigerator to store cold drinks while farming. In response, we proposed EcoCabin as a private room. However, the product–market fit was not good, because commercial vehicles such as vans can be used for the same purpose. Nevertheless, we considered that EcoCabin might be attractive as a stylish rest space for amateur farmers who come from the city to rural areas to farm on weekends or to experience farming.

The third interviewee was a worker at a resort facility. We proposed EcoCabin as a first-aid space for outdoor sporting events, music festivals, and so on. The product–market fit was not good, because it has no income-generating potential. However, the possibility of using EcoCabin as a communication tool with

Table 3.4 Interview results

Interviewee	Needs mechanism	Product–market fit	Reason for decision	Value proposition of EcoCabin derived from product–market fit
1. Full-time farmer	Wants to help elderly farmers continue farming	Poor	There is no demand for breaks, because the farm is close to home	Can be used as a shelter (mounted on a truck) by a farming association.
2. Part-time farmer	Wants to change clothes or use a refrigerator	Poor	A van can be used for the same function.	Can be used as a resting space for urban residents who come to rural areas for farming experiences.
3. Worker at a resort facility	Wants a cool space for outdoor sports and activities	Poor	Has no income-generating potential.	Can be rented for events such as sports and music festivals.
4. Person in charge of a farmers' market	Wants to support local farmers	Poor	Existing stores are sufficient; could not understand how to use EcoCabin.	Can be used as a mobile market where local farmers sell seasonal produce directly to customers.
5. Owner of a tourist farm	Wants to provide direct sales along the main street	Good	Wants to use it because the shape is cute; can communicate directly with customers.	Can be used as a mobile store that sells seasonal fruits.

customers was considered by the interviewee, including renting it for a limited time, such as for outdoor events.

The fourth interviewee was in charge of a farmers' market. The market sold agricultural products from the area and was eager to support the local farmers. The EcoCabin product–market fit was not good, because the local farmers conducted direct sales through the market. Furthermore, we were unable to clearly communicate how EcoCabin might be used for the business, and the interviewee was unable to understand its proper use. However, we learned in the interview that EcoCabin might serve as a place where farmers could directly explain and sell their agricultural products to customers.

The fifth interviewee was the owner of a farm offering fruit-picking experiences to tourists. The product–market fit was good, and the interviewee was considered a potential early adopter. She observed that, particularly because of its "cute" shape, she could use the EcoCabin as a mobile store to sell her product and to communicate directly with her customers. She stated that other tourist farms had started offering similar harvesting experiences through direct sales at nearby stores. She wished to try direct sales because her farm was off the main street, and thus it was difficult to attract new customers. Following the interview, we concluded from her statements that the value of EcoCabin lay in its distinctive round design and appearance, which could serve to encourage communication with customers.

3.4 *Post facto* Result and Analysis

3.4.1 *Consideration Using Socio-Relation Map*

In this study, the author investigated the applicability of MOA to regional revitalization by exploring potential uses for EcoCabin from the perspective of Jobs Theory. To evaluate the product-market fit of EcoCabin based on the unmet needs of area residents, five residents of Nagara were interviewed. An assessment of how social implementation of EcoCabin might contribute to regional revitalization was then undertaken. Contrary to expectation, the results indicated that members of the local community would be unlikely to use EcoCabin for agriculture or tourism, two key industries in rural areas. However, it was suggested that EcoCabin might be used as a mobile store and that it could help promote communication between residents and visitors in such areas.

Figure 3.9 shows the application of an SRMap to a tourist farm. The figure on the left is an SRMap without EcoCabin; the figure on the right is an SRMap with EcoCabin used as a mobile sales store, which was recognized as a value proposition based on Jobs Theory. The tourist farm had built relationships with customers by selling fruit-picking experiences to visitors, some of whom became repeat customers (segment 1). Using EcoCabin as a mobile shop, a tourist farm can sell fruit to previously unconnected customers (segment 2). In addition, EcoCabin's round, distinctive design catalyzes face-to-face communication with customers, which may lead to segment 1, fruit-picking experiences.

3.4.2 *Significance of Regional Revitalization of MOA*

To date, no study has investigated practical ways to apply MOA to regional revitalization in Japan. However, studies of temporary emergency housing, mobile hospitals, countermeasures against slums, implementations in off-grid areas, and other studies linked to social issues are being conducted in other countries. There are several possible reasons that research on the role that MOA might play in regional

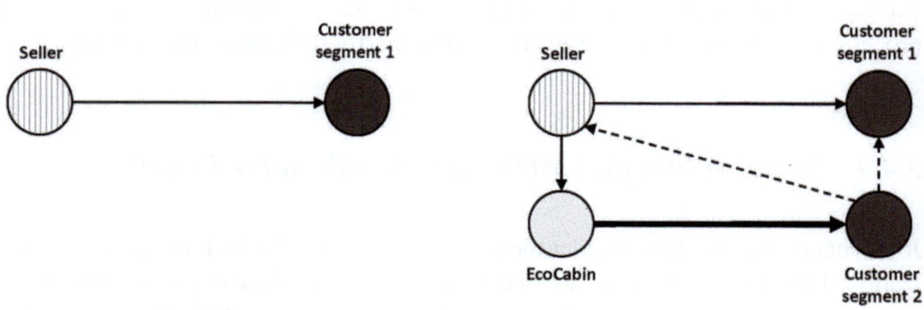

Fig. 3.9 SRMap of a tourist farm

revitalization has not been widely conducted in Japan. First, in the field of architecture and construction, mobile architecture does not fall under the category of buildings under the Building Standards Act. Therefore, the academic evaluation of mobile architecture is limited to temporary emergency housing. The author expects that there will be more active discussions on the potential application of mobile architecture, including MOA, to regional revitalization in the future. The second reason is that in areas such as Japan, where infrastructure is well developed, research is focused mainly on net zero energy buildings (ZEBs), which have an annual energy balance that is virtually zero. ZEBs are connected to the commercial power grid and differ from off-grid architecture. Approximately 733 million people worldwide do not have access to electricity [14]. The use of MOA is an important issue that should be studied for regional revitalization as well as solving global issues. The third reason is that, in terms of policy, the ambiguity of mobile architecture is an issue in rural areas. For example, some local governments have established ordinances to restrict the installation of mobile architecture because mobile architecture is not subject to property taxes. However, as this study suggests, mobile architecture might be used to respond to regional needs that can aid regional revitalization.

It was shown in this study that MOA for regional revitalization has potential, as well as problems to be solved. By continuing to refine and extend this research in the future, the author intends to chart new territory as a frontier that incorporates the perspective of regional revitalization into the burgeoning academic field of MOA.

3.4.3 Research Limitations

This study investigated the possible application of MOA to meet the needs of local farmers, a resort facility, an agricultural product direct sales shop, and a tourist farm in Nagara. From the perspective of Jobs Theory, more targets need to be included and multifaceted verification will be required to elucidate the various mechanisms of needs (i.e., jobs-to-be-done) of local residents. Moreover, the product–market fit evaluation results obtained from interviews conducted over such a short period are clearly insufficient for broad generalization. It should also be noted that none of the interviewees indicated an essential need for EcoCabin in times of disaster, which was the original purpose of its development. The author will continue the interview process, adding more interviewees in order to clarify their needs mechanisms.

3.4.4 Social Values that MOA Can Provide to the Region

Jobs Theory was used to consider the possibility of using MOA for regional revitalization. Jobs Theory offers a way to assess customer needs when developing products and services by clarifying the needs mechanism. Although the product-market fit for EcoCabin was found to be not suitable for many presumed customers, satisfactory results were obtained to verify regional needs.

In this research, by using an SRMap together with Jobs Theory, it was suggested that the needs of residents for MOA and the effect of regional revitalization by MOA could be verified at the same time. The effect of regional revitalization through the use of MOA that emerged from the SRMap analysis is an increase in the relevant population. However, the residents targeted in this study had limited needs for MOA and the SRMap could be used only in the case of a tourist farm. In order to verify the social value of MOA in terms of increasing the number of people involved, we need results that increase the probability of more interviews and social implementation using Jobs Theory.

The results of this study suggested two main points regarding the expected social impact of regional revitalization through the use of MOA. The first point relates to the possibility of utilizing MOA as a new tourism tool. MOA's unique portability makes it possible to do things that are difficult to do at tourist farms in places far from a main street and that are difficult to see by tourists. The second point relates to the activation of communication. In addition to approaching local industries, the use of MOA can be discussed in terms of healthy life expectancy and cultural inheritance by contributing to active communication between people inside and outside the region.

Jobs Theory has a constructive role to play in future research focused on evaluating the use of MOA. Furthermore, in local policy planning, elucidating the mechanism of needs, Jobs Theory can be effectively used for targeted marketing in areas such as tourism, specialty product development, and immigration and settlement.

3.4.5 Additional Survey to Residents

In the fall of 2022, the author publicly unveiled EcoCabin at a local event in Nagara. Valuable opinions from a survey of more than 150 people, including local residents and visitors, were compiled (Fig. 3.10). In this additional survey, participants were asked about their needs in the time of disaster and for their impressions of EcoCabin. In responding to a question regarding what information they wanted in the event of a disaster, "warnings" was the most common answer, followed by "evacuation information from local governments" and "damage status." When asked about their means of gathering information during a disaster, "television" was the most common answer, followed by "internet" and "email." In their open-ended answers, the following comments were made: "I want to borrow it," "It seems to be useful in times of disaster," "It looks cool," "I want you to post event information," and "I want a little smaller one."

In the future, the author will conduct more interviews and verify the product's compatibility with the market.

Fig. 3.10 Open to residents at a town event

3.5 Conclusion

This study investigated the applicability of mobile off-grid architecture (MOA) to regional revitalization by applying Jobs Theory and a socio-relation map, using EcoCabin, a prototype developed by the author as an example of an MOA. The author selected Nagara, a town in Japan's Chiba Prefecture, to explore the social potential of implementing MOA. The product-market fit of EcoCabin was assessed based on the needs of participants in the study. The results indicated that MOA should promote communication between residents in rural areas and visitors to rural areas in order to contribute to regional revitalization. Based on these results and the statement made by one of the interviewees indicating that she would use EcoCabin to communicate with people, the author will begin operating an EcoCabin in Nagara as a way to catalyze communication among residents and visitors.

Acknowledgements This work was supported by JSPS KAKENHI Grant Number JP22K04489. I want to express my gratitude to the local government staff of Nagara, Chiba who cooperated in carrying out this research, to everyone who participated in the interviews, to Mr. Tsutsumi who taught basic knowledge of Jobs Theory, and to the researcher and the students who conducted the interviews.

References

1. Ministry of Land, Infrastructure, Transport and Tourism. (2020). *White paper on land, infrastructure, transport and tourism in Japan, 2020*. Retrieved from https://www.mlit.go.jp/hakusyo/mlit/r01/hakusho/r02/pdf/kokudo.pdf. Accessed 17 Nov 2022
2. Tajima, S. (2018). *Efforts that take advantage of the characteristics of the university: University-linked CCRC in Nagara*, Regional Development, vol. 625, Japan Center for Area Development Research, pp. 29–32.
3. Tajima, S., Hanazato, M., & Nishigaki, M. (2021). Design of a walking track aimed at realizing a town that makes residents want to walk. *Chiba University Journal of Liberal Arts and Sciences, 5*, 153–169. https://doi.org/10.20776/s24326291-5-p153
4. Tajima, S., & Nasu, S. (2020). ARCHITETTURA MOBILE OFF-GRID Uno strumento possibile per la resilienza delle comunità rurali in caso di calamità naturali | MOBILE OFF-GRID ARCHITECTURE A potential tool for the resilience of rural communities in the event of natural disasters. *AGATHÓN | International Journal of Architecture Art and Design, 8*, 118–127. https://doi.org/10.19229/2464-9309/8112020
5. Tsuchiya, S. & Ishida, T. (2019). *The report on functional alteration of trailer house used as the disaster support in the case of Kumamoto Earthquake*. Summaries of technical papers of annual meeting. Architectural Institute of Japan, pp. 987–988.
6. Tsuchiya, S. & Ishida, T. (2021). *A report of temporary housing using trailer house in dispersive location after 2018 Hokkaido Eastern Iburi Earthquake*. Summaries of technical papers of annual meeting in Hokkaido. Architectural Institute of Japan, pp. 272–275.
7. Omi, Y. & Shutou, K. (2019). *Research on classification of tiny house and actual condition of trailer house in Japan*. Summaries of technical papers of annual meeting, Architectural Institute of Japan, pp. 929–930.
8. Ministry of Land, Infrastructure, Transport and Tourism. (2018). *Fiscal 2018 vacant land model survey*. Retrieved from https://www.mlit.go.jp/totikensangyo/totikensangyo_tk2_000124.html. Accessed 17 Nov 2022
9. Cabinet Office. (2022). *The 5th survey on changes in lifestyle awareness and behavior under the influence of the new coronavirus infection*. Retrieved from https://www5.cao.go.jp/keizai2/wellbeing/covid/pdf/result5_covid.pdf. Accessed 17 Nov 2022.
10. Alonso, E., Sherman, M. S., Wallington, T. J., Everson, M. P., Field, F. R., Roth, R., & Kirchain, R. E. (2012). Evaluating rare earth element availability: A case with revolutionary demand from clean technologies. *Environmental Science and Technology, 46*(6), 3406–3414. https://doi.org/10.1021/es203518d
11. Hankammer, S., Brenk, S., Fabry, H., Nordemann, A., & Piller, T. P. (2019). Towards circular business models: Identifying consumer needs based on the jobs-to-be-done theory. *Journal of Cleaner Production, 231*, 341–358. https://doi.org/10.1016/j.jclepro.2019.05.165
12. Christensen, C. M., Cook, S., & Hall, T. (2005). Marketing malpractice: The cause and the cure. *Harvard Business Review, 83*(12), 74–152. Retrieved from https://hbr.org/2005/12/marketing-malpractice-the-cause-and-the-cure. Accessed 17 Nov 2022.
13. Tajima, S. (2022). Action research on a locally oriented sustainable product. *International Journal of Automation Technology, 16*(6), 845–852. https://doi.org/10.20965/ijat.2022.p0845
14. United Nations. (2022). *The sustainable development goals report 2022*. Retrieved from https://unstats.un.org/sdgs/report/2022/The-Sustainable-Development-Goals-Report-2022.pdf. Accessed 17 Nov 2022

Part II
Challenges and Opportunities of Ocean-Link Industries

Chapter 4
Challenges Facing Ocean Education in Japanese Schools

Sachiko Oguma

Abstract To investigate the state of ocean education in Japanese schools and suggest future actions, a text analysis of the practice reports submitted by 988 schools participating in the Ocean Education Pioneer School Program (PSP) was conducted. Text-mining techniques were used to extract words describing the characteristics of the aims, results, and issues of ocean education in elementary junior high, and high schools. As a result of the analysis, it is suggested that continuation and improvement of ocean education will require cooperation among teachers within schools, with the prospect of teacher transfers, and coordination with related organizations. It is also pointed out that identifiers are needed to evaluate the contribution of universities to the schools and communities as a part of university social responsibility. Finally, a support network for ocean education is proposed as a way to address the problems identified in the practice reports, taking into consideration curriculum management as emphasized in the Courses of Study.

Keywords Ocean education · Hands-on activity · Community cooperation · Curriculum management · SDG14

4.1 Introduction

The Earth's oceans face a number of grave threats, including rising sea temperatures and ocean acidification caused by global warming, environmental pollution caused by marine debris including microplastics, declining marine resources, progressive coastal erosion, and serious maritime accidents. To realize the global goal of protecting the marine environment and promoting sustainable use of the oceans, it is important not only to develop professional human resources such as managers, administrators, and researchers who can manage the oceans appropriately, but also

S. Oguma (✉)
Ocean Policy Research Institute, The Sasakawa Peace Foundation, Tokyo, Japan
e-mail: s-oguma@spf.or.jp

M. C. Huang et al. (eds.), *Innovative Social Practice and Community-Based Approach to the Ocean*, https://doi.org/10.1007/978-981-96-9104-3_4

to promote a better understanding of the oceans among the public through activities designed to broadly disseminate ocean-related knowledge.

In Japan, "to contribute to the coexistence of the oceans and mankind," the Basic Act on Ocean Policy was enacted in 2007, which serves as the legal basis for the promotion of ocean education. Article 28 seeks "to promote school education and social education with regard to the oceans" for "that citizens shall have a better understanding of and deeper interests in the oceans" [1].

Although recommendations, opinions, and proposals [2] were put forward for implementing systematic ocean education teaching and learning based on the Courses of Study, no specific "ocean" unit was included in the 2017 revised Courses of Study [3] (hereinafter referred to simply as "the Courses of Study"). Rather, "education on the ocean" was included in the commentary on the General Provisions as one of the educational contents that should be treated across subjects related to contemporary issues [4]. In response, the Third Basic Plan for Oceans states that the Courses of Study for elementary, junior high, and high schools has been enhanced to provide more guidance on education related to the ocean. However, what should be taught as "ocean education" is not systematically defined, and even the descriptions in the General Provisions of the Courses of Study are merely excerpts from the existing content of science and social studies related to the ocean. The study of the ocean itself, including hands-on activities, is currently left to the various institutions within the field of education.

Cooperation between schools and universities, museums, NPOs, and other organizations has assumed a central role in developing community-based curricula and applying overseas educational programs in various fields. Indeed, there are multiple examples of practical research on ocean education in cooperation with local communities [5, 6]. Matsumoto et al. investigated the factors influencing the settlement orientation of children and students through educational activities based on community-based life and nature experiences by comparing the effects before and after the introduction of related educational activities [5]. Sakurai compared the educational effects, such as changes in behavior, exhibited by junior high school students who, together with local fishermen, were continually involved in the maintenance and management of the local Satoumi, with results from schools in other regions and verified the efficacy of such involvement [6] (Satoumi are coastal waters that show high biodiversity and productivity through appropriate human interventions [7]). In recent years, the global dissemination of ocean literacy [8, 9] has been facilitated mainly by IOC-UNESCO, whose efforts have been promoted by universities and NPOs in Japan [10, 11].

While ocean education is currently being addressed in concert with external organizations, the lack of an effective framework to support ocean education practices at school education sites has been identified as an important reason why proactive efforts within schools have not proliferated [12]. In promoting the spread of such education, it is important to understand the crucial elements and issues in ocean education in order to formulate meaningful proposals that meet the needs of educational fields [13]. Strengthening the development of human resources such as teachers, accumulating and verifying learning examples in schools, and developing an external support system for schools would seem essential.

In this study, practice reports written by teachers teaching classes at schools participating in the "Ocean Education Pioneer School Program" (hereinafter, PSP) were used as the primary data source. PSP is a joint project of the Nippon Foundation, the Ocean Policy Research Institute of the Sasakawa Peace Foundation, and the Center for Ocean Literacy and Education attached to the Graduate School of Education, the University of Tokyo (until FY2021) [14]. The intent of the program is to expand and improve the quality of ocean education at schools by developing curricula and fostering leaders in the field. The program provides financial support for activities at schools across Japan that are (or will be) implementing such education. Grants are available in national, public, and private pre-school facilities, elementary schools (hereinafter, ES), junior high schools (JH), high schools (HS), compulsory education schools, secondary schools, special needs schools, and technical colleges nationwide. In total, there were 988 schools and pre-school facilities participating in the program over the 6 years from FY2016 to FY2021.

The analysis was conducted based on the practice reports written at the PSP-participating ES, JH, and HS over the targeted 6-year period. The methodology used follows that of a previous study [15]. First, the location of each school, the nature of the hands-on activities undertaken, and the tendency to select cooperating organizations in the implementation of PSP ocean education were established. Next, from each school's free-text practice reports, text mining techniques to extract words that described their characteristics in terms of the aims, results, and issues of ocean education were used. Similar words that appeared in the text were coded together, and an attempt was made to understand the efforts and problems of the participating PSP schools as a whole, both quantitatively and qualitatively, as indicated by the frequency of occurrence of the codes. Finally, based on the results of these analyses, the role of ocean education implemented through the cooperation between the communities and the schools was established, and the issues reported by the field regarding the implementation and continuation of ocean education, as well as their possible solutions, were identified.

4.2 Status of Implementation at PSP Participating Schools

Of the schools and pre-school facilities participating in the PSP to date, the current study included the practice reports of those schools (ES, JH, and HS) that had participated in the unit development sector between FY 2016 and FY 2021—a total of 963 schools over this 6-year period (the 25 participating pre-school facilities were not included). The location of each school is shown in Fig. 4.1.

Each individual participant in the PSP is essentially able to decide the themes, hours, and hands-on activities devoted to ocean education. Thus, the amount and nature of the information in the reports differs from school to school. To the extent possible, common information obtained from the descriptions included in the reports was tabulated. This includes (1) distance between school and ocean, (2) activity themes, and (3) cooperating organizations/schools.

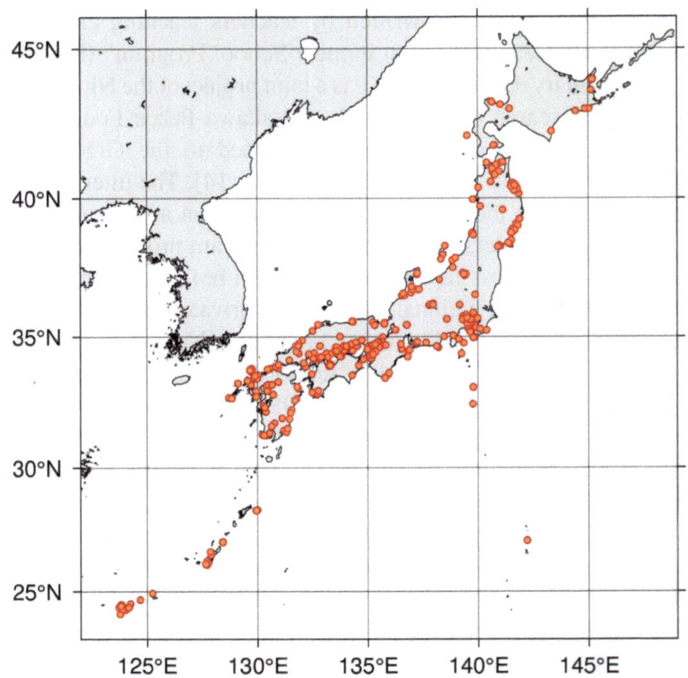

Fig. 4.1 Distribution of PSP-participating schools. Source: compiled by the author

4.2.1 Distance Between School and Ocean

The "National Survey on the Status of Ocean education Implementation in Elementary and Secondary Schools" (hereinafter, "National Survey") has indicated that there is a significant relationship between a school's distance from the ocean and the level of awareness and implementation of ocean education [16]. However, in this study, only a few practical reports directly mentioned the distance in numerical terms, and most of them used experiential expressions such as "can see the ocean from my school," "can walk to shore," or "cannot see the sea daily." Therefore, the direct distance between the school and the nearest shoreline, denoted as d_{sea}, was calculated using a map, although the distance between the school and the sea may be shorter than the length of the path.

Figure 4.2 shows the frequency distribution of d_{sea}. The d_{sea} values were classified into three levels (0–1 km, 1–5 km, and 5 km or more) using the "15-minute walk" and "1-hour walk," which are the boundaries of the "National Survey" [16] classification, as a yardstick. Excluding the duplication of schools participating in multiple years, 218 schools were in the 0–1 km category, 101 schools were in the 1–5 km category, and 111 schools were in the 5 km or more category.

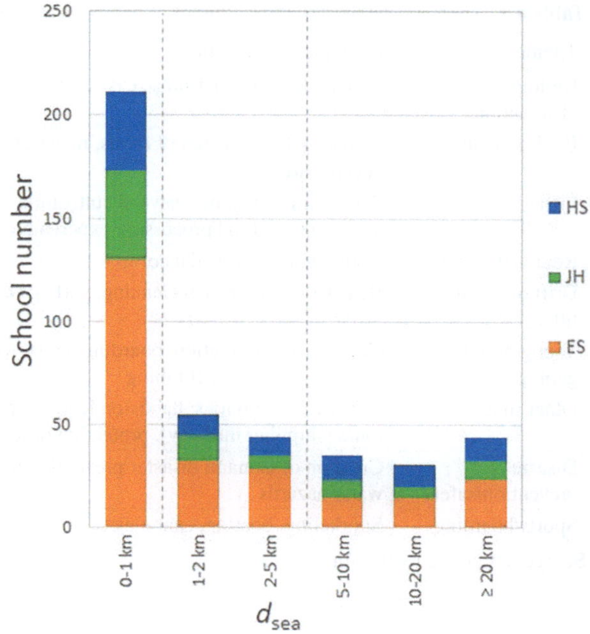

Fig. 4.2 Frequency distribution of the linear distance between the school and the sea (d_{sea}). Dotted lines indicate the 1 km and 5 km boundaries. Source: compiled by the author

4.2.2 Themes of Hands-On Activity

Many different hands-on activities are incorporated into ocean education. Among the various activities undertaken by each school, those with similar content were categorized based on the themes shown in Table 4.1.

Figures 4.3, 4.4, and 4.5 show the percentage of schools that engaged in activities in each thematic category, by school type. As indicated, the percentage of schools that engaged in "Biological observation" activities was high for all three school types. On the other hand, the percentage of schools that engaged in "Topography/Geology" to study coastal landforms and strata structure and "Disaster prevention/Safety" to prepare for tsunami and other disasters and marine accidents was low. The overall trend was that some schools cancelled or changed the content of their hands-on activities, such as group travel to the sea or cooking and eating local cuisine, because of the COVID-19 pandemic. Among the schools, the percentage of JH that were engaged in activities in the "Drift object/Marine litter" thematic category was higher than in the previous year, partly because it was a priority theme of the unit development sector of the PSP in FY2021. As for differences among school types, the percentage of schools engaged in hands-on activities was generally lower in HS.

Table 4.1 Thematic categories and examples of hands-on activities

Theme	Examples of activities
Biological observation	Observation at aquariums/seashores, biological observation in laboratories
Environment	Water quality research of rivers, material cycles between terrestrial and oceanic areas
Fisheries	Set netting, wakame seaweed cultivation experience, hatching and hatchling, seafood processing experience
Regional culture	Cooking, literature, dance
Drift object/marine litter	Beachcombing, beach cleaning, garbage collection in the bay by boat
Topography/ geology	Geological observation, boarding a boat to observe coastal landforms from offshore, mountain climbing
Other industries	Paddy field activities, hands-on learning of buckwheat cultivation, port tours (shipping industry), protection of tourism resources
Disaster prevention/safety	Creation of tsunami disaster prevention maps, swim in clothes to prevent water hazards
Sports/boarding	Snorkeling, boating, canoeing

Source: compiled by the author

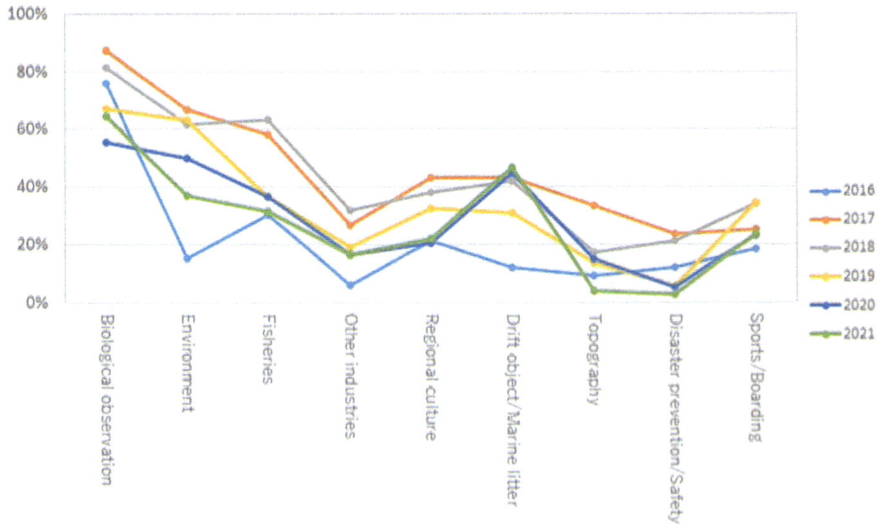

Fig. 4.3 Percentage of ES by themes of hands-on activities per year. Source: compiled by the author

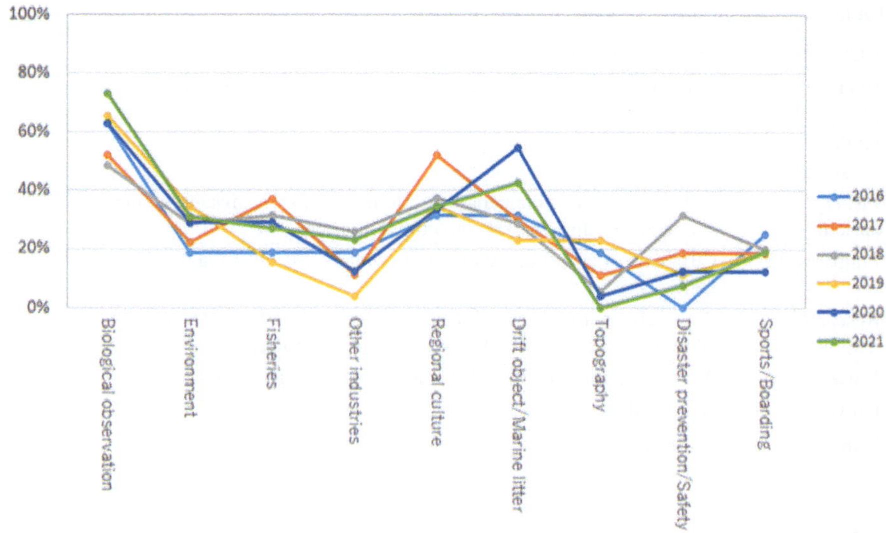

Fig. 4.4 Percentage of JH by themes of hands-on activities per year. Source: compiled by the author

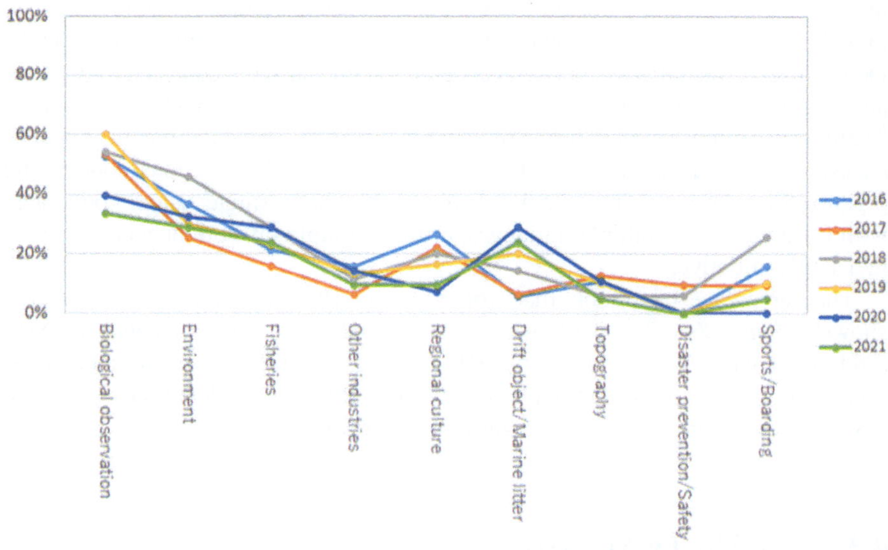

Fig. 4.5 Percentage of HS by themes of hands-on activities per year. Source: compiled by the author

Table 4.2 Classification of cooperating organizations

Classified name	Institutional examples
Regional private	Individuals, stores, private companies (excluding fisheries)
NPO organization	NPOs, foundations, incorporated associations
Fishery/ agriculture	Fishermen, fishing cooperatives, fishing groups, freshwater fishing cooperatives, agricultural cooperatives, farmers
Public agency	City halls, ward offices, community centers, MLIT-affiliated offices, public facilities
Research institute	Research institute, research center, fisheries experiment station, fisheries laboratory, research and development organization
Museum	Aquarium, museum, historical museum, exhibition hall
University	Universities

Source: compiled by the author

4.2.3 Cooperating Organizations and Schools

In Japanese schools, classes are given not only by teachers on campus, but also by invited outside lecturers. Local professionals such as fishermen or people engaged in volunteer activities are sometimes invited to speak as experts in their fields. Depending on the initiative, personal cooperation may also be requested for the pre- and post-teaching of hands-on activities; for example, cooking and marine sports. There is also cooperation in terms of using facilities for tours and practical experiences, such as aquaculture farms, ships, and factories. The various cooperating organizations are listed in Table 4.2. It is possible that a single school cooperated with institutions for multiple initiatives, or that multiple institutions were involved in a single initiative.

The percentage of schools that worked with each cooperating organization is shown in Figs. 4.6, 4.7, and 4.8. Although there was some variation between years, a relatively large number of ES and JH cooperated with local private companies, non-profit organizations, and public institutions. On the other hand, nearly half of HS cooperated with universities, regardless of the year.

4.3 Text-Mining Analysis

The PSP asks participating schools to submit practice reports summarizing their efforts during the year. The reports summarize the aims of the study, the results obtained, and the issues that arose, from the planning of the study curriculum to its implementation and review at the end of the school year. Because they are free descriptions, the reports differ in their specifics; however, it is likely that common aims, results, and issues would exist across the various reports. Therefore, a text

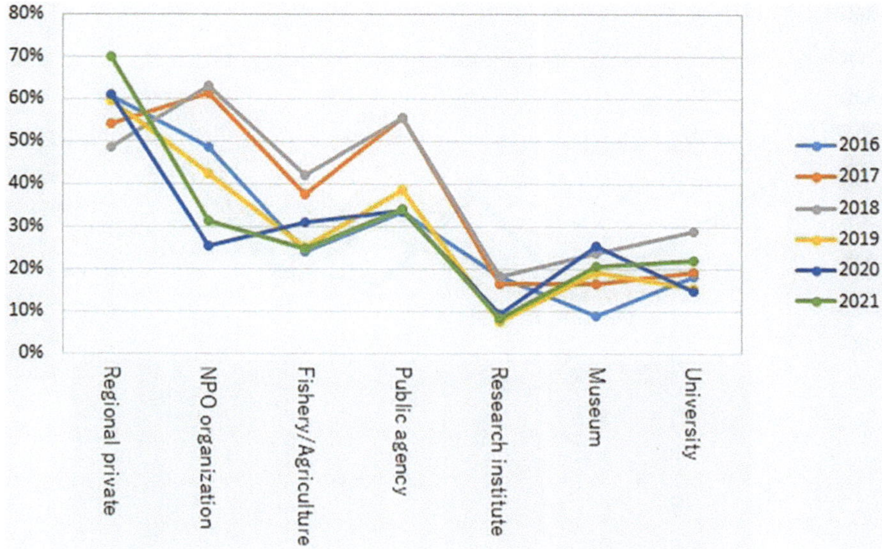

Fig. 4.6 Percentages of ES by cooperating organization as shown in Table 4.2 per year. Source: compiled by the author

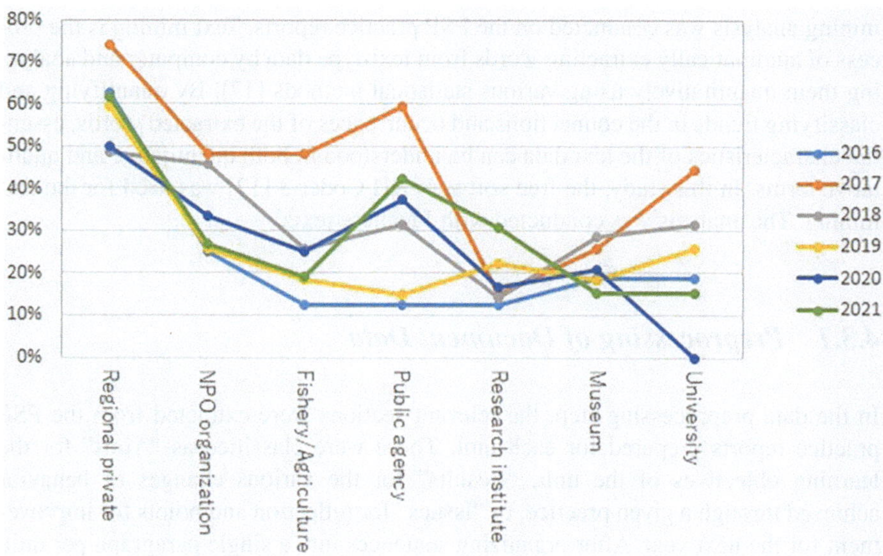

Fig. 4.7 Percentages of JH by cooperating organization as shown in Table 4.2 per year. Source: compiled by the author

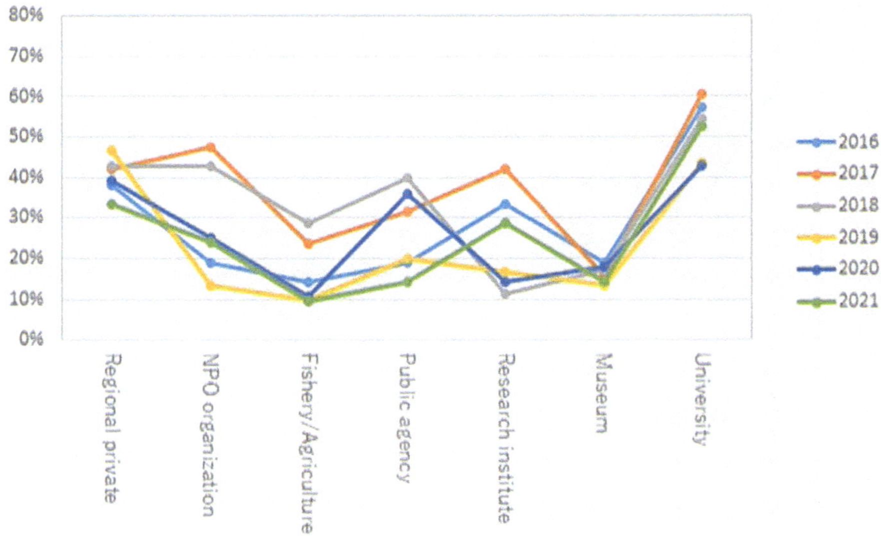

Fig. 4.8 Percentages of HS by cooperating organization as shown in Table 4.2 per year. Source: compiled by the author

mining analysis was conducted on the PSP practice reports. Text mining is the process of automatically extracting words from text-type data by computer and analyzing them quantitatively using various statistical methods [17]. By quantifying and classifying trends in the connections and occurrences of the extracted words, essential characteristics of the text data can be understood in both quantitative and qualitative terms. In this study, the free software KH Coder 3 [17] was used for the text mining. The analysis was conducted with Japanese texts.

4.3.1 Preprocessing of Document Data

In the data preprocessing step, the relevant sections were extracted from the PSP practice reports prepared for each unit. These were classified as "Aims" for the learning objectives of the unit, "Results" for the various changes of behavior achieved through a given practice, or "Issues" for reflection and points for improvement for the next year. After organizing sentences into a single paragraph per unit, the documents were divided into "Aims," "Results," and "Issues" by school type (ES, JH, or HS).

In addition, to prevent the occurrence of a word from affecting the frequency of other words that occur at the same time within a sentence (word co-occurrence), the names of places to be visited and organisms to be observed were excluded to the extent that the context was not broken. Furthermore, synonymous words were replaced with typical words with the same meaning, while taking the context into consideration.

Next, a morphological analysis was performed to extract words from the documents using KH Coder 3. A morpheme is the smallest meaningful constituent within a given word; for example, in Japanese, "kaiyoukyouiku" (ocean education) contains two morphemes, kaiyou (ocean) + kyouiku (education). The document was broken down into morphemes and converted into a form that could be analyzed quantitatively. However, words that are often used in compound, such as "ocean education," were not separated into morphemes, but were set to be extracted as the entire compound. Among morphemes, proper nouns, names of organizations, people, places, interjections, negative auxiliary verbs, adverbs, and adjectives were excluded before the final analysis. Tables 4.3, 4.4, and 4.5 summarize the numbers of sentences and paragraphs used and the number of words found in the text mining analysis of each document. The 30 most frequent words in the "Aims," "Results," and "Issues" documents for each school type are shown in Tables 4.6, 4.7, and 4.8.

Following the morphological analysis, a co-occurrence network analysis to capture document features was performed on a sentence-by-sentence basis; coding was performed on a paragraph-by-paragraph basis, allowing paragraphs to have multiple features (codes).

Table 4.3 Numbers of sentences and paragraphs used in text mining analysis

	Aims		Results		Issues	
School types	Sentence	Paragraph	Sentence	Paragraph	Sentence	Paragraph
ES	1271	631	2584	666	1834	633
JH	579	228	908	248	672	229
HS	683	253	981	255	831	236

Source: compiled by the author

Table 4.4 Number of total words used in text mining analysis. Numbers within brackets indicate words used for analysis, which do not contain particles and auxiliary verbs

School types	Aims	Results	Issues
ES	49,781 (21,130)	87,002 (33,979)	54,726 (21,103)
JH	21,261 (9175)	31,057 (12,442)	19,943 (7733)
HS	24,793 (2436)	31,953 (12,949)	25,552 (10,295)

Source: compiled by the author

Table 4.5 Numbers of different words used in text mining analysis. Numbers within brackets indicate words used for analysis, which do not contain particles and auxiliary verbs

School types	Aims	Results	Issues
ES	2763 (2134)	4390 (3383)	3391 (2635)
JH	1920 (1510)	2693 (2078)	2144 (1677)
HS	2436 (1912)	3038 (2365)	2660 (2036)

Source: compiled by the author

Table 4.6 Thirty most frequent words in "Aims." Paragraphs were classified by school type (ES, JH, and HS) for the analysis. Note that the analysis was conducted in Japanese.

ES			JH			HS		
Extracted words			Extracted words			Extracted words		
Japanese	English	Frequency	Japanese	English	Frequency	Japanese	English	Frequency
海	Sea	1019	海	Sea	323	海	Sea	214
地域	Regional	546	地域	Regional	234	海洋	Ocean	156
考える	Think	320	生徒	Pupil	148	地域	Regional	143
学習	Learn	291	学習	Learn	118	理解	Understanding	139
自分	Myself	279	活動	Activity	108	生物	Living thing	134
活動	Activity	257	学ぶ	Study	105	生徒	Pupil	132
児童	Children	245	考える	Think	91	学習	Learn	126
生き物	Living thing	230	知る	Know	87	考える	Think	115
環境	Environment	208	理解	Understanding	79	学ぶ	Study	110
自然	Nature	206	海洋	Ocean	74	行う	Do	110
知る	Know	175	自然	Nature	74	環境	Environment	81
調べる	Examine	164	環境	Environment	73	活動	Activity	79
学ぶ	Study	136	自分	Myself	72	研究	Research	76
理解	Understanding	136	生物	Living thing	65	生態系	Ecosystem	70
身近	Familiar	133	生活	Life	64	育成	Training	64
守る	Secure	130	育成	Training	62	保護	Conservation	60
関心	Concern	127	行う	Do	62	資源	Resource	58
生活	Life	123	保護	Conservation	60	問題	Problem	58
気付く	Aware	119	深める	Deepen	49	海洋環境	Ocean environment	50
育成	Training	115	体験	Experience	46	深める	Deepen	49
大切	Cherish	110	身近	Familiar	43	解決	Resolve	47
行う	Do	109	育てる	Rear	42	調査	Survey	45
川	River	107	持つ	Have	42	興味	Interest	44

育てる	Rear	105	自然環境	Natural environment	42	知識	Knowledge	44
高める	Enhance	104	学び	Study	39	基礎	Basis	42
豊か	Rich	103	海洋教育	Ocean education	37	授業	Lesson	42
関わる	Affect	101	観察	Observation	36	自然	Nature	41
持つ	Have	99	実践	Practice	35	実習	Practice	41
問題	Problem	98	単元	Teaching unit	35	力	Power	41
体験	Experience	92	関心	Concern	33	関心	Concern	40

Source: compiled by the author

Table 4.7 Thirty most frequent words in “Results” (Table 4.6 notes apply)

ES			JH			HS		
Extracted words			Extracted words			Extracted words		
Japanese	English	Frequency	Japanese	English	Frequency	Japanese	English	Frequency
児童	Children	863	海	Sea	327	生徒	Pupil	341
海	Sea	831	生徒	Pupil	295	活動	Activity	162
学習	Learn	595	学習	Learn	172	研究	Research	140
活動	Activity	503	地域	Regional	170	海	Sea	131
地域	Regional	474	活動	Activity	160	行う	Do	126
自分	Myself	443	考える	Think	117	考える	Think	120
考える	Think	335	学ぶ	Study	105	地域	Regional	117
知る	Know	229	行う	Do	96	学習	Learn	107
体験	Experience	205	体験	Experience	95	理解	Understanding	95
見る	See	202	海洋教育	Ocean education	91	授業	Recture	79
行う	Do	192	自分	Myself	87	学ぶ	Study	78
環境	Environment	190	環境	Environment	69	実習	Practice	78
生き物	Living thing	190	生物	Living thing	67	海洋	Ocean	74
感じる	Feel	176	見る	See	65	発表	Presentation	65
学ぶ	Study	156	理解	Understanding	62	調査	Survey	63
関心	Concern	152	知る	Know	58	実施	Implementation	62
自然	Nature	148	海洋	Ocean	57	感じる	Feel	59
調べる	Examine	148	自然	Nature	56	見る	See	57
身近	Familiar	142	実践	Practice	56	生物	Biology	57
発表	Presentation	142	持つ	Have	50	興味	Interest	56
意識	Awareness	139	機会	Opportunity	49	観察	Observation	54
理解	Understanding	137	意識	Awareness	48	関心	Concern	53
取り組む	Initiative	128	感じる	Feel	48	自分	Myself	53

意欲	Will	125	調査	Survey	46	取り組む	Initiative	50
ゴミ	Litter	118	観察	Observation	45	問題	Social distance	49
興味	Interest	116	関心	Concern	44	環境	Environment	48
高める	Enhance	114	思う	Think	42	思う	Think	48
持つ	Have	114	取り組む	Initiative	41	内容	Think	45
気付く	Aware	113	授業	Lecture	40	海洋教育	Ocean education	43
守る	Secure	113	学校	School	39	体験	Experience	43

Source: compiled by the author

Table 4.8 Thirty most frequent words in "Issues" (Table 4.6 notes apply)

ES			JH			HS		
Extracted words			Extracted words			Extracted words		
Japanese	English	Frequency	Japanese	English	Frequency	Japanese	English	Frequency
活動	Activity	397	生徒	Pupil	134	生徒	Pupil	171
学習	Learn	381	必要	Necessity	128	活動	Activity	140
必要	Nessesity	377	学習	Learn	120	必要	Necessity	139
児童	Children	371	考える	Think	113	行う	Do	123
考える	Think	262	海	Ocean	100	研究	Research	117
海	Ocean	250	活動	Activity	95	考える	Think	114
地域	Regional	162	行う	Do	82	今後	Hereafter	80
行う	Do	151	地域	Regional	67	時間	Time/period	79
時間	Time/period	141	海洋教育	Ocean education	63	実施	Implementation	77
計画	Plan	133	時間	Time/period	63	地域	Regional	63
今後	Hereafter	126	今後	Hereafter	58	連携	Cooperation	63
海洋教育	Ocean education	121	継続	Continuation	45	学習	Learn	61
自分	Myself	121	実施	Implementation	45	実習	Training	57
感じる	Feel	115	計画	Plan	42	授業	Lecture	54
連携	Cooperation	112	学ぶ	Study	41	海洋	Ocean	53
内容	Contents	102	次	Next	41	継続	Continuation	52
教員	Teacher	100	授業	Lecture	39	次	Next	51
単元	Teaching unit	98	内容	Contents	38	教員	Teacher	49
学校	School	95	学年	Grade	37	計画	Plan	48
環境	Environment	93	教員	Teacher	36	指導	Guidance	47
実施	Implementation	91	思う	Think	36	内容	Contents	47
学年	Grade	90	指導	Guidance	36	海	Sea	46
学ぶ	Study	85	連携	Cooperation	35	調査	Survey	46
体験	Experience	82	感じる	Feel	34	発表	Presentation	42

意識	Awareness	81	取り組む	Initiative	34	事前	Prior	41
実践	Practice	81	体験	Experience	34	生物	Living thing	39
工夫	Device	77	実践	Practice	33	テーマ	Theme	38
取り組む	Initiative	75	学校	School	32	観察	Observation	38
生き物	Living thing	75	情報	Information	30	環境	Environment	37
発表	Presentation	71	生物	Living thing	30	十分	Necessity	36

Source: compiled by the author

4.3.2 Co-Occurrence Network

Co-occurrence networks were created to show the characteristic connections among the extracted words in the "Aims," "Results," and "Issues" documents. A co-occurrence network indicates the co-occurrence between extracted words at the sentence level. Visually, the number of occurrences is proportional to the size of the circle shown in the network diagram; the strength and relevance of the co-occurrence are expressed by the presence or absence of lines connecting the circles. These connections between extracted words provide an effective visual representation of the characteristic themes of the document.

The Jaccard coefficient, which can be used as a basic measure of similarity between texts [18], was applied to quantify the strength of the association or co-occurrence relationship between words. In general, the Jaccard coefficient measures the similarity between two sets. For example, let set $A = \{x, y, v, w\}$ and set $B = \{x, y, z\}$. The Jaccard coefficient is calculated as the number of members common to both sets, divided by the number of members in either of the two sets, including any members in both. Here, the Jaccard coefficient would be calculated as

$$\frac{number\left(A \cap B\right)}{number\left(A \cup B\right)} = \frac{2}{5} = 0.4$$

Frequency in the co-occurrence network diagram is the number of times the extracted word appears in a sentence; the subgraphs are groupings of words that are automatically detected when they form relatively strong connections to each other.

4.3.3 Coding

Extracted words with high frequency of occurrence, words that are similar to them in meaning and usage, and words that are closely related in the co-occurrence network are summarized as "feature words" that represent characteristics of the document. These are grouped together and assigned as "codes," and their grouping rules were defined as "coding rules." The coding rules are then used to classify paragraphs that referred to a certain subject or matter by automatically assigning a code to the extracted words in the document. In this study, the same coding rules were applied to the "Aims," "Results," and "Issues" documents. The percentages of occurrence for each code in a paragraph were compared in order to quantify the difference in content between them. However, since KH Coder 3 gives multiple codes when multiple coding rules apply to an article, each paragraph is represented by a combination of multiple codes, and co-occurrences of codes are expected.

4.3.4 Cross-Analysis

To assess d_{sea} as an external factor, a cross-tabulation was conducted between the number of paragraphs of each code and d_{sea}. d_{sea} was set at three levels, bounded by 1 km and 5 km, as indicated by the dotted lines in Fig. 4.2. The chi-square (χ^2) test is often used as a method for cross-tabulation. However, for some codes, the expected frequency was less than five. For this reason, the p-values from Fisher's exact test [19, 20] were used for the evaluation.

4.4 Results

4.4.1 Co-Occurrence Network

The co-occurrence networks for the "Aims," "Results," and "Issues" documents for each school type are shown in Figs. 4.9, 4.10, 4.11, 4.12, 4.13, 4.14, 4.15, 4.16, and 4.17. The words used in the network diagram were limited to the top 20–30 words included in Tables 4.6, 4.7, and 4.8 so that the distribution of lines among the extracted words would not become too complicated. It should be noted that all co-occurrence frequencies were estimated using extracted words in Japanese.

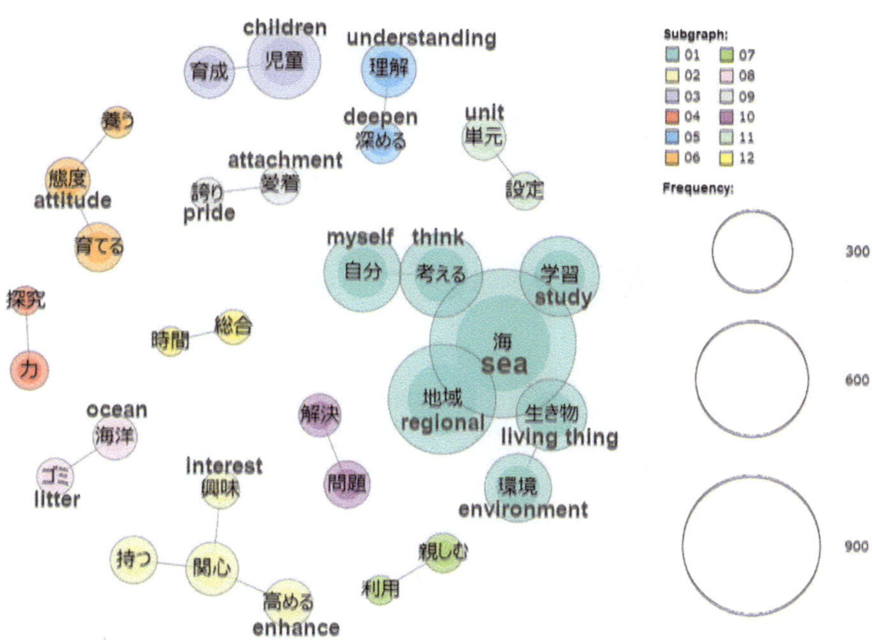

Fig. 4.9 Co-occurrence networks for "Aims" in ES. Note that Japanese words are used to estimate the Jaccard coefficients for drawing the co-occurrence network. Source: compiled by the author

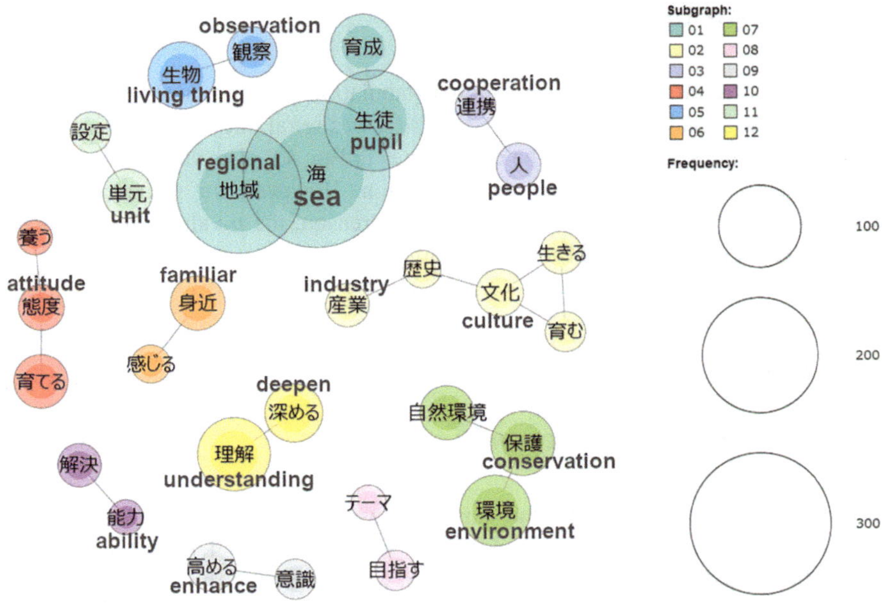

Fig. 4.10 Co-occurrence networks for "Aims" in JH (Fig. 4.9 notes apply). Source: compiled by the author

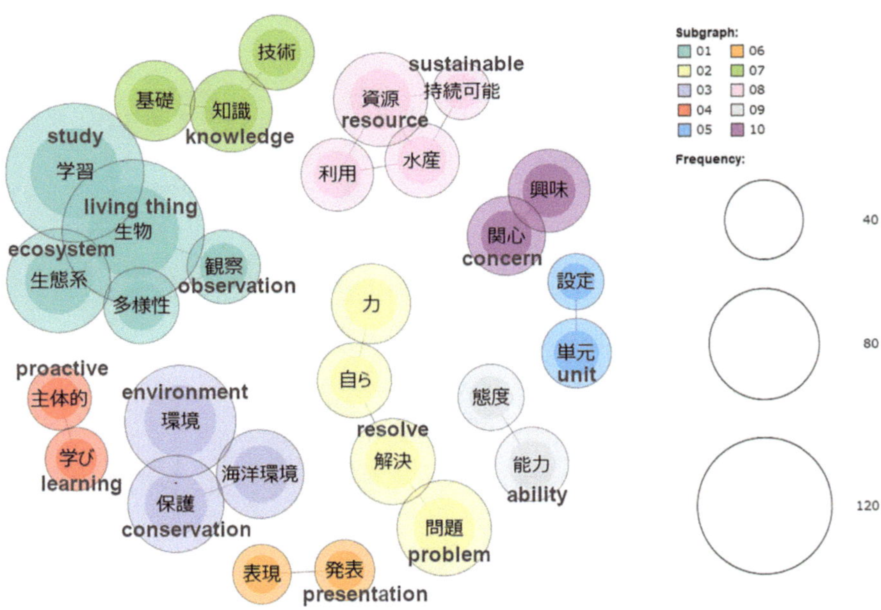

Fig. 4.11 Co-occurrence networks for "Aims" of HS (Fig. 4.9 notes apply). Source: compiled by the author

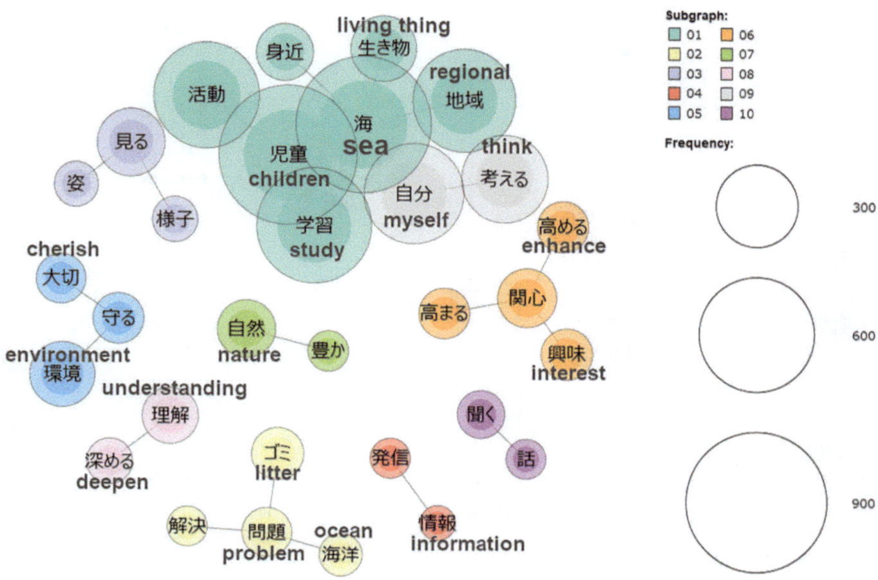

Fig. 4.12 Co-occurrence networks for "Results" in ES (Fig. 4.9 notes apply). Source: compiled by the author

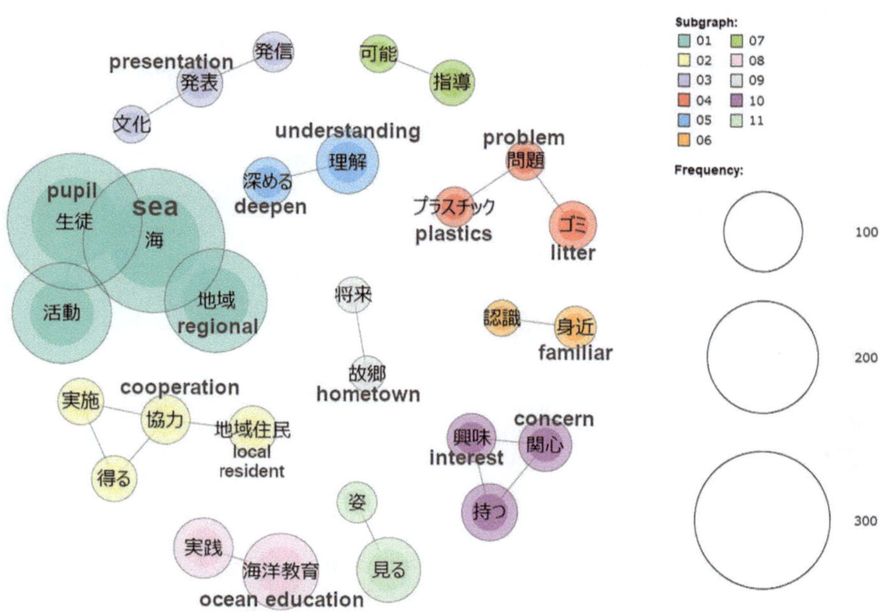

Fig. 4.13 Co-occurrence networks for "Results" in JH (Fig. 4.9 notes apply). Source: compiled by the author

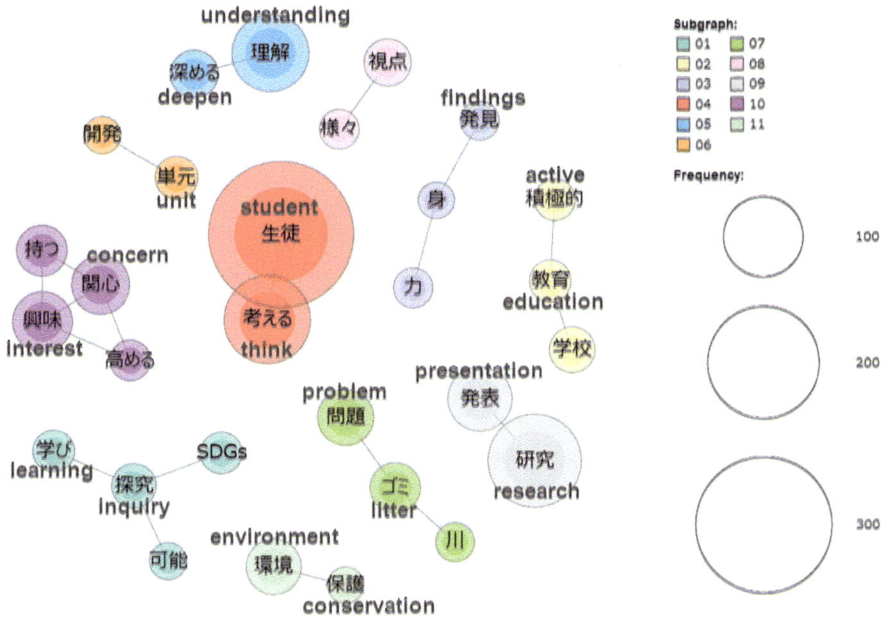

Fig. 4.14 Co-occurrence networks for "Results" in HS (Fig. 4.9 notes apply). Source: compiled by the author

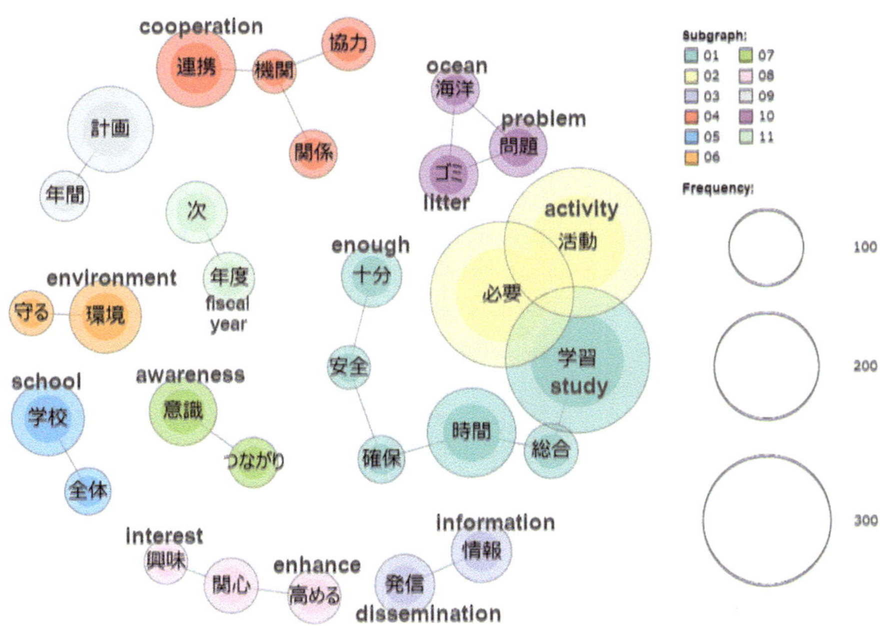

Fig. 4.15 Co-occurrence networks for "Issues" in ES (Fig. 4.9 notes apply). Source: compiled by the author

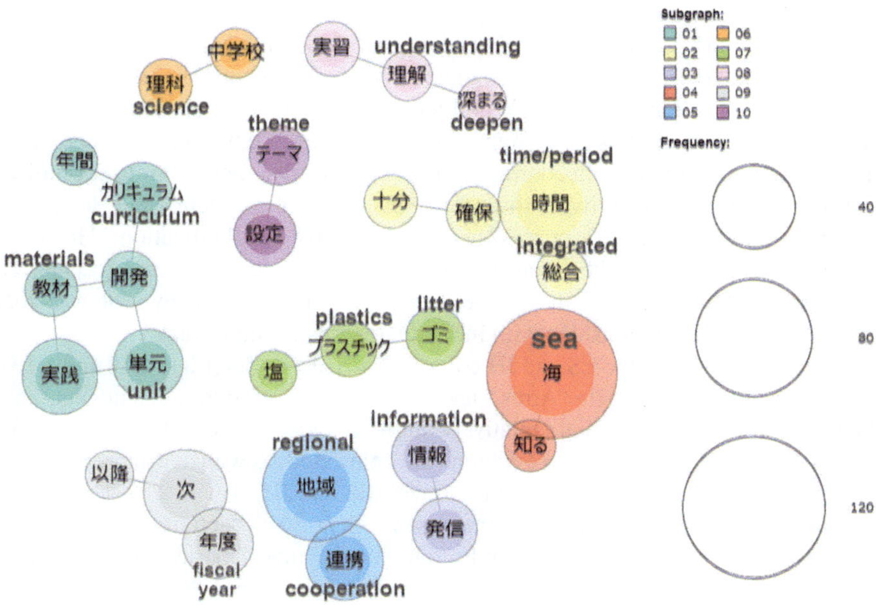

Fig. 4.16 Co-occurrence networks for "Issues" in JH (Fig. 4.9 notes apply). Source: compiled by the author

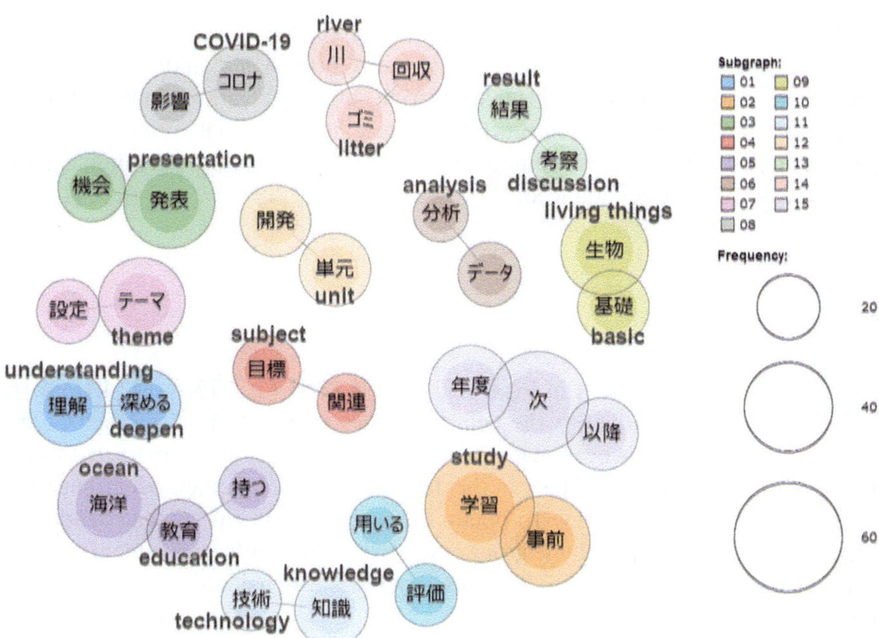

Fig. 4.17 Co-occurrence networks for "Issues" in HS (Fig. 4.9 notes apply). Source: compiled by the author

In the co-occurrence networks of the extracted words for the "Aims" of ES and JH (Figs. 4.9 and 4.10), words such as "region," "student," and "myself" are connected around "sea," which has the highest frequency of occurrence (see Table 4.6). In ES, "ocean" is linked to "litter," "problem," "solution," and "proactive," while in JH, "conservation" is linked to "environment," "natural environment," and "attitude," among other words. In contrast, in the HS networks, there is more specialization as a unit theme, from "living things" to "diversity," "ecosystem," and "learning," and from "fisheries" and "resources" to "sustainability" and "utilization." However, the extracted words with the greatest occurrence frequencies, "sea" and "ocean," do not appear in Fig. 4.11. This may be because they appear in so many sentences that the co-occurrence relationships with individual words become weak.

As for "Results," in the ES and JH co-occurrence networks (Figs. 4.12 and 4.13), "sea" is the main word, as in "Aims," and "community," "children," "students," and "activity" are connected with relatively high frequency (see Table 4.7). In HS (Fig. 4.14), "research" and "presentation" are connected, as well as "interest," "concern," "litter," and "problem," in common with ES and JH.

On the other hand, for "Issues," "necessity," "learning," "activities," "children," and "students" appear more frequently than "ocean" and "marine" for all school types (see Table 4.8). Around them, connections such as "time," "secure," "information," "transmission," "next," and "year" are formed. Connections such as "collaboration," "institution," and "cooperation" are also found in ES, "region," "cooperation," "unit," "development," and "practice" in JH, and "knowledge" and "technology" in HS.

Thus, the words that co-occur and are central to the connections among "Aims," "Results," and "Issues" documents are different. While "Aims" and "Results" have strong co-occurrence relationships that describe children's learning in the local sea, "Issues" has more frequent occurrence of words related to school initiatives, such as cooperation with the local community and in-school instructional planning, and the connections are more pronounced.

4.4.2 Coding

The co-occurrence networks in Figs. 4.9, 4.10, 4.11, 4.12, 4.13, 4.14, 4.15, 4.16, and 4.17 allow us to identify the central themes in the "Aims," "Results," and "Issues" documents. However, many extracted words similar to the extracted words with the highest frequency appear in the documents, although their occurrence frequency may be relatively low. To obtain the actual document content trends, the documents were coded to include groups of such similar words, and content changes were quantified for the "Aims," "Results," and "Issues" using the occurrence frequency of the codes.

To code the "Aims," "Results," and "Issues" documents, coding rules for extracted words such as those shown in Table 4.9 were developed based on the connections among the extracted words in the co-occurrence network and the extracted words included in Tables 4.6, 4.7, and 4.8. To reflect the content of the original

Table 4.9 Coding rules applied to keywords extracted from the documents. Note that the analysis was conducted in Japanese

コード群 code group	Code	Feature words (excerpts)
校内対応 In-school coordination	Teachers	Teacher, mentor
	School/grade support	School, grade, system, continuation
	Syllabus and contents	Plan, syllabus, curriculum, subject
	Learning environment	Materials, fundings
	Training and preparation	TRAINING, preparation
	Weather	weather, season
校内外の連携 Cooperation inside and outside school	Cooperation	Cooperation, burden, schedule
	External organization and university	External, organization, research institute, university
	Local community and hometown	Region, local, local residents
児童の学び Children's learning activities	Hands-on activity	Hands-on activities, experience
	Children's learning	Study, understanding, think
	Inquiry-based learning	Inquiry, research
	Information dissemination	Information, dissemination
児童の変容 Children's change of behavior	Qualities, abilities, attitudes	Qualities, abilities, attitudes
	Interests and concerns	Interests, concerns
	Attachment, mind, pride	Attachment, mind, pride
活動テーマ Activity theme	Sea/ocean	Sea, ocean, ocean environment, shore
	Other nature	Forest, river, mountain
	Living things	Living things (fish, mollusk, etc.), ecosystem
	Environmental issues	Environment problem/conservation
	People, culture, history	People, culture, history, local cuisine
	Industry and resource	Industry, resources, fisheries
	Global warming and acidification	Global warming, carbon dioxide, acidification
	Marine litter, plastics, cleaning	Litter, plastics, cleaning
	Sea grass (blue carbon)	Sea grass, seaweed, eel grass
概念·専門性 Concept and expertise	Science	Science, technology
	Global	Worldwide, global
	Sustainability	ESD, SDG, sustainable
	Infectious disease control	COVID-19, infectious disease control
	Ocean education	Familiar with/know/utilize/protect the ocean, ocean education
	Disaster prevention and safety	Disaster prevention (bosai), tsunami, evacuation

Source: compiled by the author

sentences and paragraphs as much as possible, some codes, such as "learning environment," "attachment, mind, pride," and "weather," were additionally set. Feature words grouped as code "attachment, mind, pride" were necessary to consider that school learning could change student minds regarding the local community [5]. However, these words did not appear in Tables 4.6, 4.7, and 4.8 or the co-occurrence networks, because of their relatively low occurrence frequency or co-occurrence. There were no restrictions or rules regarding the number of extracted words that could be included in a single code.

The 31 codes in Table 4.9 were classified as code groups according to location (school or community), change in pupils (learning or behaviors), and theme or concept of learning. The percentage of paragraphs in the "Aims," "Results," and "Issues" documents for each code is shown in Figs. 4.18, 4.19, and 4.20 by school type. The three school types have in common that the percentage of the codes "syllabus and contents," "hands-on activity," "children's learning," "sea/ocean," and "other nature" are significantly high. In addition, "interests and concerns" and "people, culture, history" tended to be high in "Aims" and "Results." On the other hand, the codes "living things" and "marine litter, plastics, cleaning," which are included in the code group "activity theme," appear relatively lower, at approximately 10%. The occurrence frequency of the code "local community and hometown" is around 70% for "Aims" in ES and JH, but only about 40% in HS. The frequency of the code "attachment, mind, pride" tends to decrease since emotional attachment to the community becomes less important in the higher grades.

4.4.3 Cross-Analysis

The previous section describing coding by paragraph (unit) for "Aims," "Results," and "Issues" indicated that the most frequently appearing codes differ among school types; however, past national surveys have shown that efforts and interest in ocean education vary with the distance of the school from the ocean [16]. Therefore, a cross-analysis using Fisher's exact probability test [19, 20] was conducted for the codes and d_{sea} to evaluate the null hypothesis that "there is no relationship between the theme of the report and d_{sea}." The hypothesis was tested at the 5% significance level with the number of schools of each code.

Figure 4.21 gives the results of the cross-analysis. As shown in the figure, relatively many codes for ES produced significant results at the 5% level, with the code group "children's change of behavior" and the codes "local community and hometown" and "hands-on activities" showing significance at the 1% level. The indication is that the occurrence of these codes, particularly in the "Aims" and "Results" documents of ES, is related to the school's distance from the sea. Among ten codes for "Aims" documents of ES with significance at the 1% level, percentage of d_{sea} of the schools where the units were developed were compared. As shown in Fig. 4.22, more than 40% of the units coded as "global" and "sustainability" were developed in ES more than 5 km from the sea, while over 70% of the units assigned other codes were in ES less than 5 km from the sea.

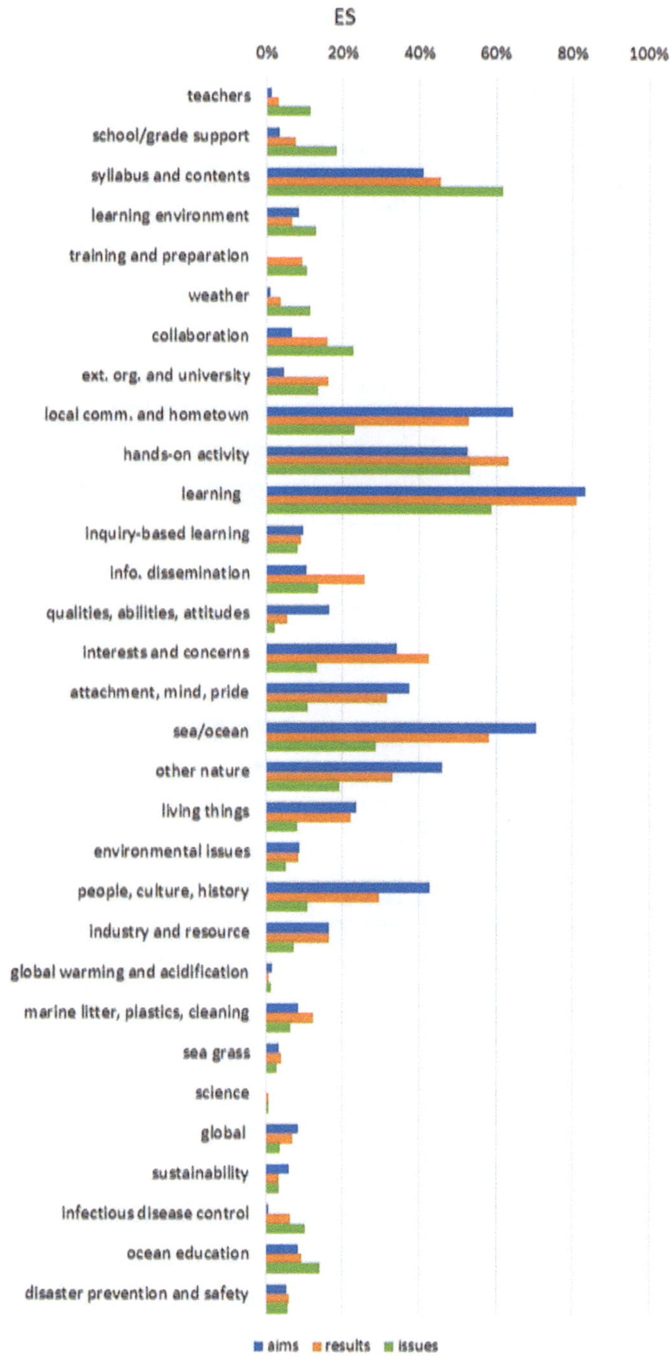

Fig. 4.18 Paragraph ratio of each code for "Aims"/"Results"/"Issues" in ES. Source: compiled by the author

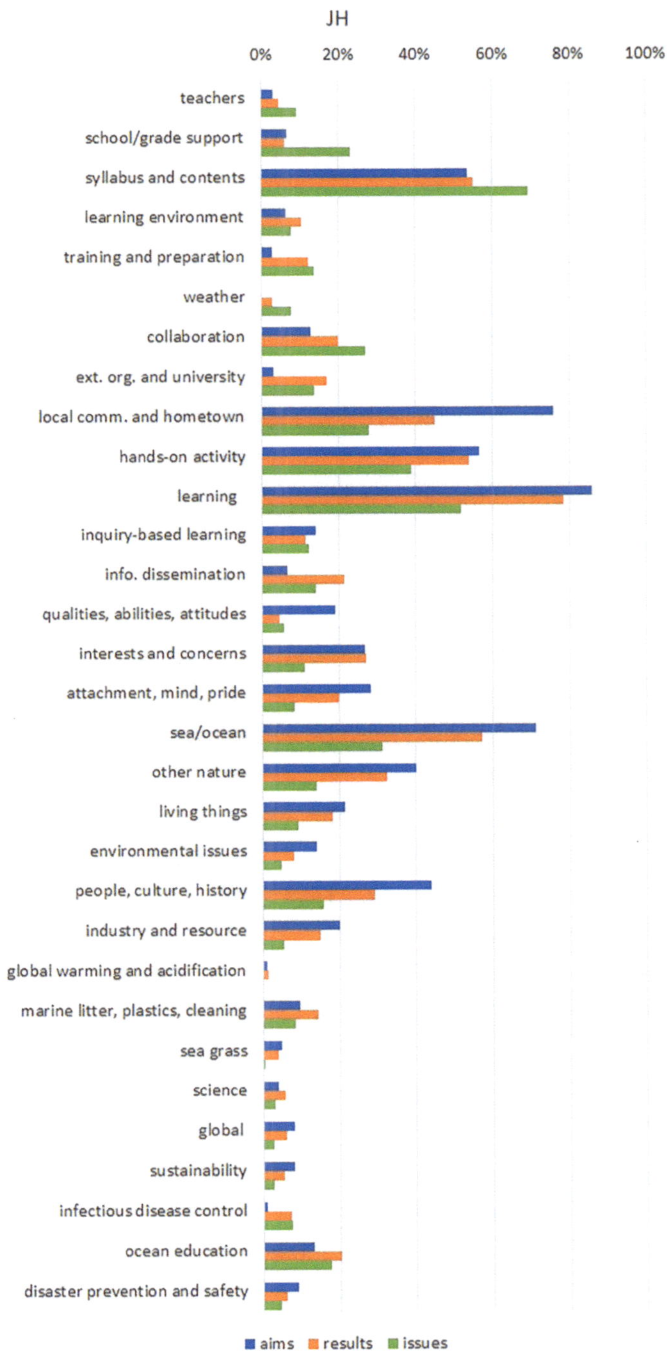

Fig. 4.19 Paragraph ratio of each code for "Aims"/"Results"/"Issues" in JH. Source: compiled by the author

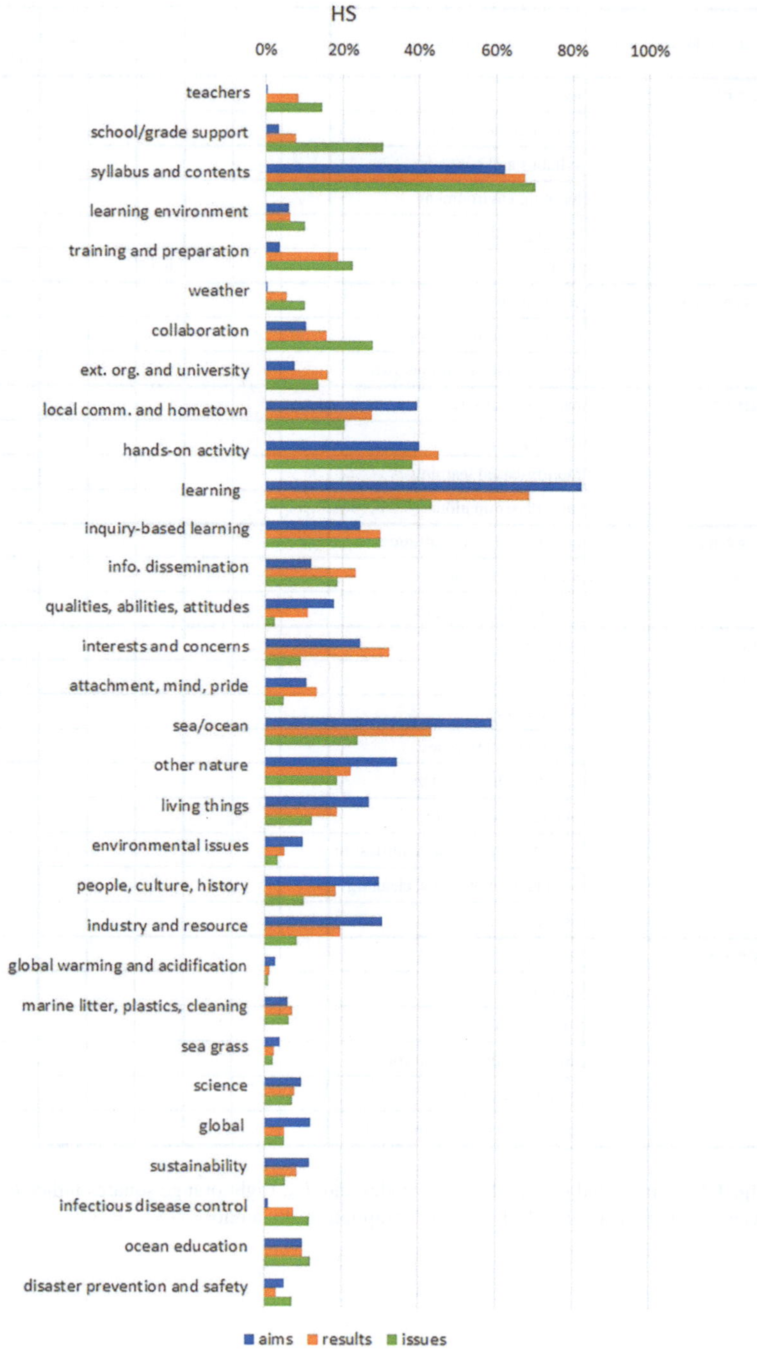

Fig. 4.20 Paragraph ratio of each code for "Aims"/"Results"/"Issues" in HS. Source: compiled by the author

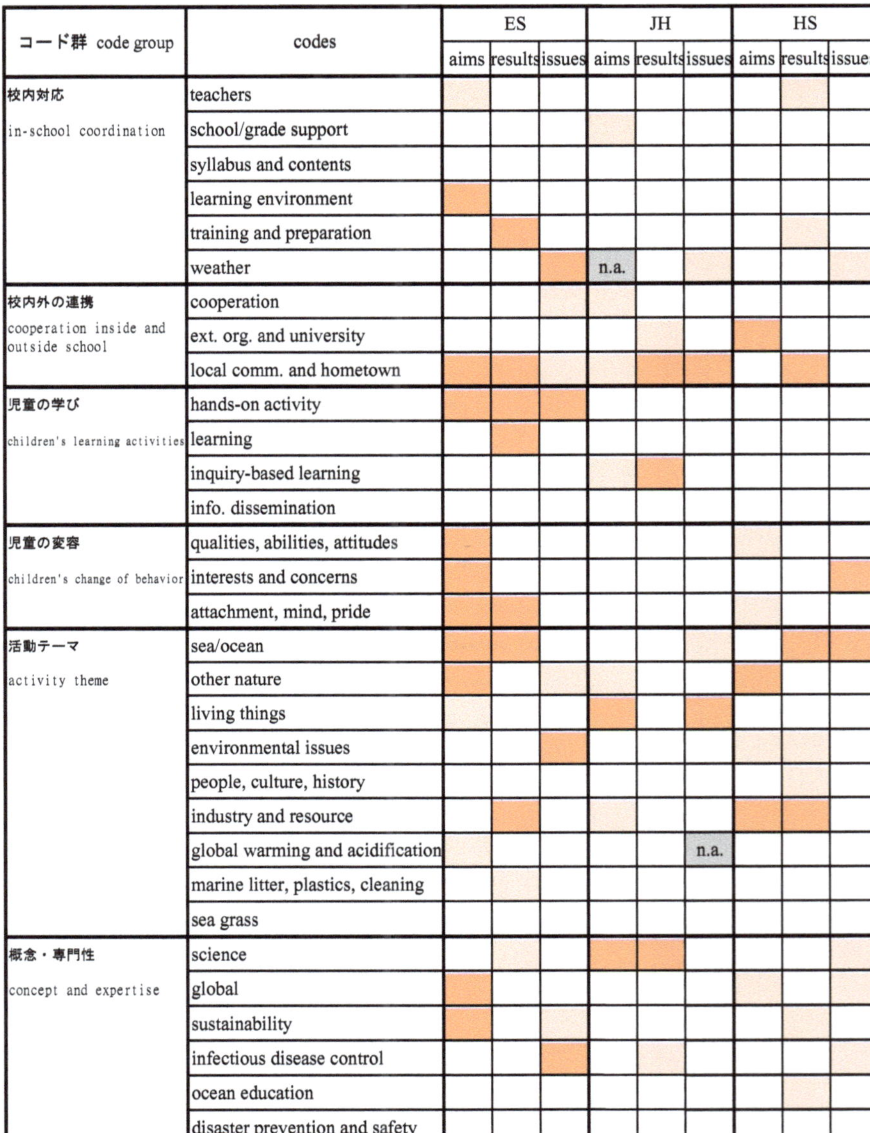

Fig. 4.21 Cross-analysis results of the codes and d_{sea}. Light orange squares indicate $p \leq 0.05$ and deep orange indicate $p \leq 0.01$. Source: compiled by the author

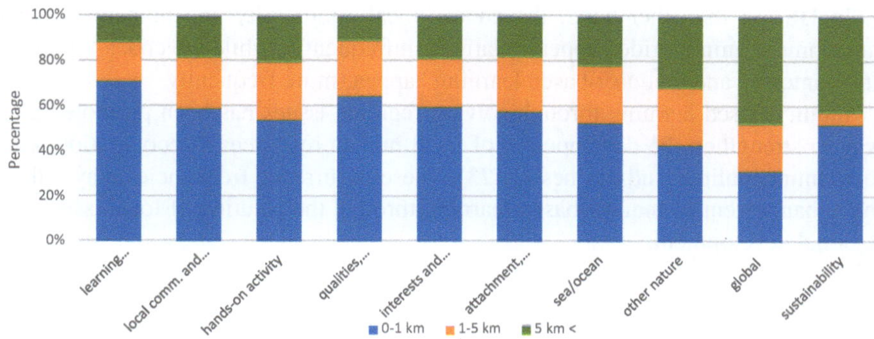

Fig. 4.22 Percentage of d_{sea} of ES where "Aims" document of unit assigned each code. Source: compiled by the author

4.5 Discussion

4.5.1 Regional Cooperation and Ocean Education

In Japan, regional cooperation in child rearing has been emphasized for more than a quarter of a century, particularly in rural areas. Establishing a local identity has been advocated to instill community pride and a sense of attachment in all its members [21]. In such a community, the adults were expected to work hand in hand to raise their children [21].

Given the declining birthrates and aging populations in Japan's rural areas, education that fosters attachment to and pride in the community is being promoted through educational activities [22]. As a core element of local development, schools are encouraged to cooperate and to collaborate with the local community using local resources [22].

In high schools, initiatives to build curricula with inquiry-based learning through solving regional issues in cooperation with local municipalities and businesses are being actively promoted [23]. The intent is to create opportunities for students to experience local attractions through enhanced internships, and to strengthen the development of locally based human resources. [23]. As can be seen in Figs. 4.18, 4.19, and 4.20, such school-community partnerships and cooperative relationships can be considered as a factor in explaining the high occurrence frequency of the code groups "cooperation inside and outside school" and "children's change of behavior" especially in the "Aims" and "Results" documents. The code "attachment, mind, pride" produced $p \leq 0.01$ in the test of its relationship to d_{sea}, indicating that the occurrence frequency tends to be higher in schools near the sea. Earlier research finding that cherishing the local sea leads JH students to an attachment to and pride in their community [24] supports the results of the present study.

In HS, on the other hand, the codes "local community and hometown" and "attachment, mind, pride" appear relatively infrequently, while the codes "syllabus and contents" and "inquiry-based learning" appear more frequently.

Inquiry-based learning through solving regional issues has been promoted as a way to strengthen the development of local human resources in cooperation with local municipalities and businesses [23]. These occurrence frequencies may reflect the enhancement of inquiry-based learning through the solution of local issues for regional development.

4.5.2 High School–University Cooperation

The "Results" section of the practice reports of many of the schools indicated that presentations by external lecturers from universities helped broaden the scope of learning among students. In particular, it was reported that their lessons and experiments promoted student awareness of ocean environmental conservation. Figure 4.8 shows that nearly half of all HS in the study cooperated with universities; however, there were few descriptions that clearly separated the contributions of universities from those of other institutions. In most cases, the contributions of universities to the overall practices were not clear, as they were partial responses to some of the "Aims." It was also difficult to evaluate the effectiveness of the specialized learning provided by the university from the descriptions in the "Results."

In Japan, the linkage between HS and universities has been promoted for education appropriate to the abilities of individual students [25]. On the other hand, university social responsibility (USR), including cooperation with local schools and/or communities, has also been discussed [26]. One of the expected social impacts of cooperation with universities is capacity building that can contribute to local communities. In addition to working on local issues jointly with university laboratories as an example of high school–university cooperation, stimulating interest in the community can be considered as a process of capacity building. The viewpoint of experts can encourage ES and/or JH students to consider their own actions in terms of their contributions to the community.

To effectively evaluate the contribution of universities to PSP-participating schools and communities as USR, it is necessary to survey identifiers that can be used as key performance indicators for not only HS but also ES and JH.

4.5.3 Challenges in the Field of Ocean Education

The various hands-on learning experiences shown in Table 4.1 are implemented through a cooperative effort involving the schools and the local cooperating organizations shown in Table 4.2. However, it has been pointed out that to continue these efforts, cooperation among teachers within schools, possible teacher transfers among schools, and coordination with cooperating organizations are necessary [15]. In the present study, which broadened the scope of analysis, the codes "correspondence of grade and school," "syllabus and contents," and "cooperation" appeared more frequently in the "Issues" for all school types in Figs. 4.18, 4.19, and 4.20.

The most frequently appearing code in the "Issues" document, "syllabus and contents," encompasses the words "plan," "syllabus," and "curriculum" and is related to curriculum management, which is emphasized in the Courses of Study, making it a particularly important issue in the "Issues" section of each school. As suggested by other codes, "cooperation" between "external organizations and universities" for "ocean" "learning," the direct support of teachers by those with specialized knowledge and skills related to the ocean and by people living in the community who are involved with the ocean has proven to be effective [27]. In addition to human resources such as external lecturers, teachers, for whom it is difficult to secure time to collect appropriate learning materials, would greatly benefit from the provision of such materials. The desired cooperation includes not only the connection of initiatives with local JH and HS and cooperation with local institutions in terms of information dissemination outside the school but also cooperation within the school among teachers and across grade levels. However, in terms of coordination and cooperation for hands-on activities and teaching content, public support to promote organic cooperation, which is suggested in the Third Basic Plan for Ocean Policy, is currently insufficient.

Many studies have focused on the educational effects of "collaboration and cooperation" with "local communities and hometowns" and "external institutions and universities" [5, 6]. However, the continuation of cooperation with the local community and other cooperating organizations also involves school management, such as schedule coordination, budget, and community-specific connections. To solve the problems faced by the educational field, it is necessary to understand the situation from the school and teacher point of view and to support them in a way that is appropriate for both the school and the community.

With regard to ocean education in the future, learning about the global ocean, in contrast to the local ocean, will need to be emphasized. The PSP listed global warming and SDG14, along with marine litter issues, as priority themes for FY2020; however, as shown in Figs. 4.18, 4.19, and 4.20, the occurrence frequencies of codes related to these themes were low. To this point, ocean education in Japan has tended to focus on the formation of attachments to the local community. In the future, an education that enables and encourages students to look at the world from a regional perspective, focused through the ocean, will be required. Ocean Literacy, as promoted by the IOC–UNESCO, calls for "an understanding of the ocean's influence on us and our influence on the ocean" [8, 9]. This means that we will all need to learn about the ocean.

To continue ocean education across school types and to expand student views to a global scale, it is suggested that local support organizations such as those shown in Table 4.2 become support networks for school-based ocean education. The development of desirable teaching content, coordination of hands-on activities, and the dispatch and placement of lecturers must be done in cooperation with the schools.

In order to properly respond, support networks that are not only familiar with local conditions but also have significant ocean-related expertise are needed. To improve curriculum management, it will be important to facilitate the sharing of knowledge among local sectors, as well as information on the educational outcomes of each school and community. The development and implementation of an appropriate system to accomplish this would encourage schools to proactively engage in ocean education.

4.6 Conclusion

In this study, the implementation of ocean education and its challenges were analyzed using practice reports from schools participating in Japan's PSP. The distance between the school and the ocean was treated as an external factor affecting such matters as the content of hands-on activities and the tendency to select cooperating organizations. Frequently used words were extracted from the free text reports on the "Aims," "Results," and "Issues" of each participating school using text mining analysis. Based on co-occurrence networks, words that appeared simultaneously in the text were coded together, and the contents of the initiatives and the issues of the schools were analyzed. It was suggested that ocean education, which is positioned as an exploratory study to build attachment to the local community and to develop human resources for local development, faces issues in "syllabus and contents" and "cooperation" with the "local community and hometown." Approximately half of the participating high schools cooperated with universities to develop expertise through classes and experiments. However, it was difficult to evaluate the university's contribution as USR separate from that of other institutions. As a means to expand the perspective of ocean education from the local to the global scale, the establishment of a local support organization, one that would serve as a support net for ocean education in schools, was proposed.

While educational activities can influence settlement orientation [5, 24], it will be necessary to evaluate their impact on a broader scale than the town level by conducting follow-up surveys of children and students who have experienced ocean education aimed at forming local attachment and promoting industry.

Given that the issues and discussions of ocean education extracted from the "Issues" documents were obtained only from PSP-participating schools in various regions of Japan, they are limited in their scope. In the future, reports of other unique ocean education programs will be analyzed to develop a system that is suited to each region.

To align the region's unique ocean learning with the Courses of Study [3, 4] and Ocean Literacy [8, 9] remains a challenge. For the subsequent promotion of Ocean Literacy as an international standard, a textual analysis will be conducted to determine whether the seven principles of Ocean Literacy are mentioned in the practice reports in future studies.

In Japan, the stated goal is to have ocean education practiced in all municipalities by 2025. If ocean education is to spread to both coastal and inland areas, it will be necessary to organize the knowledge needed to promote "the coexistence of the oceans and mankind" [1], as well as community-based learning, and to develop an ocean education environment and support system having a broad perspective.

Acknowledgements I would like to express my sincere gratitude to the reviewers and the chair of the editorial committee for their valuable time and useful suggestions in the preparation of this chapter.

The Ocean Education Pioneer School Program is jointly sponsored by the Nippon Foundation, Ocean Policy Research Institute of the Sasakawa Peace Foundation, and the Center for Ocean Education attached to the Graduate School of Education, the University of Tokyo (until FY2021). We, the PSP secretariat, would like to express our sincere appreciation to all students, faculty members, and staff of the schools participating in this program, as well as to all related community organizations for their understanding and cooperation in the initiatives of each school.

References

1. Cabinet Office, Basic Act on Ocean Policy (Act No. 33 of April 27, 2007). https://www8.cao.go.jp/ocean/policies/law/pdf/law_je.pdf
2. Oceanographic Society of Japan. (2016). *Proposal for the establishment of a new 4th grade elementary school science unit*, "The Ocean's Particulars". Available at: https://kaiyo-gakkai.jp/jos/archives/topic/4989 (published in Japanese).
3. Ministry of Education, Culture, Sports, Science and Technology. (2017). *Elementary School Courses of Study* (published in Japanese).
4. Ministry of Education, Culture, Sports, Science and Technology. (2017). *Commentary on the Courses of Study for Elementary Schools, General Provisions* (published in Japanese).
5. Matsumoto, K., Takeno, K., Urata, S., Matsubara, M., Kato, T., Suzuki, N., & Hayakawa, K. (2017). Research on children's settlement intention in rural areas through community-based Education: A case study of marine education in Noto Town, Ishikawa Prefecture. *Environmental Education, 27*(1), 16–22. (published in Japanese). https://doi.org/10.5647/jsoee.27.1_16
6. Sakurai, R. (2018). Effectiveness of marine education program on junior high school students with a specific focus on Satoumi. *Environmental Education, 28*(1), 12–22. (published in Japanese). https://doi.org/10.5647/jsoee.28.1_12
7. Yanagi, T. (2006) *Satoumi Ron (Satoumi theory)*. Koseisha Kosei-Kaku., 102p (in Japanese).
8. Centers for Ocean Science Education Excellence, National Geographic Society, National Oceanic and Atmospheric Administration, and College of Exploration. (2005). *Ocean literacy: The essential principles of ocean sciences grades K–12, a jointly published brochure*. https://www.coexploration.org/oceanliteracy/documents/OceanLitConcepts_10.11.05.pdf
9. Santoro, F., Santin, S., Scowcroft, G., Fauville, G., & Tuddenham, P. (2017). *Ocean literacy for all — A toolkit*. IOC/UNESCO & UNESCO Venice Office. (IOC Manuals and Guides, 80 revised in 2018).
10. Sasaki, T. (2017). Outcomes and issues of aquatic marine environmental literacy education promoting program. *Bulletin on Coastal Oceanography, 55*(1), 23–32. (published in Japanese with English abstract).
11. Tsuzuki, A., Imamiya, N., Fujita, Y., Hirai, K., & Strang, C. (2013). The role of MARE as educational resources for ocean science education and ocean science communication. *Japanese Journal of Science Communication, 14*, 32–43. (published in Japanese) http://hdl.handle.net/2115/53767
12. Ocean Policy Research Foundation. (2015). *Heisei 26 nendo "Waga kuni no gakkou kyouiku ni okeru kaiyou kyouiku kakuju ni muketa torikumi (Nihon Zaidan kaiyou kyouiku suishin*

puroguramu)" (FY2014 Report on "Efforts to expand ocean education in Japanese school education (Nippon Foundation ocean education promotion program)", 9–10. (published in Japanese).
13. Sakai, E. (2009). 21-seiki no kaiyou kyouiku towa – Kaiyou kihon hou seitei go no kaiyou kyouiku ni kansuru teian (Ocean education in the 21st century: A proposal on ocean education after the enactment of the Basic Act on Ocean Policy). *Maritime Transport Research, 58*, 15–31. (published in Japanese).
14. The Ocean Education Pioneer School Program website, https://www.spf.org/pioneerschool/.
15. Oguma, S. (2021). Challenges facing ocean education in Japanese elementary schools: Text mining result of practice reports. *Oceanography in Japan, 30*(4), 57–83. (published in Japanese with English abstract). https://doi.org/10.5928/kaiyou.30.4_57
16. The Nippon Foundation and Ocean Policy Research Foundation. (2012). *"Shou-chuu gakko no kaiyo kyouiku jisshi joukyo ni kansuru zenkoku chousa" houkoku sho* (Report for "National Survey on the Status of Ocean education in Elementary and Junior High Schools"), 45–49. (published in Japanese).
17. Higuchi, K. (2020). *Quantitative text analysis for social researchers: A contribution to content analysis* (2nd ed.). Nakanishiya Publishing. (published in Japanese).
18. Nanba, H. (2020). Tekisuto kan no ruiji-do no sokutei (Measurement of similarity between texts). *Joho no kagaku to gijutsu (Science and Technology of Intormation), 70*, 373–375. (published in Japanese).
19. Fisher, R. A. (1922). On the interpretation of χ^2 from contingency tables, and the calculation of P. *Journal of the Royal Statistical Society, 85*(1), 87–94.
20. Fisher, R. A. (1934). *Statistical methods for research workers* (5th ed.). Oliver and Boyd.
21. Central Council for Education. (1996). *Dai-san sho: Korekara no chiikishakai ni okeru kyoiku no arikata* (Chapter 3: The Future of Education in Local Communities), Ministry of Education, Culture, Sports, Science and Technology (ed.), The Future of Education in Japan in the 21st Century (The First Report of the Central Council for Education), Ministry of Education, Tokyo. https://www.mext.go.jp/b_menu/shingi/chuuou/toushin/960701j.htm (published in Japanese).
22. Ministry of Education, Culture, Sports, Science and Technology. (2018). *Dai-san ki kyoiku sinko kihon keikaku* (the Third Basic Plan for the Promotion of Education). (published in Japanese).
23. Machi-Hito-Shigoto Sousei, H. Q. (2018). *Machi-Hito-Shigoto Sousei Sogo Sen-ryaku 2018* (Comprehensive Strategy for the Creation of Towns, People, and Work 2018) (published in Japanese).
24. Sakurai, R., Uehara, T., Kondo, K., & Fujita, K. (2022). Attitudes toward the sea and conservation of students at a junior high school offering marine education: A comparison among Likert-scale items, open-ended questions, and drawing. *Japanese Journal of Conservation Ecology*. (published in Japanese with English abstract). https://doi.org/10.18960/hozen.2108
25. Ministry of Education, Culture, Sports, Science and Technology. (2007). "*Daigaku eno souki nyugaku oyobi koutou gakkou/daigaku kan no setsuzoku no kaizen ni kansuru kyougikai*" (Early entry for university and high school-university cooperation).
26. Chile, L. M., & Black, X. M. (2015). University–community engagement: Case study of university social responsibility. *Education, Citizenship and Social Justice, 10*(3), 234–253. https://doi.org/10.1177/1746197915607278
27. Research Institute for Ocean Economics (2011) *"Kaiyo kyoiku no genjo ni kansuru chosa" Hokokusho ("Survey on the Current State of Ocean Education" Report)*. Survey by the Secretariat of the Headquarters for Ocean Policy, Cabinet Secretariat, FY2010. (published in Japanese).

Chapter 5
Regional Revitalization Through Development of Taiwan's Yachting Industry: Challenges and Opportunities

Hsueh-wen Chow, Weilin Lee, and Jyh-Yeuan Lo

Abstract Although Taiwan is a yacht manufacturing center, hardware planning and software management in Taiwan's leisure yacht industry are in need of improvement. Many of Taiwan's marinas have been rebuilt from fishing ports and lack international certification. Such a condition fails to meet the needs of international consumers and ignores the potential of local resources. Through a series of interviews with local yacht operators, this study identifies the bottlenecks in the development of Taiwan's yacht industry. It also examines the methods used in neighboring Japan, South Korea, and Singapore to develop and expand their leisure yacht industries. The principal aim of the study is to enable Taiwan's marinas to effectively integrate resources into the operation and management process, adapt measures to local conditions, and align with the international community. It is expected to provide guidelines for marina management and governmental participation. Future research should track and monitor the sustainable development of Taiwan's overall yacht service business and leisure marine activities.

Keywords Blue Economy · Marinas · Fishing Port · Yachting Industry · Tourism · SDG8 · SDG 9 · SDG 14 · SDG 17

5.1 Introduction

As island states, both Taiwan and Japan are home to an ever-changing coastal landscape and diverse marine ecology that enables them to engage in a wide range of marine activities. In recent years, yacht tourism has emerged as a significant marine leisure activity. Since 2014, Taiwan has promoted marine affairs as one of the mainstays of national governance and adopted a vision of Taiwan as a marine country.

H.-w. Chow (✉) · W. Lee
National Cheng Kung University, Tainan, Taiwan
e-mail: hwchow@gs.ncku.edu.tw

J.-Y. Lo
LOHAS Ocean Leisure, Tainan, Taiwan

M. C. Huang et al. (eds.), *Innovative Social Practice and Community-Based Approach to the Ocean*, https://doi.org/10.1007/978-981-96-9104-3_5

Both the public sector and private enterprise have committed to this vision and see developing hydrophilic spaces as tourism development goals.

Taiwan is an island of only 36,197 km^2, with a coastline stretching some 1566 km. The economic zone around Taiwan consists of 83.231 km^2 within a 200 nautical mile radius, with a territorial sea of 12 nmi (22.2 km; 13.8 mi) [1]. Taiwan is rich in marine resources and environments, making it highly suitable for the development of various marine industries and activities. Although, in the early years, Taiwan imposed many restrictions on marine activities due to political and national defense concerns, it has more recently signaled its intention to seek marine development by establishing the Council of Ocean Affairs, formulating laws and regulations, and promoting a variety of marine activities under various ministries.

Taiwan's commitment to marine development is reflected in a number of papers and policies. The South China Sea Policy Guidelines in 1993 [2], the White Paper on Ocean Policy in 2001 [3], the National Marine Policy Program in 2004 [4], the Ocean Policy White Paper in 2006 [5], the Marine Education Policy White Paper in 2007 [6], and National Ocean Policy White Paper in 2020 [7] all promote the vision and policy objectives of Taiwan's marine affairs. Together they constitute a blueprint of the government's marine policy and serve as the basis for administrative departments to advance marine affairs. Relevant organizational laws and regulations have also been enacted, including the Wetland Conservation Act in 2013 [8], the Coastal Zone Management Act in 2015 [9], and the Spatial Planning Act in 2016 [10]. In addition, four organizational laws related to the Ocean Council—the Organizational Act of the Ocean Affairs Council in 2015 [11], the Organization Act of Coast Guard Administration in 2015 [12], the Organization Act of Ocean Conservation Department of the Ocean Council in 2015 [13], and the Organization Act of the National Agency for Ocean Research in 2015 [14]—have helped establish the basic framework of Taiwan's marine governance [15] and laid the groundwork for the Ocean Basic Act [16] in 2019.

Notwithstanding the enactment of such policies, regulations, and systems, the act of supporting the development of related industries and marine activities requires cooperation among the relevant ministries and commissions. At a time when Taiwan's traditional industries such as primary aquaculture, secondary manufacturing, and tertiary marine services are gradually declining, the development of a marine leisure and tourism industry appears promising. According to marine economy-related data of the Organization for Economic Cooperation and Development (OECD), the annual output of the marine economy reached 1.7 trillion US dollars (USD) in 2010, and that of maritime and coastal tourism, including beach recreation, coastal recreation, yachts, cruise ships, and leisure fisheries, was 44.2 billion dollars—much higher than other activities, such as port activities, maritime facilities, aquatic processing, shipping, and fishing. The output of the marine leisure sports and tourism industry is also substantial, with its economic scale increasing every year [17].

The yacht industry enjoys a huge market share globally. According to the Yacht Charter Market Size & Trends Analysis Report, 2021–2028 [18], the world yacht market was valued at 850 million USD in 2021 and is expected to reach 1.216

billion USD in 2028. Not surprisingly, there is a positive correlation between the development of the yacht industry and the national economy. When a country's gross domestic product (GDP) reaches 5000 USD, the yacht economy starts to grow rapidly. The yacht industry is already fully developed in Europe, the United States, and Australia. More recently, the yacht leisure industry has become a focus of development in Asian countries. Both government and private enterprise are making every effort to support the industrial transformation and operation management of the yacht industry, pressing ahead with the construction of software and hardware infrastructure such as marinas, and giving priority to talent training and regular policy amendment to create a high-quality yachting ecosystem. Given this strong impetus, this study used field interviews with local yacht operators to take stock of the existing bottlenecks in the development of Taiwan's yacht industry and examined the development of the yacht industries of neighboring Japan, South Korea, and Singapore. Results suggest that Taiwan's yachting industry can effectively integrate resources in the operation and management process, leverage local advantages, and keep pace with the international community.

5.2 Yacht Service Industry Development Across Countries

As noted above, the yacht leisure industry has become the focus of development in several Asian countries. Both governments and private enterprises have been fully engaged. The following sections describe the development of the yacht leisure industry in Taiwan, Japan, the Republic of Korea, and Singapore.

5.2.1 The Yacht Industry in Taiwan

Due to its exquisite craftsmanship, cheap labor, manufacturing costs, and the advantages of Kaohsiung's production chains, Taiwan's yacht and shipbuilding industry thrived in the 1960s and 1990s [19]. The export of yachts from 2012 to 2017 was nearly 246 billion New Taiwan Dollars (NTD) [20]. According to the Ship and Ocean Industries R&D center, in the 3-year period 2018–2020, yacht exports totaled 52.3, 69.8, and 5.84 billion NTD, respectively [21]. In recent years, the government has also actively assisted in building Taiwan into a "kingdom of yachting," as seen in the increasing willingness of international buyers to purchase Taiwan-built yachts and in the industry's hosting of the biennial Taiwan International Boat Show in Kaohsiung [22].

Although Taiwan's yacht industry once flourished, the international environment was always highly competitive. In the late 1980s, many businesses collapsed due to factors such as the appreciation of the Taiwan dollar, the shrinking market, the ending of US preferential tariffs, and the implementation of new labor laws. As a result, many manufacturers moved their production overseas to reduce labor costs as the manufacturing-based industrial model could not stay competitive. In order to reinvigorate its yachting industry, Taiwan not only needs to focus on the niche high-end market [23], but also must broaden its base by expanding the market and the overall yachting industry.

Due to regional security concerns, Taiwan implemented Measures for Taiwan Provincial and Regional Authorities and People to Apply for Entering and Exiting Coastal Areas and Important Areas with Military Facilities during the Martial Law Period in the early 1950s. Coastal control was strict, and citizen access to the sea was restricted. Accordingly, the development and participation of the Taiwanese people in marine leisure activities were limited. More recently, a number of policy measures, such as the 2020's *Salute to the Seas*, have been introduced, with the aim of encouraging the public's embrace of the ocean and expanding public perspectives and experiences. The expectation is that Taiwan can gradually develop its marine recreation and yachting industries, improve economic benefits, and ultimately achieve the goal of sustainable marine development [24].

At present, the primary focus is on marine activities in Kenting National Park, the East Coast, Penghu, Dapeng Bay, the Southwest Coast, the North Coast, Kuanyin Mountain, and other national scenic spots. The principal infrastructure of Taiwan's yachting industry is its marinas. (Taiwan's major marinas are shown in Table 5.1) There are multiple administrative departments responsible for these marinas. The Maritime and Port Bureau of the Ministry of Transportation and Communications serves as the main port authority, while the Sports Administration of the Ministry of Education is responsible for water sports; the various aspects of yacht recreation, use, berthing, and driving are the responsibilities of central departments such as the Maritime and Port Bureau of the Ministry of Transportation and Communications, Taiwan International Ports Corporation, the Fisheries Agency of the Council of Agriculture, the Coast Guard Administration of Ocean Affairs Council or local governments, such as the Marine Bureau of Kaohsiung City Government, the Tainan City Fishing Harbor and Coastal Fisheries Management Office. This multi-sided situation has led to confusion among yachting enthusiasts with respect to their rights and responsibilities [20].

In addition, the development of Taiwan's yacht activities is also restricted by factors such as underdeveloped laws and regulations and a substandard yachting environment. Because yachts are registered differently from other vessels, it is difficult to manage and supervise them. Yacht audit procedures are complicated and ineffective. To manage yachts, the main standards were encapsulated in "Yacht Management Measures" [25]. Following the abolition of these Measures in 2007, the management of yachts was added to the Law of Ships regulatory system [26], where vessels are divided into large and small classes based on their tonnage, with no specific classification for yachts. The Law of Ships was subsequently revised in 2010. In the revised version, yachts were better defined, yacht inspection provisions were relaxed, and issues such as yacht registration and license issuance were clarified. Since 2000, the government has played a role in the yacht industry and encouraged the public to embrace the marina environment by developing marinas and promoting marine leisure activities.

Table 5.1 Taiwan marinas

Type	Location	Yacht marina	Authorities
Public marina	Keelung	Yacht Berthing Area, Badouzi Fishing Port	Keelung City Government
	Taoyuan	Entertainment Fishing Boat Wharf, Zhuwei Fishing Port	Taoyuan City Government Agriculture Bureau
	Hsinchu	Hsinchu Fishing Port	Hsinchu City Government
	Tainan	Anping Fishing Port	Tainan City Government
	Tainan	Tainan Jiangjyun Fishing Port	Tainan Fishing Port and Offshore Management Office
	Kaohsiung	Yacht Recreation Area, Gu-shan Fishing Port	Kaohsiung City Government
	Kaohsiung	Floating Wharf, Xingda Fishing Port	Kaohsiung City Government
	Pingtung	Hou-Bi Lake Fishing & Yacht Port	Kenting National Park Management Office
	Pingtung	Binwan Wharf	Dapeng Bay National Scenic Area Management Office
Private marina	New Taipei	Longdong Marina	Kiwano Yule Co., Ltd
	New Taipei	Exclusive Yacht Berth Marina	Royal Regal Waterfront Development Co., Ltd
	New Taipei	Tamsui Yacht Wharf	Dazhou Yacht Co., Ltd
	Yilan	Wushi Yacht Wharf	LeaLea Wushih Marina Co., Ltd
	Chiayi	Princess Budai Marina	Taiwan Princess Yacht Co., Ltd
	Tainan	Anping Argo Yacht Wharf	Anping Branch, Argo Yacht Development Co., Ltd
	Kaohsiung	KhaSihing Pier 22	Khasihing Yacht Co., Ltd
	Kaohsiung	Horizon City Marina	Ya-peng Yacht Development Co., Ltd
	Penghu	Penghu Argo Yacht Wharf	Ya-peng Yacht Development Co., Ltd

Source: Maritime Port Bureau, Taiwan (https://yacht.motcmpb.gov.tw/)

To better understand the current issues facing the yachting industry, we made field visits to several yachting marinas in Taiwan, including the Horizon Marina in Kaohsiung, Pier 22 in Kaohsiung, Budai Princess Yachts in Chiayi, and Anping Argo Yacht Warf in Tainan, and conducted interviews with the chief managers of these yachting service providers in Spring 2022. The main questions put to the interviewees related to their overall development of the yachting service, the challenges and issues they faced, regulations pertaining to marina development, and the acquisition and training of yachting service personnel. Each interview lasted approximately 2 h.

Based on our field investigations and interviews, it is clear that Taiwan's commercial yacht services continue to face a number of obstacles—(1) *Facilities*: Several yachting marinas were reconstructed from traditional fishing ports; consequently, their design and environment do not necessarily meet the needs of those engaged in yachting activities. Furthermore, due to high berthing costs and a sharp increase in the number of yachts in recent years, marinas in Taiwan have been unable to provide sufficient berths. Because of the shortage, some yachts are berthed at common fishing ports, causing considerable chaos; (2) *Authorities:* As the yachting service is new to much of the public as well as to yachting authorities such as the Maritime and Port Bureau, some authorities are reluctant to facilitate development of the service out of concern that it will benefit only a very small group of people. Additionally, too many authorities are responsible for various tasks, meaning that there is no central point of contact. The yachting service or marina providers are forced to contact multiple authorities regarding an issue, which is time-consuming and lacks coordination; (3) *Investment*: The government does not invest sufficiently in building basic infrastructure; (4) *Personnel*: Yachting services require a wide range of professionals, such as engineers, service personnel, and managers, and there are not enough professional personnel with the necessary skills available.

5.2.2 The Yacht Industry in Singapore

Located at the southern tip of the Malay Peninsula, Singapore is a tropical island in Southeast Asia. It covers an area of 710 km^2 and has a coastline of 193 km. Both Taiwan and Singapore serve as important maritime hubs. Singapore is a yacht development pioneer in Asia, tracing back to the British colonial period. In 1956, the United Kingdom established the first modern yacht club (Royal Singapore Yacht Club, RSYC) in Asia, which flourished after the War. Historically, locals regarded the sea as a trade route rather than a leisure space, rendering the government generally indifferent to the marine leisure industry and yacht tourism. Given the primary economic importance of the sea as a trade route, the Singaporean government did not give high priority to the development of marine leisure activities like yachting or boating for recreation or tourism. Like Taiwan, Singapore, as a small island nation, faces the issue of limited land resources. The lack of infrastructure for yachting and marine leisure activities only heightened this pressure as land could not be readily allocated for these purposes since it was needed for housing, industry, and other essential uses. With the growth of Singapore's economy, plans for integrated development in coastal areas were implemented. This included decentralization, livable buildings for the elderly and the young, fewer private vehicles, and mixed zones for both housing and business. Such measures markedly improved the living standards of Singaporeans. As a consequence, yacht activities gradually began to attract attention in the local area, and many yacht-related sideline industries have been developed [27].

Today, yacht wharfs have evolved beyond simple functions, such as boat berthing and replenishment, to open spaces featuring diversified services, including catering, entertainment, accommodation, business, maintenance, sailing courses, and clubs. As the hinterland is too small, the government has had to attach importance to the overall development of the marina and tourism industries and has regarded tourism as an unlimited resource. In 1964, the Tourism Promotion Bureau was established to act as the planner, promoter, and developer responsible for leading Singapore's tourism industry [28]. Today, the tourism industry contributes roughly 4% of Singapore's GDP and provides approximately 160,000 jobs. With the fully-fledged development of the country's economy, the tourism industry can play a more effective role; as an economic source, tourism has some unique characteristics, with the potential to consolidate Singapore's image as a dynamic global city and serve as a magnet for capital, talented personnel, and entertainment and business exhibitions [29]. Large sporting events have become a recent phenomenon in Asia, targeting specific interest groups or attracting more general groups [30]. In 2005, the International Yacht Race was held by the Singapore Tourism Bureau, RSYC, Sentosa, and other partners, sponsored by well-known international brands, in a display of Singapore's soft power. Moreover, in order to promote the sporting spirit and expand the public's interest in navigation, the government authorized the Singapore Yachting Federation to give an on-site demonstration of sailing during the 2005 International Yacht Race, encouraging interested sailors to participate. The Sports Council also provided a first-time display of cutting-edge navigation simulators, allowing the public to experience sailing through such instruments without getting wet [31].

Over the years, Singapore has taken a number of actions to better protect marine recreation, including the Fisheries Act (1966) [32] on the Protection of Fishery Resources; the Prevention of Pollution of the Sea Act (1990) [33] to prevent marine pollution; the Merchant Shipping Act (1995) [34] to promote the safety and welfare of seafarers, protect the marine environment and ensure the smooth and efficient operation of shipping and related activities; and the Maritime and Port Authority of Singapore Act, (1996) [35] which established the Maritime and Port Authority of Singapore as the national maritime agency responsible for the development, promotion, and regulation of Singapore's maritime industry. The government also regulates maritime and port-related businesses and provides maritime commercial services. The Singapore Marine Guide (2020) is the first online platform to continuously provide up-to-date guidelines and to offer consultation services to ship users, brands, suppliers, service providers, and leisure enthusiasts in Singapore's marine leisure sector [36].

5.2.3 The Yacht Industry in South Korea

In 1953, The Republic of Korea Naval Academy (ROKNA) (해군사관학)published *Dominance of the Sea*, which described yacht operation, education, and navigation at the Academy. Two decades later, the 1970s marked the beginning of South Korea's private yacht voyage. For the first time, yachts produced in South Korea met the standard for traversing the Pacific Ocean. At that time, South Korea opened yacht training grounds and began to establish yacht associations or clubs. In 1977, the Ministry of Commerce and Industry listed the yacht industry as a strategic export project, enabling shippers to participate, which significantly boosted the domestic yacht building industry. In 1988, South Korea hosted the Seoul Olympic Games, utilizing the Yacht Sports Arena of Busan Suyeongman Bay Yachting Center (수영만 요트경기장) for several international yacht events. At that time, yacht courses and experiential activities also came on the scene in the Han River. All this indicates that the yacht leisure industry had taken root in South Korea. In the 1990s, the Republic of Korea engaged in various international events, including the Beijing Asian Games and the Bangkok Asian Games, and achieved impressive results, further prompting the country to focus on such events as competition targets [37, 38].

Beyond competition, the South Korean government understands and attaches great importance to the potential of the marine leisure industry for domestic economic and social development and has intensively studied and discussed the sector. Related maritime leisure laws have been enacted, such as the Excursion Ship and Ferry Business Act in 1993 [39], the Installation and Utilization of Sports Facilities Act in 2007 [40], the Act on the Development and Management of Marinas in 2009 [41], the Aquaculture Industry Development Act in 2019 [42], the Beach Utilization and Management Act in 2014 [43], the Act on Prevention of Accidents at Coastal in 2014 [44], the Framework Act on Fisheries and Fishing Villages Development in 2015 [45], and the Water-Related Leisure Activities Safety Act in 2005 [46]. The intent is to establish a comprehensive system of multiple cooperation networks that connect locals and foreigners. In addition to the legal framework, the Ministry of Oceans and Fisheries (해양수산부) recognizes that wharfs are the most important infrastructure for leisure vessels such as yachts. By upgrading the wharfs' software and hardware, the country can develop an industrial cluster characterized by efficient port operation and management, such as clubs, yacht trade, ship maintenance, and spare parts. The formation of such a cluster encourages neighboring businesses to provide a variety of tourism and leisure services, such as catering, accommodation, and entertainment, and its high industrial-added value will create more employment opportunities within the country. However, given the growing demand for marine leisure, there is a shortage of infrastructure [47]. Keenly aware that the construction of wharfs and other infrastructure is crucial to support the development of the yacht leisure industry across the board, South Korea published its development plans for yacht wharfs and marinas in 2010, 2015, and 2016. It continues to construct facilities and to promote comprehensive activities for marine tourism. In 2015, the government unveiled the Cruise Industry Development and Support Act aimed at developing the cruise industry and underpinning the construction and modernization of yacht marinas [48]. Various government agencies work with other entities to support such development. South Korea made significant efforts to attract three million cruise tourists in 2020 and encouraged tourists to engage in marine leisure activities. It sought to increase the popularity of the yachting industry and create approximately 12,000 new jobs.

Since 2019, nearly three billion USD has been invested to promote the "300 New Fisheries Policy" plan, which is expected to complete the infrastructure revitalization of 300 fishing villages [49]. The plan calls for investing in infrastructure projects that include the construction of new fishing ports, the renovation of existing facilities, the installation of new equipment, and the improvement of transportation and communication networks. Government officials in South Korea have expressed their commitment to addressing the issues of aging fishing villages and population outflow, believing that young people are more likely to return to their hometowns if land and water planning can be used to revitalize their economies. A revitalized and modernized fishing village will serve to promote economic growth and improve the quality of life of local residents [49].

Responding to international trends and a loosening of national security concerns, the South Korean government opened the sea to the public in 2010 and has since been committed to promoting related hardware facilities and software services. Benefiting from the government's strong support and a favorable environment for developing yachting, there has been a rapid increase in yacht registrations and driving licenses. From 2008 to 2013, yacht registrations showed an annual growth rate of 15.9%, covering 15,285 yachts. Over that same period, a total of 140,137 yacht licenses were issued, representing an annual growth rate of 7.2%. According to statistics published by the Republic of Korea Coast Guard [50], the number of registered yachts was approximately 30,000 in July 2020, and the number of registered maritime leisure institutions had reached nearly 40,000. Given that the population of South Korea is 51.64 million, this roughly equates to 6 yachts per 10,000 people. The South Korean government has recently proposed a solution to the imbalance between supply and demand for yacht berthing spaces [51]. Under the Harbor Act [52], the country allocates funds and offers policy support for overall marine leisure development planning. As of 2020, 46 wharfs have been built to provide up to 1500 berths [53]. It is estimated that 58 wharfs and 15,000 berths will have been built by 2029. The construction of these marinas will be primarily based on the Build–Operate–Transfer (B.O.T.) model.

5.2.4 The Yacht Industry in Japan

Japan's first yacht was built in 1861 in Nagasaki, when a British shipbuilder received an order for the boat's construction. The ship was due to participate in the Nagasaki Yacht Race that same year. In 1882, Japan began manufacturing yachts in Yokohama and sailing them in Kanagawa. Yeshan Port in Kanagawa subsequently became a place for the development of Japanese yachts. In the 1950s, Japan emerged from the war making every effort to bolster its social recovery and economic progress. In addition to becoming the world's leading shipbuilder at that time, the country also witnessed an increase in the number of domestic participants in yachting activities, and actively engaged in international events and exchanges. In the 1970s, the Yokohama Yacht Association aggressively promoted infrastructure (i.e., a clubhouse), construction of a harbor, and education on matters related to marinas after being granted legal status by the Kanagawa County Education Committee.

The yachting economy is an important part of Japan's marine industry. Yachting services that support the yachting economy are a tertiary industry, in addition to research, design, and manufacturing in its core areas. The economic drivers in this sector include ship operation, maintenance, and management, which has led to the rapid development of yacht marinas, yacht education and training, yacht transport, aquatic entertainment, catering services, and other related industries. To strike a proper balance between the yacht leisure industry and fisheries, Japan has improved the overall quality of marine recreation, revamping old fishing port hardware and service on a large scale, planning coastal corridors for sightseeing, strengthening the emergency aid system for marine activities, and coordinating the overall development of coastal areas. In 2007, the Ministry of Land, Infrastructure, Transport and Tourism proposed working with local public and non-governmental organizations, with the government as the core, to formulate the Sea Station plan (海の駅 [umi no eki]), whose central concept is "all railway destinations are equipped with a station that enables people to gather and interact, and the sea should also have stations which serve as a hub between sea and land, and are provided for yacht users and marine leisure tourists" [54].

Under the Sea Station Plan, nearly everyone will have access to marine leisure activities. In addition to serving as hubs between land and sea, Sea Stations provide an educational base for citizens. As a result of the Japanese government's promotion of the Sea Station concept, many fishing ports and marinas have joined the Sea Station plan. By August 2019, there were 168 Sea Stations available for citizens in Japan. The number of stations is gradually expanding. In the future, the stations will mainly operate in core sea areas, enriching the local culture and revitalizing the regional economy [54–56].

Not only are there temporary berthing zones for yachts, sailboats, and other ships, but also basic facilities for ship maintenance and operations such as refueling, water filling, and emergency repair. Moreover, the area offers the information and services needed by tourists for ocean leisure, such as sea condition advisories, toilets, accommodations, and catering.

While the Sea Station network in Japan has been generally well-received by both locals and visitors, there have been issues and challenges associated with its development, especially with regard to environmental impact. Some Sea Stations are located in environmentally sensitive areas, such as coastal wetlands and fisheries. The increased tourism and development associated with the stations can have negative impacts on these ecosystems, including damage to habitats and overfishing [56]. Other issues include overcrowding during peak travel seasons, which makes it difficult for visitors to enjoy the facilities and services that the Sea Stations offer. In addition, the facilities at some stations may not always be well-maintained due to limited resources and funding. This can affect the overall experience of visitors and impact the long-term sustainability of the facilities [57].

The White Paper on Tourism published by the Japan Tourism Agency under the Ministry of Land, Infrastructure, Transport and Tourism forecasts that the tourism and leisure industry will become the core industry in Japan's economy. In particular, the marine leisure industry is expected to be a driving force for regional economic transformation, creating new employment opportunities [58]. The correlation between sports and the leisure industry is a crucial basis for sustainable operation. The correlation among different industries creates an economic multiplier effect, making other related industries more profitable.

5.2.5 *Summary*

Japan, South Korea, and Singapore have each adopted unique marine policies that reflect their geographical, economic, and social contexts, which significantly influence their yacht industry success. For instance, Japan has heavily invested in infrastructure such as the Sea Station plan, which integrates marine leisure hubs with local tourism and business sectors, thereby enriching regional economies. South Korea, on the other hand, has focused on building a robust legal framework and supporting infrastructure to promote marine leisure and tourism, illustrated by the Act on the Development and Management of Marinas. Singapore's approach has emphasized high standards for marina operations and environmental sustainability, turning its limited space into high-value marine leisure hubs that attract international visitors.

These strategies underline the critical factors contributing to the successful development of the yacht industry in these countries. They include strong governmental support, strategic infrastructure investment, comprehensive legal frameworks, and a focus on integrating marine leisure with broader economic development goals.

For Taiwan, learning from these examples could involve adopting a more integrated approach to policy-making where infrastructure, legal frameworks, and international standards are aligned to support the yacht industry comprehensively. This could include policies that reduce bureaucratic hurdles, foster international collaborations, and promote Taiwan as a destination for marine leisure. Additionally, Taiwan could benefit from creating a more cohesive brand for its yacht industry, leveraging its existing strengths in yacht manufacturing to attract a global clientele.

5.3 Conclusion

Although Taiwan, Singapore, South Korea, and Japan have long coastlines and rich resources for marina development, they have all encountered challenges. First, as these Asian countries are densely populated, with limited space, finding suitable sites for marina development can be difficult. Second, the development of marinas in these countries is subject to numerous regulations, including those related to zoning, land use, and environmental protection. Such regulations can be complex and vary by region, which can make the development process more challenging. Third, coastal areas are often home to delicate marine ecosystems, which means that marina development must be undertaken with care to minimize its impact on the environment. This can involve measures such as environmental assessments, habitat restoration, and wastewater management. Fourth, some local communities may oppose marina development due to concerns about environmental impact, changes to the local landscape, or increased traffic and noise. Finally, developing a marina requires significant investment in infrastructure, such as docks, breakwaters, and onshore facilities, which can be expensive. This can make it difficult to secure the necessary funding, especially for smaller marinas.

The exploration of yacht industry development strategies in Japan, South Korea, and Singapore has provided significant insights that can be instrumental for Taiwan as it seeks to revitalize its own yacht sector. These countries demonstrate varied yet effective approaches to leveraging marine resources for economic and recreational benefits, underpinned by robust governmental support, strategic policy frameworks, and substantial infrastructure investments. All four of the countries studied have a developed maritime industry and are popular destinations for boating and water-based activities. However, there are some differences in their approaches to marina development and management. Japan is known for its extensive network of small, community-based marinas and its Sea Stations, which are often operated by local municipalities. The development of marinas in Japan is typically tied to regional revitalization efforts, with an emphasis on promoting local culture and tourism. South Korea has made significant investments in marina development in recent years, with a particular focus on attracting high-end luxury yachts and superyachts. There has been a particular emphasis on developing marinas near major cities and tourist destinations, such as Busan and Jeju Island. Singapore is a major center for maritime commerce and has a well-developed marina industry catering to both local and international sailors. It is known for its strict regulations and high standards for marina management and environmental sustainability. Taiwan has a rapidly growing leisure boating industry, with a focus on developing marinas in areas with high potential for tourism and economic growth. However, the development of marinas in Taiwan has been hindered by a lack of available land and regulatory challenges. Overall, the approaches to marina development and management in these countries are shaped by a combination of economic, cultural, and environmental factors, as well as government policies and regulations.

The international tourism industry has become a key development project in many countries—one that can deliver significant economic benefits. The development of the maritime yacht business can play a highly significant role in promoting a country's economic growth. Besides providing job opportunities, such a business can stimulate the entire industrial ecosystem.

Through an extensive collection and analysis of literature across many countries, it was found that the yacht industry has gradually shifted from the Western market to Asia and that governments in Asia have set marine development as a key goal, vigorously promoting policies such as the Singapore Blue Plan [59], measures to activate marine leisure tourism in South Korea [60], and Sea Stations in Japan [54]. Through administrative laws and regulations, these governments have supported the upgrading of commercial yacht services and tourism, and the transformation of declining fishing ports and fishing villages, thus effectively developing the yacht industry.

For Taiwan to capitalize on these insights, it is crucial to implement a multifaceted strategy that encompasses governmental support, industry-specific regulations, and international standard compliance. Enhancing infrastructure, fostering public-private partnerships, and promoting Taiwan as a premier destination for yacht tourism are essential steps. Such efforts should be supported by data-driven policies and a commitment to continuous improvement and adaptation to the evolving global marine leisure landscape. By systematically applying the lessons learned from these regional neighbors, Taiwan can not only enhance its yacht industry but also contribute to broader economic growth and the enrichment of its marine leisure sector.

Taiwan's yacht industry has slowly evolved from an earlier industrial production model centered around manufacturing into an all-round and diversified yacht marine tourism and recreation industry that integrates upstream and downstream industrial chains, exhibitions, dock operations, leisure tourism, cultural innovation, etc. These efforts have a significant impact on regional revitalization, particularly in fishing villages that are attempting to improve living standards, enhance local economies, and promote sustainable development. One example of this in Taiwan is the Anping Argo Yacht Wharf in Tainan. The National Cheng Kung University (NCKU), located in Tainan, has partnered with the Lohas Ocean Maritime Academy in Anping to foster long-term industry-academic cooperation. A human resource framework and the competencies of marina services personnel will be identified and developed through the collaboration.

By using analytic hierarchy processes, NCKU researchers will identify the most optimal yacht pier management and talent cultivation system in Taiwan. The aim is to train yacht service professionals who will stay in Tainan. Given the diverse development of the yacht leisure industry chain, this approach should not only lead to the development and retention of professional talent resources, but also promote the surrounding community's overall development. In this way, the development disparities between northern Taiwan, such as the Taipei municipalities, and southern Taiwan can be reduced or eliminated. Declining fishing ports will become vibrant hubs for regional regeneration, transforming them into thriving centers. Long-term industry-academic cooperation has the potential to make Tainan the flagship for commercial yacht services. It would then be possible to expand to other ports throughout Taiwan that wish to develop yacht businesses or transform fishing ports and promote the spirit of regional revitalization as a model for other cities.

It will be important for Taiwan's marinas and yachting services to improve their facilities and services so that they comply with international marina standards, such as Gold Anchor Global Marina Accreditation by the Global Marina Accreditation [61] or the International Maine Certification Institute's CE certification of watercraft and their components in the European Union [62].

The importance of the human factor in recreational activities and navigation safety, particularly in the context of yacht recreation, cannot be ignored. The management system for yacht driving licenses by the authorities is a step towards ensuring the safe and responsible operation of yachts, especially in cases where they are used for commercial purposes. By regulating non-self-use or commercial behavior in yachting recreation, the authorities can help prevent accidents and ensure the safety of those who participate in such activities. Overall, it is a positive move towards promoting safe and responsible recreation and navigation practices, while also protecting the well-being of individuals involved in such activities.

Establishing appropriate marina development plans and yachting service programs and maintaining appropriate standards will require the collaboration of government authorities, practitioners, marina experts, and scholars. Through such collaboration, Taiwan's yachting industry will grow, the market will be expanded, and complementary economic and social benefits will be realized. With the proper approach, Taiwan can become a world-class maritime region, fulfilling the vision embodied in its *Salute the Seas*.

References

1. Wikipedia. (2023). *Geography of Taiwan*. Wikimedia Foundation. https://en.wikipedia.org/wiki/Geography_of_Taiwan. Accessed 10 August 2023.
2. 中華民國內政部. (1993). 南海政策綱領, 中華民國, (Ministry of the Interior, R.O.C. Taiwan, *Policy Guideline for The South China Sea*) https://www.land.moi.gov.tw/law/Resultdet1/105?LCID=224&lawname=%E5%8D%97%E6%B5%B7%E6%94%BF%E7%AD%96%E7%B6%B1%E9%A0%98 Accessed 10 August 2023.
3. 行政院研究發展考核委員會. (2001). 海洋白皮書, 臺北. (Research, Development and Evaluation Commission, Executive Yuan, *Ocean White Paper*, Taipei) https://books.google.de/books?id=PZM2sMKb2iQC&printsec=frontcover&hl=zh-TW&source=gbs_ge_summary_r&cad=0#v=onepage&q&f=false Accessed August 10, 2023.
4. 海巡署企劃處. （2004）. 國家海洋政策綱領 (Coast Guard Administration Planning Division, *National Oceans Policy Guidelines*). chrome-extension://efaidnbmnnnibpcajpcglclefindmkaj/https://www.cga.gov.tw/GipOpen/wSite/public/Attachment/f1260928833977.pdf Accessed 10 August 2023.
5. 行政院研究發展考核委員會. (2006). 海洋政策白皮書, 臺北(Research, Development and Evaluation Commission, Executive Yuan *Ocean Policy White Paper.* Taipei). https://books.google.de/books/about/%E6%B5%B7%E6%B4%8B%E6%94%BF%E7%AD%96%E7%99%BD%E7%9A%AE%E6%9B%B8.html?id=VKuiKwW-1zkC&redir_esc=y
6. 教育部. (2007). 海洋教育政策白皮書, 臺北(Ministry of Education, *A White Paper on the Marine Education Policy,* Taipei) chrome-extension://efaidnbmnnnibpcajpcglclefindmkaj/https://ws.moe.edu.tw/001/Upload/3/relfile/6315/55805/40f900df-a70b-4e1f-847f-e53ed94b4c77.pdf Accessed 10 August 2023.
7. 海洋委員會. (2020*)* 國家海洋政策白皮書, 高雄 (Ocean Affairs Council, *2020 National Ocean Policy White Paper)*. https://www.oac.gov.tw/ch/home.jsp?id=232&parentpath=0,2. Accessed 10 August 2023.
8. 內政部. （2013）. 濕地保育法 (Ministry of the Interior, *Wetland Conservation Act*). https://law.moj.gov.tw/ENG/LawClass/LawAll.aspx?pcode=D0070209. Accessed 10 August 2023.
9. 內政部. （2015）. 海岸管理法 (Ministry of the Interior, *Costal Zone Management Act*). https://law.moj.gov.tw/ENG/LawClass/LawAll.aspx?pcode=D0070222. Accessed 10 August 2023.
10. 內政部. （2015）. 國土計畫法 (Ministry of the Interior, *Spatial Planning Act)* https://law.moj.gov.tw/ENG/LawClass/LawAll.aspx?pcode=D0070230. Accessed 10 August 2023.
11. 海洋委員會. （2015）. 海洋委員會組織法 (Ocean Affairs Council, *Organization Act of the Ocean Affairs Council)*. https://law.moj.gov.tw/ENG/LawClass/LawAll.aspx?pcode=D0090030 Accessed 10 August 2023.
12. 海洋委員會 (2015) 海洋委員會海巡署組織法 (Ocean Affairs Council, *Organization Act of Coast Guard Administration*). https://law.moj.gov.tw/ENG/LawClass/LawAll.aspx?pcode=D0090031 Accessed 10 August 2023
13. 海洋委員會（2015）海洋委員會海洋保育署組織法 (Ocean Affairs Council, *Organization Act of Ocean Conservation Administration*). https://law.moj.gov.tw/ENG/LawClass/LawAll.aspx?pcode=D0090032 Accessed 10 August 2023
14. 海洋委員會 (2015) 國家海洋研究院組織法 (Ocean Affairs Council, *Organization Act of National Academy for Ocean Research*). https://law.moj.gov.tw/ENG/LawClass/LawAll.aspx?pcode=D0090033 Accessed 10 August 2023

15. 邱文彥. (2016). 海洋立法與海洋治理的挑戰. 航運季刊 (Chiau, Wen-Yan, *Marine Legislation and Challenges of Ocean Governance*, Maritime Quarterly), 25(1), 1–25.
16. 海洋委員會. (2019). 海洋基本法 (Ocean Affairs Council, *Ocean Basic Act*). 2019. https://law.moj.gov.tw/ENG/LawClass/LawAll.aspx?pcode=D0090064. Accessed 10 August 2023.
17. The Organisation for Economic Co-operation and Development. (2016). *The Ocean Economy in 2030*. https://www.oecd.org/environment/the-ocean-economy-in-2030-9789264251724-en.htm. Accessed 10 August 2023.
18. Grand View Research. (2021). *Yacht market size, share & trends analysis report by type (Super Yacht, Flybridge Yacht, Sport Yacht, Long Range Yacht), by length, by propulsion, by region, and segment forecasts,* 2021–2028.
19. 鄭春發, 鄭國泰, 吳連賞. (2008). 遊艇產業聚集之空間群聚與網絡的分析. 環境與世界 (Cheng, Chun-Fa, Cheng Kuo-Tai, Wu Lien-sheng. Yacht Industrial Cluster of Space and Network), (18): p. 75–102.
20. 李伯言,陳妤岑. (2021). 從硬體邁向軟體, 台灣遊艇服務產業的發展策略. 臺灣經濟研究月刊, *44*(3), 121–126.
21. 財團法人船舶暨海洋產業研發中心. (2021). *2021*全球遊艇訂單與*2020*產值統計. Available from: https://www.soic.org.tw/2021%e5%85%a8%e7%90%83%e9%81%8a%e8%89%87%e8%a8%82%e5%96%ae%e8%88%872020%e7%94%a2%e5%80%bc%e7%b5%b1%e8%a8%88/. Accessed March 10, 2023.
22. 台灣國際遊艇展. (2021). *2022*年台灣國際遊艇展 明年*3*月高雄港都揚帆啟航. (Taiwan International Boat Show); Available from: https://www.boatshow.tw/zh-tw/index.html. Accessed March 10, 2023.
23. 陳振杰, 吳連賞. (2014). 台灣遊艇產業轉型之研究: 基於路徑依賴觀點. 正修通識教育學報 (Chen, Jen-Jie and Wu, Lien-Shang. The Transformation of Taiwan's Yacht Industry on the Perspective of Path Dependence), (11), 109–133.
24. 行政院新聞傳播處. (2020). 鼓勵人民「知海、近海、進海」 蘇揆:向海致敬留下美好記憶. (Department of Information Services, Executive Yuan, *Encourage the people to "Know the sea, Approach the sea, and Enter the Sea" Su Kui: Pay tribute to the sea and leave a good memory*]. https://www.ey.gov.tw/Page/9277F759E41CCD91/f3e6fd5d-4337-44ca-b1ec-d0f2c0cd604a. Accessed Aug 10, 2023.
25. 交通部. (1993). 遊艇管理辦法 (Ministry of Transportation and Communications, *Management Measures for Yachts*). https://law.moj.gov.tw/LawClass/LawAll.aspx?pcode=K0070039. Accessed Aug 10, 2023.
26. 交通部. (2018). 船舶法. (Ministry of Transportation and Communications, *The Law of Ships*) 2018. https://law.moj.gov.tw/ENG/LawClass/LawAll.aspx?pcode=K0070004. Accessed Aug 10, 2023.
27. Hockney, K. (2020). *The current landscape for cruising in South East Asia*.
28. Ukessays. (2018) *Various impacts of tourism in Singapore tourism essay*. Available from: https://www.ukessays.com/essays/tourism/various-impacts-of-tourism-in-singapore-tourism-essay.php?vref=1. Accessed March 10, 2023.
29. Centre for Liveable Cities Singapore. (2015). *Planning for tourism Creating a vibrant Singapore*. (1st edn). Urban Systems Studies. p. 125.
30. Dolles, H., & Söderman, S. (2008). *Mega-sporting events in Asia — Impacts on society, business and management: An introduction.* Asian Business and Management, 7.
31. Singapore Tourism Board. (2005). *Ready with a uniquely Singapore welcome*. Available from: https://www.stb.gov.sg/content/stb/en/media-centre/media-releases/ready-with-a-uniquely-singapore-welcome.html. Accessed March 10, 2023.
32. *Fisheries Act.* (1966). https://sso.agc.gov.sg/Act/FA1966. Accessed March 10, 2023.
33. *The Prevention of Pollution of the Sea Act*. (1990). https://sso.agc.gov.sg/Act/PPSA1990. Accessed March 10, 2023.
34. *Merchant Shipping Act*. (1995). https://sso.agc.gov.sg/Act/MSA1995. Accessed March 10, 2023.
35. *Maritime and Port Authority of Singapore Act*. (1996). https://sso.agc.gov.sg/Act/MPASA1996. Accessed March 10, 2023.

36. *Singapore Marine Guide*. (2020). Available from: https://sgmarineguide.com/. Accessed March 10, 2023.
37. 강동균, 한국 요트의 변천과정에 관한 연구 (2019). https://hdl.handle.net/10371/151230. Accessed August 10, 2023.
38. Kang, N., & Kim, N. (2013). Based on as-is analysis about marine leisure and super-yacht industry. 대한인간공학회 학술대회논문집, 99–104.
39. *Excursion Ship and Ferry Business Act*. (1993). https://elaw.klri.re.kr/eng_mobile/viewer.do?hseq=47747&type=part&key=10. Accessed March 10, 2023.
40. *Installation and Utilization of Sports Facilities Act*. (2007). https://elaw.klri.re.kr/eng_mobile/viewer.do?hseq=60374&type=lawname&key=Installation+and+Utilization+of+Sports+Facilities+Act. Accessed March 10, 2023.
41. *Act on the Development and Management of Marinas*. (2009). https://elaw.klri.re.kr/eng_mobile/viewer.do?hseq=55353&type=sogan&key=55. Accessed March 10, 2023.
42. *Aquaculture Industry Development Act*. (2019). https://elaw.klri.re.kr/eng_mobile/viewer.do?hseq=57307&type=lawname&key=Aquaculture+Industry+Development+Act. Accessed March 10, 2023.
43. *Act on the Use and Management of Bathing Beaches*. (2014). https://elaw.klri.re.kr/eng_mobile/viewer.do?hseq=55791&type=sogan&key=55. Accessed March 10, 2023.
44. *Act on Prevention of Accidents at Coastal Sea*. (2014). https://elaw.klri.re.kr/eng_mobile/viewer.do?hseq=56573&type=lawname&key=Act+on+Prevention+of+Accidents+at+Coastal. Accessed March 10, 2023.
45. *Framework Act on Fisheries and Fishing Villages Development*. (2015). https://elaw.klri.re.kr/eng_mobile/viewer.do?hseq=55173&type=lawname&key=Framework+Act+on+Fisheries+and+Fishing+Villages+Development. Accessed March 10, 2023.
46. *Water-Related Leisure Activities Safety Act*. (2005). https://elaw.klri.re.kr/eng_mobile/viewer.do?hseq=55434&type=lawname&key=Water-Related+Leisure+Activities+Safety+Act. Accessed March 10, 2023.
47. Korea Coast Guard (Ed.). (2012). *2012 Korea Coast Guard White Paper*. Korea Coast Guard, Editor.
48. *Cruise Industry Development and Support Act*. (2015). https://elaw.klri.re.kr/eng_mobile/viewer.do?hseq=51737&type=lawname&key=Cruise+Industry+Development+and+Support+Act. Accessed March 10, 2023.
49. *Fishing Village New-deal 300 Project*. (2019). Available from: https://www.mof.go.kr/en/page.do?menuIdx=1487. Accessed March 10, 2023.
50. Korea Coast Guard. (2023). https://www.kcg.go.kr/search/front/Search.jsp. Accessed August 10, 2023.
51. Ministry of Land Transport and Maritime Affairs. (2010). 2010-2019 마리나항만기본계획 (1st (2010~2019) Marina Port Basic Plan). http://www.molit.go.kr/USR/I0204/m_45/dtl.jsp?gubun=&search=&search_dept_id=&search_dept_nm=&old_search_dept_nm=&psize=5&search_regdate_s=&search_regdate_e=&srch_usr_nm=&srch_usr_num=&srch_usr_year=&srch_usr_titl=Y&srch_usr_ctnt=&lcmspage=1460&idx=8698. Accessed August 10, 2023.
52. *Harbor Act*. (2020). https://elaw.klri.re.kr/eng_mobile/viewer.do?hseq=54512&type=lawname&key=Harbor+Act. Accessed March 10, 2023.
53. Korea Hydrographic and Oceangraphic Agency of Ministry of Oceans and Fisheries. (2020). *Map of Yacht sailing route 2nd edition route*. https://www.khoa.go.kr/eng/user/bbs/detailBbsList.do?bbsMasterSeq=BOARD_MST_0000000041&bbsSeq=BBS_0000000101. Accessed March 10, 2023.
54. 国土交通省海事局船舶産業課 (2022)マリンレジャーの振興拠点「海の駅」*(Shipbuilding and Ship Machinery Industries, Maritime Bureau, Ministry of Land, Infrastructure, Transport and Tourism, Marine Leisure Promotion Base "Umi no Eki")*. Available from: https://www.mlit.go.jp/maritime/senpaku/Sea_station/index.html. Accessed March 10, 2023.

55. 全国海の駅一覧 *(Overview of National Sea Stations)*. (2022). Available from: https://www.umi-eki.jp/contents/list.html. Accessed March 10, 2023.
56. 海の駅を全国マップから探す*(Tajiri Sea Station Access: Visit from the Sea)*. (2023). Available from: https://www.uminoeki.org/. Accessed March 10, 2023.
57. 近畿運輸局. (2023). 漁業者から寄せられた要望等です!!プレジャーボート (Kinki district Transport Bureau, *Requests from Fishermen! Pleasure Boat)*. Available from: https://wwwtb.mlit.go.jp/kinki/koutsu/pb/gyokou/youbou.htm. Accessed March 10, 2023.
58. Japan Tourism Agency, Ministry of Land, Infrastructure, Transport and Tourism (2022). White paper on tourism in Japan, 2022 (Summary). chrome-extension://efaidnbmnnnibpcajpcglclefindmkaj/https://www.mlit.go.jp/kankocho/content/810003404.pdf. Accessed 15 July 2025
59. 해양레저관광과. (2022). 해양레저관광 활성화 방안 발표 *(Ministry of Oceans and Fisheries. Announcement of Measures to Vitalize Marine Leisure Tourism)*. Available from: https://www.korea.kr/common/download.do?fileId=196824778. Accessed August 11, 2023.
60. Urban Redevelopment Authority. (2023). *Green and Blue Plan*. Available from: https://www.ura.gov.sg/Corporate/Planning/Long-Term-Plan-Review/Space-for-Our-Dreams-Exhibition/Steward/Green-and-Blue. Accessed March 10, 2023.
61. The Yacht Harbour Association Ltd and Marina Industries Association. (2023). *Gold Anchor: Global Marina Accreditation*. Available from: http://www.goldanchors.com/. Accessed March 10, 2023.
62. International Marine Certification Institute. (2023). *Certification of watercraft & components*. Available from: https://www.imci.org/. Accessed March 10, 2023.

Chapter 6
Creating New Industries by Blue Tech: Challenges of Marine Open Innovation in Japan

Masahiro Hashimoto

Abstract The Marine Open Innovation (MaOI) project, including marine biotechnology, has been active in Shizuoka Prefecture, Japan since 2019. This is an ambitious project to develop a platform for utilization of marine genetic resources or other marine-related technology and creation of new industries. The concept of Blue Tech Cluster, which is a base of MaOI project, aims at sustainable technology development and industrialization based on science at the urban and regional levels, and it's further spreading worldwide. It is targeting all industries related to the ocean and water and is also compatible with the Sustainable Development Goals, especially Goal 14: life below water in this region. This chapter aims to clarify the details of the MaOI project, as a new type of the industrial cluster, as an example of how to create new innovation oriented toward sustainable development originating from the region.

Keywords Blue economy · Marine biotech · Industrial cluster · SDGs14 · Economic ripple effect · Regional innovation

6.1 Introduction

The marine open innovation project (MaOI project) aimed at creating marine biotechnology and/or other marine-related industries was launched in Shizuoka Prefecture, Japan, in the fiscal year 2019. This ambitious project aims to develop new technologies, including the utilization of marine genetic resources and other marine-related technology, and establish a base for the creation of new industries such as incubations, research center, or network of venture capital (VC) and supporting experts. This project is further advanced by the Blue Tech Cluster Initiative, which is being promoted globally, particularly in the United States. The Blue Tech Cluster Initiative aims to develop and industrialize scientifically-based sustainable

M. Hashimoto (✉)
Hosei Graduate School of Regional Policy Design, Tokyo, Japan
e-mail: prof.hashimoto@office.email.ne.jp

M. C. Huang et al. (eds.), *Innovative Social Practice and Community-Based Approach to the Ocean*, https://doi.org/10.1007/978-981-96-9104-3_6

technologies at the city and regional level for all ocean-related industries and economies (Blue Economy), and is also in line with the UN's Sustainable Development Goals (SDGs).

This chapter aims to clarify the details of the MaOI project, a new type of industrial cluster, as an example of how to create new innovation oriented toward sustainable development originating from the region, and to look ahead to the future in light of global trends such as Blue Economy. Further, the discussion on the economic ripple effects analysis of the project is shown at the last session and this research is still in progress, a primary analysis is outlined.

6.2 Research Background: Industrial Clusters and Innovation

This chapter discusses a case study of industrial policy aimed at creating innovation in a region by restructuring industrial clusters.

Industrial clusters have attracted attention and prompted research since the 1990s as an important mechanism for creating innovation, with Silicon Valley at the forefront, and the 1990s as a period of dramatic growth in innovation research (Hashimoto et al., 2012 [1]). The Silicon Valley model has been studied not only in the U.S. but also in many other countries, and innovation through the construction of similar models is being pursued. Among these studies, Porter's theory of industrial clusters has played a leading role (Porter, 1998 [2]). Porter considers industrial clusters to be a powerful source of competitive advantage and, using examples of existing industrial clusters such as Italian footwear and California wine, analyzes in detail the scope, formation process, and composition of clusters, the roles of government and business, and their strong influence on innovation creation [2]. These discussions have influenced not only researchers but also innovation policy makers worldwide. Nishizawa (Nishizawa et al. 2005 [3]) analyzed in detail the process of IT high-tech industry creation that took place in Austin, USA, and elucidated the reality of the innovation cluster.

Thus, from the 1990s through the twenty-first century, the significance of industrial clusters in innovation creation became a common understanding not only in academia but also in government. And in Japanese government, the Industrial Cluster Plan (Ministry of Economy, Trade and Industry) and the Intellectual Cluster Creation Project (Ministry of Education, Culture, Sports, Science and Technology) have been promoted.

Porter's analysis includes examples of small-scale industrial clusters that originally existed but became the mothers of new innovations. On the other hand, in the Austin example (Nishizawa et al. 2005 [3]), IC^2—launched by the creator of the cluster, Professor G. Kozmetsky of the University of Texas—was an innovation network, and a great industrial cluster was built from the ground up, meaning that it was a cluster that had not previously existed. In other words, the Austin example shows that new innovation clusters are formed through the presence of innovation leaders and the role of government rather than the creation of new innovations from existing clusters. Thus, it is important to note that there are two sides to the industrial cluster theory: the development of existing (spontaneous) clusters and the creation of policy for new clusters.

This chapter analyzes the latter process of policy-driven industrial cluster creation, while positioning and analyzing the MaOI project as a model for the twenty-first century, so to speak, with a strong awareness of the SDGs.

6.3 Structure of this Thesis

This chapter first describes the background of the MaOI project, from before its establishment to its launch, and then analyzes and describes its position after organizing the background of the project's establishment. The chapter will then outline the Blue Economy, which is deeply related to the SDGs (Sustainable Development Goals proposed by the United Nations), and the Blue Tech Cluster. This chapter will also show that the project is unique in Japan. Then, it will analyze the project's policy tools used by the local government (Shizuoka Prefecture), which include to create a vision, to promote R&D, to establish a research center, and to build and to utilize databases. It will discuss the policy effects of these tools. Finally, I will discuss the possible impact on the local economy of the development of the "marine-related industries" targeted by the project, and link this to future research.

6.4 Backgrounds of the Establishment of the MaOI Project

6.4.1 Background of the Establishment of the MaOI Project 1: Shizuoka Prefecture and Marine Biotechnology

Alongside being home to Mt. Fuji, Shizuoka Prefecture is a maritime region that includes Suruga Bay. Suruga Bay is one of the steepest bays in the world and the deepest in Japan, reaching 2500 meters at its deepest point. As a result, the bay is rich in biodiversity and is said to be home to more than 40% of all fish species in Japan. In the 1990s, two sites of the Marine biotechnology Institute (the MBI) were established in Shimizu (Shizuoka Prefecture) and Kamaishi (Iwate Prefecture in the Tohoku region) at the initiative of the Japanese government and private companies and universities. The MBI was established to promote research and development and industrialization of new applications for unlimited marine biological resources. 24 private companies, including Toa Fuel Industries (now ENEOS Corporation) and Nippon Steel Corporation, and universities participated in this research and development project. The MBI was a highly advanced global effort to promote research and development of biotechnology projects on a scale of 15 billion yen (initial plan). (Shindo [1989] [4]). The MBI had been applied for more than 300 patents, including patents related to antifouling paints for ships, based on research results regarding the characteristics and genome information of various marine organisms.

At the same time, Professor Tadashi Matsunaga of the Tokyo University of Agriculture and Technology, who is one of the leaders in the field of Marin Biotechnology, also contributed to the management of the MBI, and other professors established the Marine Biotechnology Research Association (now the Japanese Society of Marine Biotechnology). The first meeting was held in May 1992 at the Faculty of Oceanography, Tokai University in Shimizu, Japan.

Around 1990, expectations for the potential of biotechnology rose rapidly worldwide, and the government established a Bioindustry Division in the Ministry of International Trade and Industry (now the Ministry of Economy, Trade and Industry) with the aim of creating a bio-industry. This was the period when genetic recombination technology became universal and was followed by genome analysis. Among these, there were many unknown genetic resources of marine organisms, and in particular, people expected unlimited possibilities from organisms living in extreme environments such as high temperatures, high pressure, or high sulfur concentration, which could not be found on the surface of the earth.

In recent years, biotechnology has made even more rapid strides. The development of next-generation sequencers has made possible high-speed and inexpensive genome decoding technology. And the development of genome editing technology that enables accurate and rapid genetic modification, coupled with advances in information analysis technology, are expected to contribute to innovation not only in the medical field but also in a wide range of industrial fields, such as agriculture, forestry, fisheries, and manufacturing. The selection of Dr. Emmanuelle Charpentier, Director of the Max Planck Institute for Infection Biology, and Professor Jennifer Doudna of the University of California, Berkeley, as the 2020 Nobel Laureates in Chemistry for the development of CRISPR Cas9, the leading genome editing technology, is symbolic of this era.

6.4.2 *Background of the Establishment of the MaOI Project 2: High-Tech Industrial Clusters and Regional Development*

Shimizu City, where the Marine Biotechnology Research Institute used to be located, merged with Shizuoka City in 2003 and became an ordinance-designated city. However, even though it is the prefectural capital, its population has begun to decline. As a result, the automobile industry, which had supported the economy of not only Hamamatsu City in the west but the entire prefecture, became concerned about future industrial decline due to the spread of electric vehicles. In response to this social and economic transition, the government of Shizuoka Prefecture was engaged in various projects to create advanced industries such as Pharma Valley (medical and health care industry cluster), Photon Valley (optical and electronics industry cluster), AOI (Agri Open Innovation Project), and CNF (cellulose nanofibers research developments).

Looking at the industrial structure of Shizuoka Prefecture, the Hamamatsu region has an industrial cluster centered on the automotive-related industry, where innovation has been created. In the Hamamatsu region, industry-academia collaboration with Shizuoka University's Faculty of Engineering is thriving, and venture companies are being actively created. In the eastern part of the region (Mishima, Numazu, etc.), there are many pharmaceutical and cosmetics manufacturers, which are ranked first or second in Japan in terms of production. Against this backdrop, the Pharma Valley Project, centered on the Shizuoka Cancer Center, has been promoted by the Ministry of Education, Culture, Sports, Science and Technology to create an intellectual cluster.

On the other hand, in the central part of the prefecture, the Shizuoka-Shimizu area, there are various industries such as food, machinery, and electricity, but there are no clusters in particular. Universities such as Shizuoka University (science, agriculture, humanities, etc.), Tokai University Faculty of Marine Science and Technology, and the University of Shizuoka Prefecture (medicine, food, management, etc.) are located in the area, but there are no nationally ranked universities in the field of science and technology, and industry-academia cooperation seems to be limited. In addition, compared to the Hamamatsu area, the city does not have a strong venture spirit, and although there is some venture support by the local government and private sector, nothing of particular note can be found.

Furthermore, a comparison of Shizuoka City's manufacturing industry with that of the 21 largest cities in Japan shows that Shizuoka City has the fourth highest concentration of the manufacturing industry (on an employee basis), following top 3. However, the percentage of "professional and technical workers" in the industry is the lowest. (14.3% according to the 2015 National Census) (Hashimoto [2018] [5]). As a point of comparison, among the 21 cities, Kawasaki City has the highest rate at 22.3%.

Given these factors, it is expected to be quite difficult to autonomously form high-tech industrial clusters with engineers and researchers, which are the key to innovation creation. Against this backdrop, and taking into account the history of the aforementioned the Marine Biotech Institute, momentum has been created and implemented by those involved to once again build a "marine biotechnology" center for the creation of high-tech innovation in Shimizu region, and to develop it into a new industry.

6.4.3 Background of the Establishment of the MaOI Project 3: Chronological Arrangement

Based on the above background, Shizuoka Prefecture established the "Marine Biotechnology Industry Promotion Vision Study Council" in November 2018 in collaboration with industry, government, and academia, to study measures to promote marine biotechnology and create new industries. And the following year, the Council compiled the "Marine Biotechnology Industry Promotion Vision." Based on this vision, the Marine Open Innovation (MaOI) Project was launched to promote not only industrial development, but also human resource accumulation and development, regional development with a marine theme, and global dissemination and deployment, with the aim of creating a world-class center in this region.

Table 6.1 summarizes the progress and history of the MaOI Project as a policy of Shizuoka Prefecture in chronological order. The starting point of contact with the prefectural government was November 13, 2017.As shown in Table 6.1, the prefectural government, immediately began to consider the budget request for the next fiscal year. In 2018, the Marine Biotechnology Study Group was launched, which continued to shift to the Marine Bio Industry Promotion Vision Review Council, and finally on February 7, 2019, I as the chairperson to the council, had handed and explained the concluded vision to Professor Kawakatsu, the Governor of Shizuoka

Table 6.1 MaOI project establishment history timeline

Year	Month	Event
2017	Nov	Courtesy call on Vice Governor Dr. Namba of Shizuoka Prefecture
	Dec	Start of project review (initial budget request for FY2018)
2018	Apr	Start of the Marine Bio Industry Promotion Project
	Jun	1st Marine Biotechnology Study Group
	Jul	2nd Marine Biotechnology Study Group
	Sep	3rd Marine Biotechnology Study Group
	Nov	Fujinokuni Marine Biotechnology Seminar
	Dec	2nd Marine Bio Industry Promotion Vision Review Council
2019	Feb	Proposal "Marine Bio Industry Promotion Vision" hand delivered to the governor, Prof. Kawakatsu
	Mar	3rd Marine Bio Industry Promotion Vision Review Council
	Apr	Adopted for regional revitalization promotion subsidy (pioneering type: 5 years)
	Jul	Establishment of Marine Open Innovation Institute
	Jul	U.S. West Coast Survey Team
	Sep	International Marine Biotechnology Conference (Shimizu)
	Oct	Marine Open Innovation Strategy Promotion Committee
	Nov	Participated in Blue Tech Week 2019 (San Diego, USA)
2020	Feb	The general meeting for the establishment of the "Society to connect the beautiful and rich seas of Shizuoka to the future"
	Mar	"Marine Open Innovation Project first Strategic Plan" formulated
	Nov	Opened MaOI-PARC

Prefecture. In fiscal 2019, Shizuoka Prefecture adopted a subsidy to promote regional revitalization, and the project began in earnest, and in July of the same year, the MaOI Institute was established.

The MaOI Project is being promoted by mobilizing excellent prefectural officials under the strong leadership of Shizuoka Prefecture Governor Heita Kawakatsu and Deputy Governor (then) Takashi Namba. Governor Kawakatsu is an expert in economic history and a former professor of Waseda University. He is known for having a unique historiographical perspective as “Bunmei no kaiyoushikan (Kawakatsu [2016] [5])” and has a strong interest and deep knowledge of the ocean. Deputy Governor Namba is a former Ministry of Transportation official who is familiar with the maritime policy such as the port policy, and he has been strongly promoting prefectural administration in various policies. With such leaders, Shizuoka Prefecture began to move toward the creation of innovation based on the ocean in a short period of time.

In general, there is always excellent leadership behind the success of regional revitalization. It can be argued that the MaOI project is a major success factor in the presence of good leaders.

In July 2019, the Marine Open Innovation Institute (MaOI Institute) was established as a project promotion and support organization. In Shizuoka Prefecture’s previous projects, a similar corporation was established with the prefecture’s investment to act as a promotional body, and has a system that undertakes various responses all at once. This MaOI project also took a similar form and became a receptacle to flexibly promote the administration of the prefecture. To establish and utilize the promotion bodies is the point to build an effective system for ensuring the flexibility and immediacy of policies promoted by the national and local governments. In promoting innovation policy at the national level in Japan, funding agencies such as NEDO and JST will create a more flexible promotion system by reducing various constraints on budget execution and complementing the inherently unpredictable nature of R&D and other important elements of innovation creation. Local governments can also promote industrial promotion measures by the private sector, which are difficult for local governments to implement on their own, by flexibly building external organizations. Professor Tadashi Matsunaga, who was instrumental in establishing the Japanese Society of Marine Biotechnology, was appointed as the first president of the MaOI Institute. (After that, he concurrently served as the president of the Japan Agency for Marine-Earth Science and Technology [JAMSTEC].)

Professor Takashi Gojobori was appointed as the director of research in the institute at the beginning of the institute. He is a world-renowned authority in the field of biotechnology, especially genome analysis, who served as Deputy Director of the National Institute of Genetics in Mishima City, and currently as Distinguished Professor at King Abdullah University of Science and Technology (KAUST) in Saudi Arabia. As a result of his appointment, the MaOI Institute has taken its first step not only as an industrial support organization, but also as a research institute that conducts its own research.

In November 2020, the core base research facility, MaOI-PARC was established in Shimizu Ward, Shizuoka City. MaOI-PARC is equipped with joint laboratories and collaborative laboratories with state-of-the-art equipment such as genome sequencers and single cell analysis systems that can be used by companies and research institutions participating in the project. MaOI-PARC plays a role as a base. In addition, MaOI coordinators provide comprehensive support for research and development and commercialization, such as matching researchers and companies and holding seminars.

6.5 MaOI Project Structure that Positions SDGs: Blue Tech, Blue Economy

In July 2019, immediately after the establishment of the MaOI Institute, the survey group, consisting of directors of the MaOI Institute, professors, and local government officials including the author, visited the West Coast of the United States to investigate innovation clusters. We visited various institutes and organization such as the UC Santa Barbara Institute of Marine Science, the Monterey Bay Aquarium, which are world-famous for its advanced marine research and cutting-edge exhibitions, and the last few days, we visited the city of San Diego, which is famous for its bio-industry cluster. The group visited universities, research institutes, and government agencies to investigate and examine the possibility of collaboration.

At that time, the group met a new movement of "Blue Tech Cluster" that we didn't know much about. Mr. Michael Jones, representative of "TMA (The Maritime Alliance) Blue Tech," when we visited in San Diego, recommended cooperation with the global network of "Blue Tech Cluster" (See Fig. 6.1). The Blue Tech Cluster has been advocated by TMA based on the concept of creating and accumulating new industries in the region, starting from "Blue Tech = technological development that contributes to all industries related to the ocean."[1] Currently, BTCA (Blue Tech Cluster Alliance [members shown in Table 6.2]) are aiming to form a marine industry clusters network. And eight countries, the United States, Ireland, the United Kingdom, Canada, Spain, Norway, France, and Portugal, are participating.

In 2017, a meeting of the world's Blue Tech clusters was held at the United Nations Headquarters. Meanwhile, the international conference "BlueTech Week," held every November in San Diego, brings together hundreds of companies, researchers, investors, and other interested parties from around the world, mainly from clusters in eight countries. In response to Mr. Jones' invitation, MaOI is the only Japanese participant in the BlueTech Week from 2019, deepening the discussion on the future of the marine industry with representatives from other countries.

The common goal of these BlueTech clusters is the concept of "Blue Economy (sustainable marine economy). Although there is no clear, unified international

[1] https://www.bluetechclusters.org/

Fig. 6.1 Blue Tech Clusters in the World. Source: The Blue Tech Cluster Alliance (2019)

Table 6.2 Blue tech cluster alliance members in 2022

Name	Country	URL
Forum Oceano	Portugal	http://www.forumoceano.pt/
Marine Institute Ireland	Ireland	https://www.marine.ie/Home/home
Oceans Advance	Canada	http://www.oceansadvance.net/
PLOCAN	Spain	https://www.plocan.eu/en/
Pole Mer Mediterranee	France	www.polemermediterranee.com
TMA BlueTech	USA	https://themaritimealliance.org/
GCE Ocean Technology	Norway	https://www.gceocean.no/
Pole Mer Bretagne Atlantique	France	https://www.pole-mer-bretagne-atlantique.com/en/
Cornwall Marine Network	UK	https://cornwallmarine.net/
Marine South East	UK	https://www.mseinternational.org/

definition of the blue economy, Mr. Jones of the TMA, at the meeting of 2019 with Japanese visitors, defines it as "the promotion of (1) marine and water-related industries, (2) based on a scientific perspective, and (3) in a sustainable manner."

The concept of the Blue Economy is in line with the SDGs, which are currently the focus of global attention. The oceans are the mother of life, and have nurtured the Earth and its people. The oceans are currently suffering from irreversible pollution and other problems. Protecting and sustainably using the ocean and its resources is an important strategy for humanity.

Coming into contact with this concept, the MaOI project originally has been focused on marine biotechnology related to conventional associated resources. However, the MaOI project has expanded the basic philosophy so that the goal is to create a blue economy in a wide range of ocean-related industrial fields. In 2020, Shizuoka Prefecture compiled the "Marine Open Innovation Project 1st Strategic

Plan (FY2019-2023)"[2] to materialize the "Marine Bio Industry Promotion Vision," a new direction with an eye on the entire blue economy was incorporated, adding breadth and depth to the project. As of November 2022, the first vision has been undergoing an interim review based on the development of various promotion systems and the progress of research after its formulation, and the new version of the vision will be setting more advanced goals. This vision aims at sustainable development of ocean and focuses on SDG14: life below water, and other goals such as SDGs 6, 7, and 17.

Shizuoka City has Shimizu Port, an international hub. It was originally a city where shipping, shipbuilding, and seafood processing were thriving. Therefore, it is thought that the marine-related industrial cluster in traditional meaning, might have existed. To discuss this point, the industrial structure of this region will be referred to in Chap. 7. The concept of the Blue Tech cluster is to promote the creation of new industries from the marine-related industrial cluster, and has great potential as an industrial policy.

6.6 Analysis of the Policy Tools in MaOI Project

The policy tools promoted as MaOI projects can be organized into policy vision, R&D subsidies, and coordination functions, original R&D, database construction and provision, and citizen network creation. These are mainly subsidized by the local government, and partly include donations from citizens, contributions from companies, and a small subsidy from the national government.

Below is a summary of the policy tools provided by the government of Shizuoka Prefecture to date, based on information from the Shizuoka Prefecture website[3] and MaOI Institute website.[4]

6.6.1 *Policy Vision and Management of the Project*

At the time of the initial launch (2018–2019), in order to formulate a vision for the promotion of the marine bio industry, Shizuoka Prefecture set up a specialized council. This council consisted of related academia, industries including marine products and fishery processing, local industrial groups, financial institutions, etc. This vision was presented to the governor and became the basis for a budget request

[2] (In Japanese)
https://www.pref.shizuoka.jp/_res/projects/default_project/_page_/001/025/738/keikaku.pdf

[3] (In Japanese)
https://www.pref.shizuoka.jp/sangyoshigoto/kigyoshien/kankyosangyo/1040481/1025704.html

[4] (In Japanese) https://maoi-i.jp/works

to the Ministry of Internal Affairs and Communications for a grant to promote regional development, which led to the acquisition of the budget.

Furthermore, in order to realize the Blue Tech cluster, which is a concept that has been further expanded from the above vision, the Marine Open Innovation Strategy Promotion Committee was established. It formulated a strategic plan based on the consideration of a wider range of members and made specific policy recommendations. The entire MaOI project is being implemented in line with this First Strategic Plan.

The First Strategic Plan is being discussed by the MaOI Strategic Promotion Committee (composed of members from academia and related industries, economic organizations, and local governments) whose secretariat is located in the Industrial Innovation Promotion Division of the Shizuoka Prefecture Department of Economy and Industry. While the management of the project is the responsibility of this division in coordination with the MaOI Institute, the overall direction of the project is determined through discussions with the above committee, especially with the chairperson of the committee, and with the author, who is MaOI's General Producer, which is the role that oversees the entire planning and execution of operations and business of the institute.

6.6.2 R&D Funds and Subsidies

Concrete research and development in the MaOI project began in 2019 in line with the above vision and strategic plan by Shizuoka Prefecture. Initially, research and development focused on marine biotechnology was carried out based on the idea of promoting the marine biotechnology industry. The following two systems, commissioned research for academia and research assistance for corporate consortiums, were started as projects of the prefecture from the beginning.

(1) *Research and development grants fund "Seeds creation research outsourcing" upper limit of 10,000,000 yen/year (within 3 years):*

These are the tools to promote seeds creation research outsourcing (publicly recruited research outsourcing unique to Shizuoka Prefecture), and it is for mainly universities, and research institutes. This is an open-recruitment type commissioned research with the aim of creating Shizuoka Prefecture's own technology seeds that will lead to the promotion of industry in the prefecture. Research on the control of blindness disease by components derived from fish from Shizuoka Prefecture," Tokyo University of Marine Science and Technology and Prefectural Fisheries and Marine Technology Research Institute, "Establishment of alfonsino breeding technology," University of Shizuoka, Hagoromo Foods Co., Ltd., Prefectural Industrial Technology Research. The MaOI project has been conducting research such as "Search for carotenoid-producing microorganisms derived from Suruga Bay and their application to supplement development" by a consortium.

(2) *Commercialization support "Marine open innovation commercialization promotion project subsidy" upper limit 20,000,000 yen/single year (within 3 years, subsidy rate 2/3)*

In this subsidy system, it is aimed to support the commercialization efforts of private companies, and these efforts that are close to commercialization have started. Examples of this are, the development of foods with fermented mackerel seasonings that use microorganisms derived from the ocean, and the development of cosmetics using ingredients such as Akamoku (A type of macroalgae) from Suruga Bay.

Through these systems in the fishery sector, the MaOI project will develop marine products with brand power using biotechnology, and develop seedling production and aquaculture businesses. In the fields of drug discovery and cosmetics, the search for novel functional substances derived from the ocean and their application to pharmaceuticals and cosmetics are expected. In the field of the environment and energy, the MaOI project is promoting the development and evaluation of biodegradable plastics, and is also implementing the development of marine-related mechanical technology, including fisheries.

In addition, from FY2020, the new type of subsidized projects have been started with an awareness of Blue Tech and with R&D themes other than bio- and fisheries-related research and development themes in mind.

(3) *Research and development support "Marine technology development promotion project subsidy" upper limit 10,000,000 yen /year (within 2 years, subsidy rate 2/3)*

The third subsidy system is focusing on various areas of research and development in the field of marine-related technology.

In addition to these three types of funds and subsidies, the MaOI Institute's own feasibility study system has realized flexible support. This funding system was proposed as a tool for the coordinator of the MaOI Institute, and they are in charge of prior consultations before the start of each research project by the local government. Although the amount of each financial support of the funds is small (two million yen per project), it functions as an effective tool for subsequent joint research and research grants.

The MaOI Institute has coordinators with expertise in manufacturing, fisheries, food, finance, etc. They actively visit companies in the prefecture to discover or organize research projects that will lead to MaOI projects and provide commercialization support to private companies which are interested in research development to realize the marine-related new industry. From around 2022, the MaOI Institute will strengthen coordination activities with the cooperation of financial institutions such as local banks.

6.6.3 Research Facilities and Research Development by MaOI Institute

The research capabilities of the MaOI Institute have been established under the leadership of Institute Director Professor Takashi Gojobori, and advanced research capabilities in biotechnology, including single-cell analysis equipment, have been developed in MaOI-PARC. In addition, the MaOI Institute has taken the lead in conducting various joint research projects on the oceans at MaOI-PARC in cooperation with prefectural public research institutes and universities. From the beginning, in collaboration with Waseda University, which possesses unique single-cell technology, advanced research has also been initiated to collect and analyze environmental DNA from Suruga Bay. In the future, this research is expected to lead to the understanding of the abundance of Sakura shrimps and other fish species in Suruga Bay, whose catch is declining rapidly.

6.6.4 Development of MaOI Institute's Own Database: BISHOP

The MaOI Institute is also collecting its own marine-related data. For example, in collaboration with the Shizuoka Prefectural Institute of Fisheries and Ocean Technology, the MaOI Institute collected the completion of whole genome decoding of aquatic organisms collected in the prefecture, such as the Sakura shrimp, at a conference of the Society of Evolution in 2022. The decoding is expected to be used to elucidate the ecology of these organisms and for resource management in the future. The marine data (physical data such as sea conditions and weather, fishery-related data such as catches of fish and fish diseases, biological or chemical data such as metagenomes, environmental DNA, etc.) collected in this region will be stored in the data platform, "BISHOP (Blue Innovation of Shizuoka Open data Platform)" and utilized as open data of Shizuoka's sea, which will contribute to industrial promotion and environmental conservation. In addition, a marine microorganism library, which collects and organizes information on marine-derived microorganisms, lactic acid bacteria, yeasts, etc. collected in Suruga Bay and other Shizuoka seas, has been established within the platform and is available for use by companies and research institutions.

6.6.5 *Promoting Innovation Network through the MaOI Forum*

Since its establishment, the MaOI Institute has provided a variety of information and business support to its member companies through the MaOI Forum, with the aim of supporting marine-related industries. Through seminars and face-to-face salons, a wide range of topics have been covered, including marine vitamins, ocean-based medicine, and aquaculture. In addition, the coordinators mentioned at Sect. 6.2, have been vigorously supporting businesses using the MaOI project. Apart from corporate members, the MaOI Forum has national and local governments and research institutions participating as supporter members. In this way, it has been actively connecting businesses and researchers. By building such a network between industry, academia, government, and banks, the forum aims to create Blue Tech innovation.

6.6.6 *Creation of a Community-Based Citizen Network: Connecting the Beautiful and Abundant Shizuoka Sea to the Future*

After exchanging views with Blue Tech clusters in advanced overseas locations, the MaOI project has decided to become a global project that will advance not only local industries, but also Japanese and international perspectives. At the same time, based on the concept of the blue economy, which places emphasis on sustainability, it was decided to not only promote industry, but also to actively address the conservation of the marine environment and protection of marine resources.

One of these efforts is the establishment of "The Association for Linking the Beautiful and Abundant Sea of Shizuoka to the Future." The association was established with the support of 140 local businesses and organizations, and the Governor of the prefecture became its chairman.

The association covers a wide range of fields, including industry, the environment, tourism, marine leisure and sports, education, and community development. By horizontally linking individuals, NPOs, businesses, local governments, educational and research institutions, and others engaged in various ocean-related activities, the association will form a large network under the theme of "Shizuoka's Oceans" to learn about, become familiar with, protect, and connect the oceans to the future.

The MaOI Institute serves as the secretariat for this association, which will enable them to establish contacts with people through the industrial approach, and to further promote the MaOI project. It is hoped that the MaOI project will provide an opportunity to further connect with local communities.

6.7 Discussion on Policies

Porter (1998 [2]) lists "promoting cluster development and upgrading" as the fourth role of government in the economy, alongside its overall macro and microeconomic roles. It also indicates a fifth role: "development and implementation of an active and well-defined long-term economic action program." It also presents a detailed menu of policies on the government's impact on the upgrading of specific clusters.

In light of Porter's thesis, the policies outlined above for the MaOI project are first of all consistent with the strategic vision for the development and implementation of a long-term action program. Simultaneously, the support for R&D and the development of R&D centers alongside the development and provision of a database (BISHOP) are positioned as "input resources."

The activities of the Forum and the Citizen Network, which have been explained on Sects. 6.5 and 6.6, are explicitly identified in the "Related and Supporting Industries" section in the Porter's diamond (Porter [1998] [2]). In this paper, Porter describes the government's influence on the upgrading of industrial clusters as spilling over throughout the Porter Diamond, and he explicitly indicates that the government will sponsor a forum to bring together industrial cluster participants.

On the other hand, for the cluster to take off, it is important to promote the matters indicated in the "Corporate Strategies and Competitive Relationships" section, and "Establish a research system at local universities in technological fields closely related to the cluster." This can be a major theme and project of "input resource." In addition, policy support for "reducing regulatory uncertainty" and "stimulating early adoption of innovations," as indicated in the "Demand Conditions" section, for example, there is a plan to make Shimizu Port "a test bed" for the development of various marine-related technologies, and further progress can be expected in this area.

Regarding Porter's discussion of the government's role in the cluster, I offer two arguments. The first is that governments should encourage the growth of existing clusters rather than creating new clusters from scratch. In this regard, it should be noted that this project follows Professor Kozmetsky's attempt to create new clusters, as described in Research Background: Industrial Clusters and Innovation (Nishizawa et al., 2002 [4]). However, as will be discussed in a later section, the ratio of marine-related industries in the Shizuoka region is higher than in other regions, and it is possible to hypothesize that a cluster of marine-related industries existed in the region to begin with. We will leave this point to future research.

The second is for the government to develop and implement a proactive and clear long-term economic action program. In this project, a 5-year strategic plan has been developed and there is a clear vision. This is by no means a long-term plan, but the policies are based on the assumption that they will be developed into a second and third phase plans in the future. Regarding the implementation of the policies, the MaOI's Strategic Promotion Committee established by the prefecture and chaired by Prof. Hashimoto, the author, which formulated the plan, determines overall policy, while implementation is handled by the responsible departments in the prefecture and the MaOI Institute. Therefore, the success or failure of this project depends on the management and strategy of this committee and the local government.

6.8 Discussion on the Economic Ripple Effects Analysis of the MaOI Project

In June 2022 the "Blue Economy Study Group" was established in MaOI Institute to examine the economic ripple effects of industrial policies in the MaOI project, and a study is underway, led by the researcher, Shigeki Aoki, who has a substantive track record of analyzing input-output tables. The research is still in progress, and as such the details will not be discussed in this chapter, but a primary analysis is outlined below.

First, referring to previous domestic and international studies (OECD, EU, TMA Blue Tech, Cabinet Office of Japan, Japan Maritime Center, etc.), the study group analyzed the definition and production scale of marine-related industries in Shizuoka City. Marine-related industries have a cross-sectional spread from primary to secondary and even tertiary industries, and the study group estimated the scale of production from a broad perspective. The production value of marine-related industries in Shizuoka Prefecture (in 2015, when statistical data were available), that was estimated in this study group, is 2,509,246 million yen which accounts for 7.5% of Shizuoka Prefecture's production value, this percentage is more than triple of the national average.. And the value-added is 3,521,213 million yen and which means the production induction factor is 1.4 (Aoki et al. 2024 [6]).

Next, an economic ripple effect analysis was conducted to estimate the impact (multiplier) of Shizuoka City's marine-related industries on the city's economy using Input-Output Tables. In the economic ripple-effect analysis, the scale of production of marine-related industries in Shizuoka City is defined as the "direct effect," and this affects the local economy through two routes:

$$\text{Economic ripple effects} = \text{direct effects} + \text{indirect effects}\left(\text{primary and secondary}\right)$$

The indirect primary effect is the magnitude of the ripple effect through the procurement activities of goods and services required for the business activities of marine-related industries in Shizuoka City. On the other hand, the indirect secondary effect is the magnitude of the ripple effect of a portion of employment income paid to workers in marine-related industries becoming consumption expenditures, thereby increasing production activity in the local economy. According to our calculations, the economic ripple effect of marine-related industries in Shizuoka City is 641.3 billion yen, and the magnitude of the multiplier for the production value of marine-related industries reaches 1.31 times of her marine-related industries. The magnitude of the economic ripple effect will largely depend on the following two elements. First is measures to improve the activities of marine-related industries, which is called the direct effects. And the second is the concentration of industries in the region, such as the degree of concentration of goods and services needed by marine-related industries. The percentage of consumption expenditure by employees that is spent in the region, and regional revitalization measures also need to be considered from these two major perspectives.

The industrial structure of Shizuoka City is comprised of a wider range of industries than the Hamamatsu area, where it is concentrated in the automotive industry. However, there seems to be a significant concentration of marine industries, and the economic ripple effects of the prefecture's MaOI project are expected to be substantial. The study group plans to continue analyzing the industrial relations table and conduct an analytical study in FY2023 to determine what effect this industrial policy could have on the prefecture as a whole. This is a groundbreaking policy that includes the quantitative measurement of policy effects right from the start of the project.

6.9 Conclusions and Future Development of the MaOI Project

6.9.1 Conclusions

This chapter has dealt with the case of the MaOI project, which is underway in Shizuoka Prefecture, and discusses the policy to create a new type of industrial cluster promoted by the local government, its background, analysis of policy tools, economic ripple effects, and future challenges. Regarding the success or failure of the project, it is mentioned the importance of leadership and management in addition to policy. However, other factors, especially social aspects, also seem to play a large role. In this regard, it is possible that the United Nations Decade of Ocean Science for Sustainable Development, will have a positive impact, such as rising global expectations for a "blue economy," which will become one of the key areas attracting the attention of global investors, who are sensitive to environmental investment.

In September 2019, the year of the project's launch, the International Marine Biotechnology Conference (MBC2019) was held. During the conference, which was a great opportunity to announce the start of the MaOI project both domestically and internationally, President Matsunaga of the MaOI Institute presented its Declaration. The declaration stated, "We will learn more about Mother Ocean, discover new blessings through Blue Tech, and work to create new value and solve problems in a variety of industries. Through these efforts, we aim to realize a more prosperous, healthy and long-lived society, and to connect our lives with the ocean into the future. We look forward to the endorsement and cooperation of many like-minded people."

6.9.2 Future Work

Regarding the (potential) indicators, and the expected cluster impact, we formulated the above-mentioned study group to examine the economic ripple effects of industrial policies in the MaOI project. The study group aims to clarify the size of ocean-related industries to date and to quantitatively measure the potential impact of blue economy policies. We hope that in a future study, at the start of the second phase of the MaOI project, we will be able to visualize the results of individual policies and measure quantitative economic effects.

6.9.3 Future Development

It is argued that there are strong leaders of Shizuoka Prefecture, Governor, Prof. Kawakatsu and other executives. Adding to people in the prefecture, the significant leadership from the policy makers, such as parliament members in the region, Yoko Kamikawa, Member of the House of Representatives, has been promoting this project which aims to build a Test Bed for the development of various marine-related technologies in this area. In January 2022, the Suruga Bay Open Ocean Diet Members Caucus (chaired by House of Representatives member Yoko Kamikawa), consisting of volunteer Diet members from the Liberal Democratic Party, the ruling party of the Japanese government, was established to promote the creation of a digital rural city concept in the ocean around Shizuoka Prefecture, centering on Suruga Bay. In response to this, the Council for the Promotion of Marine Culture Research Center was established in July 2022, by private companies in the region. Further to this, moves to promote a blue economy in Suruga Bay are accelerating in step with the Diet Members Caucus. This is not just the work of one local government, Shizuoka Prefecture, but has great potential to become an extremely useful program for the creation of innovation in Japan. With the support of the Japanese government, it can be expected that this trend will accelerate in the future. The year 2021, when the MaOI project had been fully operational, was coincidentally the first year of the United Nations Decade of Ocean Science for Sustainable Development (2021-2030). Through the MaOI project, it is hoped that Suruga Bay will progress as a global center for the promotion of marine industries and the conservation of the marine environment.

References

1. Hashimoto, Kajikawa, Sakata, Takeda and Matsushima. (2012). Academic landscape of innovation research and national innovation policy reformation in Japan and the United States. *International Journal of Innovation and Technology Management, 09.*

2. Porter, M. E. (1998). *On competition*. Harvard Business School Press. Japanese edition: Porter, M. E. (2018). *Kyousousenryaku Ron (On Competision) II*. p-141, fig 2-11, Diamond Press.
3. Nishizawa, A., & Fukushima, M. (2005). *Daigaku hatsu bencha to kurasuta senryak (University spinoff companies and cluster strategy)*. Gakubunsha.
4. Shindo, H. (1989). *Journal of the Seawater Society of Japan, 43*(3).
5. Kawakatsu, Heita. (2016). Bunmei no Kaiyoushikan. *Chuoukouronshinhsa.*
6. Aoki, S., & Shi, L. (2024). Project report. *MaOI Institute Blue Economy Study Group Seminar, 2024*(3), 21.

Part III
Innovative Forms of Blue Impact

Chapter 7
A People-Centered Approach: The Case of Community-Based Ecotourism in Palau

Li-Yun Hsu and Hideyuki Shiozawa

Abstract In 2015, the Sasakawa Peace Foundation (SPF) launched an initiative to promote environmentally sustainable tourism in Palau, where rapid growth in inbound tourism had begun to pose significant social and environmental challenges. The project introduced tourism carrying capacity assessments and community-based ecotourism models aimed at balancing local economic benefits with the preservation of Palau's natural and cultural heritage. In collaboration with the International Cooperation and Development Fund (TaiwanICDF), which implemented a circular agriculture project, the initiative also supported capacity building through workshops and training programs. Amid the socio-economic vulnerabilities exposed by the COVID-19 pandemic, particularly in small island developing states (SIDS), this initiative offers an ecotourism model for enhancing resilience. By promoting sustainable tourism diversification alongside the conservation of cultural and natural resources, the project contributes to the development of more adaptive and resilient island societies.

Keywords Sustainable tourism · SDG8 · SDG12 · People centered approach · Resilient island society · Palau · Ecotourism

7.1 Introduction

Palau is a small island country located on the westernmost edge of the Micronesian region of the Pacific Ocean. It has a land area of approximately 444 km^2 and an exclusive economic zone of roughly 600,000 km^2. It comprises approximately 340 islands, islets, and atolls. About 18,000 people live on eight islands, mostly in Koror,

L.-Y. Hsu (✉)
International Cooperation and Development Fund, Taipei, Taiwan
e-mail: l.y.hsu@icdf.org.tw

H. Shiozawa
Ocean Policy Research Institute (OPRI), Sasakawa Peace Foundation, Tokyo, Japan
e-mail: h-shiozawa@spf.or.jp

M. C. Huang et al. (eds.), *Innovative Social Practice and Community-Based Approach to the Ocean*, https://doi.org/10.1007/978-981-96-9104-3_7

the former capital of the country [1]. The country consists of 16 states that evolved from traditional villages, where a modern democratic society coexists with a traditional society that includes a long-established chieftaincy system, which today has no political authority (Fig. 7.1).

Palau became part of the United Nations Trust Territory of the Pacific Islands in 1947 and gained independence as a Freely Associated State with the United States in 1994. The following words appear in the preamble to Palau's Constitution: "We renew our dedication to preserve and enhance our traditional heritage, our national identity and our respect for peace, freedom and justice for all mankind. In establishing this Constitution of all the sovereign."

The Government of the Republic of Palau is responsible for implementing national policies to achieve the "conservation of a beautiful, healthful and resourceful natural environment and promote the national economy." At the same time, "Each state shall have exclusive ownership of all living and non-living resources, except highly migratory fish, from the land to 12 nautical miles seaward from the traditional baselines."

Palau's main industry is tourism. Indeed, according to the World Bank, prior to the COVID-19 pandemic, approximately 70% of the country's $311 million gross domestic product (GDP) in 2019 was tourism-related [1]. As noted earlier, the national government has the role of pursuing both economic promotion and conservation of the natural environment. In 1915, Palau enacted the Palau National Marine Sanctuary (PNMS) Act. The PNMS Act prohibits fishing in 80% of the EEZ and imposes on visitors entering the country a $100 Palau Environmental Fee (PPEF) and requires the signing of the Palau Pledge. The PPEF is intended to supplement the reduced revenues from the sale of fishing rights in the EEZ, which had been distributed to each state, and to finance the management of the terrestrial and marine protected areas established by each state and registered in the Protected Areas Network (PAN) by the national government. This has defined Palau as an environmental tourism country.

Palau's EEZ is relatively small in the region, and revenues from the sale of fishing rights, which amount to about $ten million, are not expected to increase significantly. On the other hand, the PNMS Act allows member countries to maintain revenues from the sale of fishing rights without the need to operate in their own EEZ by selling fishing rights to member countries under the Vessel Day Scheme (VDS) of the Parties to the Nauru Agreement (PNA), introduced in 2009.

The COVID-19 pandemic in 2020 caused a major contraction in the tourism industry, which led to a sharp decline in PPEF revenues. Both government finances and the private sector economy were in crisis, prompting calls to restore the economic spillover effect (approximately $three million) to the private sector from fishing vessel activities in the country lost due to the implementation of the PNMS. With this background, the Government of Palau announced the Blue Prosperity Plan at the Our Ocean Conference held in Palau in April 2022. As of July 2023, the country has been strengthening relationships with development partners to implement the plan and is working to revive its tourism industry through aggressive promotion, especially in Asian countries.

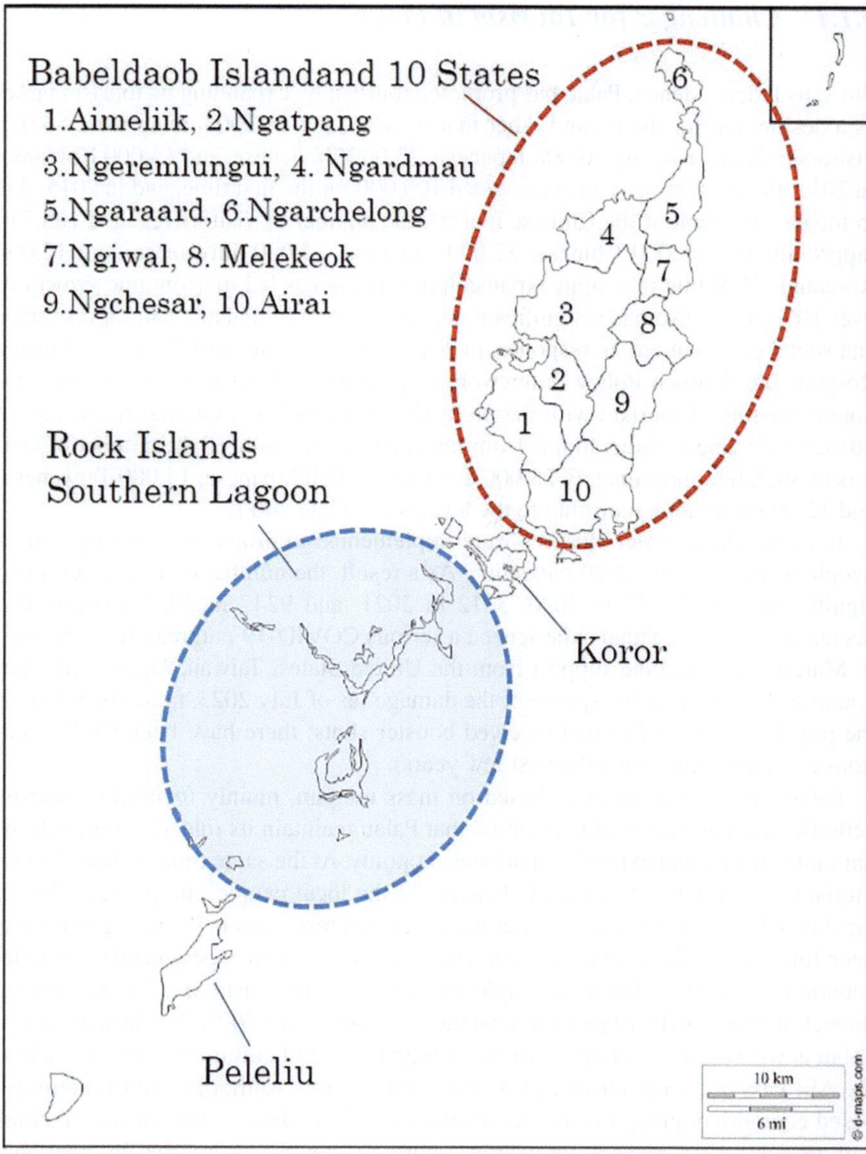

Fig. 7.1 Map of Palau

7.1.1 Challenges for Tourism in Palau

Since its independence, Palau has promoted tourism by expanding its tourist market as a destination for diving and other marine activities. In 2008, there were 83,075 visitors to Palau (roughly 30,000 Japanese, 23,000 Taiwanese, and 15,000 Koreans). In 2011, the number of visitors exceeded 100,000 for the first time, and in 2015, due to the development of the Chinese market, the number of visitors reached 168,770 (approximately 91,000 Chinese, 32,000 Japanese, 15,000 Taiwanese, and 12,000 Koreans) [2]. While this rapid expansion in tourism has led to economic growth of over 10%, it has also had a significant negative impact on Palau's natural resources and social environment. In response, in 2017, the Government of Palau developed a Responsible Tourism Policy Framework to promote policies that balance the economic benefits of tourism with the protection of natural and cultural resources. In 2019, the decline in direct flights from Japan and China reduced the number of visitors to 89,726 (approximately 28,000 Chinese, 20,000 Japanese, 14,000 Taiwanese, and 12,000 Koreans), returning to the levels of the late 2000s.

In early 2020, border closures were implemented to protect the country and its people from the COVID-19 pandemic. As a result, the number of visitors dropped significantly, to 41,753 in 2020, 3412 in 2021, and 9247 in 2022. Despite this decrease in visitors, Palau experienced a serious COVID-19 outbreak from January to March 2022; vaccine support from the United States, Taiwan, Japan, and other countries helped limit the spread of the damage (as of July 2023, more than 70% of the population of 18,281 had received booster shots; there have been 6160 infections and nine deaths over the past few years).

Palau's tourism industry is based on mass tourism, mainly focused on marine activities such as diving. It is essential that Palau maintain its role as a tourist destination to sustain and expand its national economy. At the same time, although mass tourism brings indirect economic benefits to the local people, the participation of local people as the stewards of natural and cultural resources in its management has been limited. In this context, between 2014 and 2022, Palau experienced substantial economic instability due to the rapid rise and fall of tourism and the devastating impact of the COVID-19 pandemic on the economy. As of 2023, the Government of Palau is working to diversify tourism through the use of cultural resources, such as the Alii Pass program introduced by the Palau Visitors Authority, the Community-based ecotourism project of the Sasakawa Peace Foundation, and various ecotourism projects that respect indigenous cultures conducted by the International Cooperation Development Fund (TaiwanICDF).

7.1.2 Environmental Protection Efforts and Cultural Heritage in Palau

BUL, a method of resource conservation and management, was originally introduced in Palau's traditional societies and has been used to promote conservation efforts since independence. In 2003, the Protected Areas Network (PAN) Act was enacted. The PAN Act is a mechanism by which state governments register their terrestrial and marine protected areas with the national Protected Areas Network, which provides technical assistance and funding to state governments that manage protected areas, funded by green fees paid by visitors to the country. Palau began charging the Green Fee in 2009 as a part of its tourism development plan. The Green Fee is now included in the Prestine Paradice Environmental Fee (PPEF). Subsequently, Palau introduced the world's first Shark Sanctuary Act in 2009, which banned shark fishing in Palau waters (Palau's Constitution gives the state ownership of resources from land out to 12 nautical miles). In 2015, the Palau National Marine Sanctuary Act was passed, which prohibits fishing in 80% of the EEZ under national jurisdiction and imposes the PPEF on those entering the country. The fee has been fully enforced since 2020 [3].

While tourism in Palau has developed primarily around marine activities, the islands are also home to archaeological sites dating back more than 2000 years. Babeldaob Island features artificial mounds and earthworks, stone monoliths, stone faces, petroglyphs, beautiful stone paths, underwater stone platforms, and traditional chiefs' meeting houses built with the traditional building method called bai. Ancient murals can be found on the Rock Islands. Palau also has a rich mythology and folklore associated with these sites. For example, the Rock Islands Southern Lagoon was added to UNESCO's World Heritage List in 2012 as a mixed heritage site in recognition of its cultural value as well as its natural resources.

Traditional societies still exist in Palau and ancient traditions are still intimately involved in the people's daily lives. For example, according to local legend, Palauan women once gave birth by having their stomachs cut open, as the Palauans had no knowledge of natural childbirth; however, according to legend, the spider demigod eventually instructed them on how natural childbirth is performed, since which time the lives of pregnant women and their children have been protected. The first-birth ceremony in Palau is still performed in the traditional way, with the mother being cared for with medicinal herbs according to each clan's recipe. In such ways, the identity of the Palauan people is closely tied to nature, and for them, the protection of natural resources is seen as protection of their identity. In Palau, myths and folklore are often passed on orally; however, it is said that some are forbidden to be passed on outside the clan, resulting in the loss of certain elements of traditional knowledge.

7.2 Sasakawa Peace Foundation's Initiative for Community-Based Ecotourism

A variety of issues surfaced in 2015 due to the rapid growth of tourism. In response, the Sasakawa Peace Foundation, in cooperation with the Nippon Foundation, launched an initiative to promote environmentally friendly tourism. To this end, the Foundation signed a tripartite MOU with the Palau government and the Nippon Foundation in February 2016. In 2019, the Sasakawa Peace Foundation established methods for the management of tourism sites based on tourism-carrying capacity surveys and the introduction of community-based ecotourism that balances economic benefits for community members with the conservation of natural and cultural resources.

This section presents the ongoing efforts to introduce community-based ecotourism after the COVID-19 pandemic in Palau.

7.2.1 Concept

The Sasakawa Peace Foundation's community-based ecotourism is based on the concept of "Traveling Like Living." In this conception of tourism, community members, who are the stewards of the natural and cultural resources, take ownership of the tours. The intent is to encourage community members to value and appropriately use existing natural and cultural resources, and provide incentive for them to create tours that will cause visitors to want to stay for a time by providing authentic experiences for a small number of visitors with local guides. Unlike mass tourism, the target tourists are those willing to pay a reasonable price for an authentic experience and interaction with the local people, even if there is some measure of inconvenience.

The community-based ecotourism initiative in Palau saw its first application in the states of Babeldaob Island. Here, to ensure that the tours could remain operational, a fee of $1000 or more per tour is required, plus profit for expenses. In addition, the number of targeted tourists is no more than 10, which would make the fee per person more than $200, a level that would be uncomfortable for local residents. To be profitable, the tours need to encourage extended visits by offering meaningful and authentic experiences. Accordingly, community-based ecotourism tours are designed to be full-day, stay-and-go tours.

Currently, these community-based ecotourism tours accept fewer than ten tourists per tour, and given the burden on local people, the tours are only conducted once or twice a week. Thus, the income brought to the community is generally only a few thousand dollars per month, and the impact on the national economy is negligible. Nevertheless, community-based ecotourism is a mechanism that generates income for the community. Moreover, through appropriate use, natural and cultural resources are sustainably conserved and passed on to future generations, along with the myths and local folklore. Such tourism is expected to contribute to the Blue Prosperity Plan of the country by empowering the local people, the rightful stewards of Palau's natural and cultural resources.

7.2.2 4-Step Introduction Process and Methodology

Although ecotourism using natural resources has existed in Palau for some time, community-based ecotourism, in which the local people play a leading role, is not a widely recognized concept. Consequently, the Sasakawa Peace Foundation has established and promoted an introduction method consisting of the following four steps (Figs. 7.2, 7.3, 7.4 and 7.5):

Step 1: Understand the concept of community-based ecotourism (key: small number of visitors, fair price, spiritual rather than material enrichment).

Step 2: Identify tourism resources ("dots") that exist in daily life through the creation of phenology calendars (key: nature, culture, heritage, history, folklore/mythology, food, etc.).

Step 3: Develop tour plans and cultivate local guides (key: turn "dots" into "lines" through stories and/or themes introduced by local guides).

Step 4: Strengthen local tour management skills (ensuring tour quality, tourist safety, pricing, organizational management, etc.).

Fig. 7.2 Community workshop

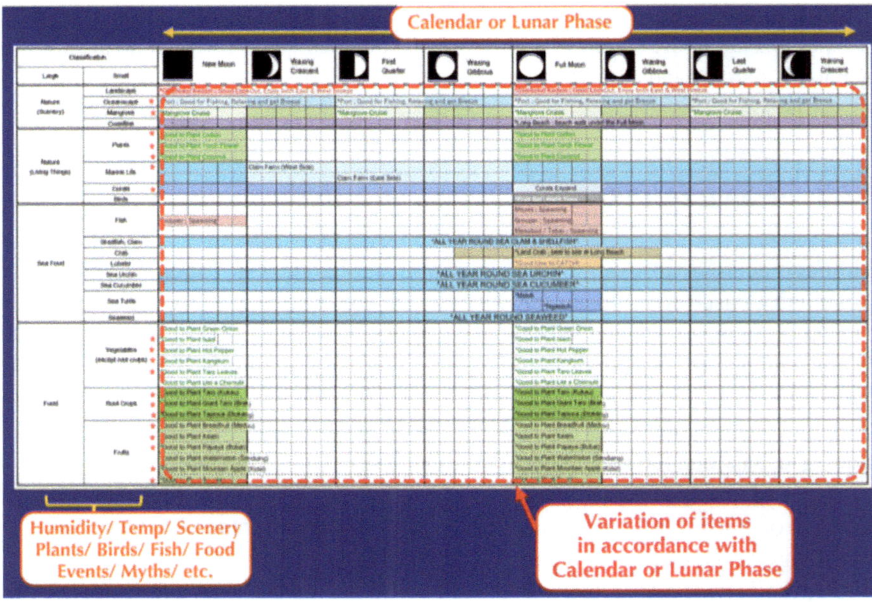

Fig. 7.3 Phenology calendar

For each step, the Sasakawa Peace Foundation uses the following methods: (1) individual dialogue with national level including cabinet ministers, (2) individual dialogue with state leadership, (3) workshops for practitioners from participating states, (4) workshops with community participation, (5) four-week training in Japan to understand the difference between community-based ecotourism and mass tourism and to learn how to create phenology calendars, (6) three-week training in Japan to create tour plans and train local guides, (7) two-week training in Japan to learn tour management, (8) on-site verification of tour plans, (9) 30-day internship training program in Japan to develop tourism human resources, (10) pilot tour implementation, (11) promotional support such as website development, etc.

Practical activities of the foundation were suspended in 2020 due to the COVID-19 pandemic; however, activities resumed in July 2022, and, as of July 2023, Airai, Melekeok, Ngatpang, Ngardmau, Ngaraard, Ngarchelong, and other states on Babeldaob Island have completed Steps 1 through 3.

This initiative by the Sasakawa Peace Foundation has been showcased at various regional conferences (Samoa in October 2018 and Cook Islands in October 2022) and UNWTO conferences (Maldives in June 2022 and Cambodia in June 2023), and information has been shared with JICA, the Japan Tourism Agency, and the Pacific Islands Center in Japan. This is not a funding or infrastructure development effort but rather an effort to transfer skills and methods to people. The Sasakawa Peace Foundation is currently working to expand activities in other Pacific Island countries interested in introducing community-based ecotourism.

Fig. 7.4 Tour planning

7.3 The TaiwanICDF Initiative

Like Palau, Taiwan is a small island nation. It is located in East Asia, along the Western Pacific Ocean. Taiwan has been actively collaborating with small island developing islands (SIDS) in the South Pacific and the Caribbean and coastal countries in Central America. Given its situation, Taiwan shares the feeling with SIDS facing multiple challenges. Taiwan is home to several indigenous Austronesian peoples, including the Amis, Atayal, Bunun, Paiwan, Rukai, and Tao. These peoples have inhabited the island for thousands of years and have contributed to Taiwan's rich cultural heritage.

Taiwan has also been involved in several cooperation and development projects in SIDS and various coastal countries. Such as horticulture and agricultural marketing project in Tuvalu (2002–2006), Papua New Guinea (2005–2010), Marshall

Fig. 7.5 On-site verification of tour plans

Islands (2011–2014) [4], and Palau (2016–2021); a small ruminant production and marketing project in Belize (2004–2009); and a fruit and vegetable production and marketing project in St. Vincent and the Grenadines (2012–2017). These and other projects proved successful in improving the well-being of residents and their economic condition with capacity reinforcement.

With the core value of "people-centered" foreign aid, TaiwanICDF promotes multi-faceted programs in agriculture, small and medium-sized enterprise development, and human resources training to help developing countries meet their economic, social, and environmental development needs and enhance their resilience and adaptability. TaiwanICDF is also actively assisting vulnerable friendly island countries and discussing with them strategies to address climate change and sustainable development.

7.3.1 Method

7.3.1.1 Problem-Solving Approach

TaiwanICDF's designs and conducts its study courses based on a problem-solving approach [5], with each class consisting of (1) Problem identification, with problems common to most countries serving as the main axis of the study; (2) Proposed problem solutions, whereby Taiwan's policies and experience are shared, and on-site visits to successful cases are arranged for participants to learn from; (3)

Comparison, which gives participants the opportunity to share the current situation in their home countries in order to better understand existing practices, and offers them the chance to interact with Taiwanese experts and scholars who can provide research guidance on appropriate technologies and policies to address country-specific situations. The ecotourism workshop organized by TaiwanICDF is designed according to this research method. With people as the starting point, the aim is to promote an understanding of the common problems of community residents and local leaders seeking to develop and sustain ecotourism.

7.3.1.2 Issue Mapping

The workshop also embraces the Issue Mapping approach of the Open Government Collaboration Conference, which emphasizes bringing together the public and private sectors and stakeholders in order to address the core issues common to the region and introduce key technical and technological tools to delve deeper into the issues and identify possible solutions. Here, TaiwanICDF colleagues lead the participants through problem construction, stakeholder definition, resource inventory, possible risks, and solution formulation, then reach a consensus through discussion.

The purpose of this solutions-oriented research method is to help participants from different countries identify commonalities in issues and policies, in the hope that this will encourage participants from industry, government, academia, and research to think differently about them, and, ultimately, to build consensus through discussions that lead to common solutions. TaiwanICDF also supplements its training with practical examples that can be applied by participants when they return home. The examples promoted by TaiwanICDF and the Sasakawa Peace Foundation serve as a reference for the promotion of ecotourism in other interested countries [6].

7.3.2 Results

7.3.2.1 Results of TaiwanICDF Ecotourism Workshop

According to the UN World Tourism Organization (UNWTO), tourism accounts for 10% of the Gross World Product and one-tenth of the world's employment opportunities, playing an important role in the realization of the United Nations Sustainable Development Goals. However, the development of tourism is often accompanied by the destruction of natural resources and the distortion of an area's native culture. Moreover, the inhabitants of tourist attractions may have to bear the damage caused by tourists while realizing little or no benefit. Thus, TaiwanICDF organizes ecotourism workshops with the aim of helping developing countries establish an approach to sustainable travel that respects the natural environment as well as the lives and culture of the local people. The course design of these workshops incorporates four key elements: (1) tourism management and sustainable development, (2) interaction between tourism and local communities, (3) preservation of local history and culture, and (4) environmental protection and resource management.

In evaluating the efficacy of these workshops, the case of the transformation of the fishing village of Badouzi in Keelung is noteworthy as it provide high value-add effect. Through the guidance of the Taiwanese government, accommodation service such as B&Bs were created in local fishing villages and marine tourism activities were introduced. Beautification of the fishing villages was initiated, coral and tropical fish stocks were restored, and activities such as beach cleaning and dive cleaning were undertaken. Participants in the workshop learned how to turn local traditions and habits into profitable tourism trips that, in turn, advanced ecological and community development.

This particular workshop also featured a lecturer from the Sasakawa Peace Foundation (Fig. 7.6), who shared successful cases of community-based ecotourism development in Palau, including how to obtain community consensus and design community-based tourism itineraries. High-level officials from the Bureau of Tourism in the Palau National Government were invited to share their expertise on how to design government policies to help manage tourism benefits and ensure sustainable environmental development.

According to the after course survey, the most influential part of the course was the "Ecotourism Itinerary Development Applied Exercise," in which an industry lecturer shared thoughts on how to ensure environmental sustainability and enhance tourism revenue from the perspective of a private company.

The lecturer also guided participants in their group discussions, clarifying the elements lacking in ecotourism in each country. He motivated the participants to think about marketing methods and targeting potential customers, while considering the on-site situation and available suppliers of hotels, transportation,

Fig. 7.6 A lecturer from the Sasakawa Peace Foundation shared introduced the case of promoting community-based ecotourism in Palau

and food and beverage, calculating the costs and benefits, and producing a practical ecotourism itinerary to enhance the professional ability of the participants. Upon returning home from the workshop, several Paraguayan participants were interviewed by the local TV program "Paraguay Noticias," where they shared not only their experiences in Taiwan but also the upcoming ecotourism trip that they had planned during their Taiwan training (Paraguayan Wetlands Tour).

7.3.2.2 Results of Tourism Training Workshop Conducted Under TaiwanICDF's Pacific Technical Program

Pacific Island countries are rich in marine resources and natural landscapes. It is not surprising, then, that they have made efforts to promote tourism development. However, the lack of systematic planning and infrastructure in the tourism industry has prevented its mature development. To address this problem, a class was designed in which travel platform manufacturers were invited to share the concept of an online travel agency (OTA) and to teach participants how to use e-commerce networks to design customized travel services that compensate for the lack of infrastructure and tourism facilities. The course plan focused on tourism activity design, itinerary planning, and accommodation management, together with analysis of the current tourism market situation and practical demonstrations of hotel catering, to train participants with professional knowledge in tour design and catering management. The intent was to enhance the abilities of participants in tourism itinerary planning and tourism service quality so that they would be prepared to successfully sell local special tourism itineraries online.

For the class, an instructor from the online travel platform KKday was asked to provide feedback on the in-depth tour designed by the workshop's participants. For the Tuvalu students, who had designed itineraries with a historical background, the instructor shared the company's approach to marketing Kinmen, arranging for local people to tell stories about scenic spots and offering costume photography as a way to more deeply engage visitors in the area and to leave with a richer impression of their trip. The instructor suggested that those participants who had little or no experience in receiving Asian tourists could open official SNS account, such as "Line" accounts to contact Northeast Asian customers and develop new markets. He also recommended that participants learn photography skills so that they could take pictures for customers as an added-value service, and noted that sending greetings on festival days was an effective way to keep in touch with customers and enhance their loyalty, possibly leading to return visits. In general, the convenience and smoothness of transportation are important elements of travel.

The instructor also offered tailored advice to participants based on their specific professional contexts. For the participants from Nauru who are employed at the country's main hotel, it was recommended that they position the hotel as a central hub for tourism activities. Surrounding scenic attractions should be thoughtfully integrated into route planning to accommodate various customer segments, such as families, couples, or solo travelers. This people-centered approach reinforces the importance of designing tourism experiences from a community-based perspective—one that not only enhances visitor satisfaction through unique and authentic experiences, but also supports the local identity and economy. By placing community interests and local context at the heart of tourism planning, the industry is reminded of the value of sustainable, inclusive development that leaves a lasting positive impression on both visitors and host communities.

After the workshop, participants reported that they were able to see the human and landscape features of their home island from a variety of perspectives through this in-depth course in tour design. The participants from Tuvalu, who already received Asian tourists, also found the training very useful and stated that they will consider adding traditional costumes and photo-taking services to enhance the uniqueness of their tours and services.

7.4 Discussion

The interaction of Taiwan and Palau has motivated the development of partnerships in many areas through networking. For example, Penghu, Taiwan's island county, and Palau have signed a memorandum of cooperation on marine culture and sustainable development, hoping to learn from Palau's experience in expanding marine reserves to maintain ecological resources, which will contribute to the sustainable development of the tourism industry; Palau has also learned from Penghu on" water supply system management." The TaiwanICDF's workshops continue to support circular economies in partner countries by showing governments and communities how to work together to build transformative ecotourism models.

For inspiration, TaiwanICDF looks inward to Taiwan's own successes in sustainable tourism. At the 2019 Workshop on Ecotourism Promotion, for example, TaiwanICDF guided participants along the Danlan Trail to see how Taiwan preserves history, culture, and the environment through tourist-friendly practices. Attendees studied how New Taipei City's Tourism Bureau and local historians complement each other, with the former protecting the trail and the latter acting as docents to introduce it to travelers. At the same time, they saw how the Shen-ao Rail Bike interlinked the trail with neighboring counties and cities, encouraging more people to visit. The workshop also explored the Meixi tribe's Green Birth Farm, where indigenous people preserve and promote their culture through travel, cuisine, and farming programs. Here, participants learned how to transform traditional lifestyles into profitable tourism ventures.

Based on this successful case study and know-how heritage, TaiwanICDF organized the Blue Economy Workshop this year, where government representatives highlighted Taiwan's renewed focus on marine tourism and leisure activities, including the emphasis by many local governments on coastal activities like environmental monitoring, beach cleanups, and marine education. Moreover, the workshop showed how capacity building could be integrating traditional industries such as maritime transportation and fisheries into these efforts to achieve a more sustainable approach to development. Participants also observed a new form of corporate ecotourism, which sees companies boosting their public image through activities such as beach cleanup.

In its pursuit of ocean conservation, Taiwan has not only relied on governmental efforts but has also harnessed the power of startups in the private sector. For example, the Blue Economy Workshop introduced the Taiwan Blue Ocean Alliance, which developed the Zhandouji marine trash collection vessel as an environmentally friendly solution to harbor waste problems. The alliance collaborates with local governments in places such as New Taipei City and Taoyuan County to create demonstration harbors showcasing the cleaning process. This initiative garnered the attention of Caribbean workshop participants, with a director from St. Lucia expressing interest in the Zhandouji vessel and acknowledging the benefits of harbor cleaning for their country's tourism industry.

TaiwanICDF workshops have also demonstrated how to combine cultural festivals and traditional industries into exciting tourism models. As an illustration, the Dapeng Bay National Scenic Area leverages local cultural characteristics, such as sailing festivals, blackfin tuna seasons, and the Zhongyuan Qianggu Festival, to offer seasonal activities. The scenic area features distinct landmarks like the Goddess of the Sea Lighthouse, the sea church, the cross-sea bridge, and the Dongqing Giant Egg, constructed from 350,000 oyster shells. The Donggang Fish Market incorporates traditional fish auctions into its tourist offerings by allowing visitors to bid for sakura shrimp. Notably, since sakura shrimp are only harvested in Taiwan and Japan, the experience highlights Taiwan's national policies for managing catch to stabilize market prices and marine resources, as well as its strategy for promoting conservation among fishermen. Successful operations like these provide an invaluable reference for workshop participants, such as those promoting marine ecotourism and tribal tourism in Palau.

7.5 The Synergy of Development Fund and Think-Do-Innovative Tank

As described above, the Sasakawa Peace Foundation and TaiwanICDF recognize the importance of balancing economic development with the conservation of natural and cultural resources for the sustainable development of small island nations, and both are taking different approaches to solving these issues. As the Sasakawa Peace Foundation has developed community-based ecotourism led by people of communities on the ground and has established a methodology for its implementation. It has also succeeded in building a Sasakawa community-based ecotourism model that reflects multiple successful examples from Japan and is working to share the model with communities in Palau and other Pacific Island countries seeking to participate.

Such model that empowers local residents to design, manage, and benefit from tourism ventures. By placing decision-making in community hands, the model safeguards ecological integrity, strengthens cultural identity, and ensures that revenues circulate locally. Pilot programs in Palau and other Pacific Island countries have already demonstrated its viability.

TaiwanICDF, by contrast, approaches the same goal through capacity building and grassroots economic development. Its training workshops, technical assistance, and circular-agriculture projects equip communities with the skills, resources, and entrepreneurial mindset needed to sustain ecotourism initiatives long after external consultants depart.

The synergy between the two organizations is clear: SPF provides a tested framework for community-led ecotourism, while TaiwanICDF supplies the training, financial instruments, and on-the-ground support essential for implementation and iterative growth. Together, they offer island nations a holistic pathway to resilient, inclusive, and sustainable development—one that balances economic opportunity with stewardship of the very environments and cultures that make these destinations unique.

While the Palau National Government ranks the economy as its highest priority, it also seeks sustainable development that values the lives of each individual citizen while making appropriate use of its resources, as exemplified by the Blue Prosperity Plan. In order for the Plan to effectively reflect the efforts of TaiwanICDF and the Sasakawa Peace Foundation, it will be important to take a different perspective on the macroeconomy and the household economy, identify national and state-level tourism policies and related laws and regulations, and promote cooperation among communities, state governments, and the national government.

7.6 Conclusion

Being in the post-pandemic era has not only motivated people to travel, it has also made them willing to step outside their comfort zones for in-depth cultural and environmental experiences that differ from traditional tourism. More and more people are seeing South Asia and the Pacific Islands as desirable destinations. At the same time, there is an increased awareness of environmental issues. The growth of tourism in small island countries with underdeveloped tourism industries is likely to face many difficulties, including a lack of large hotels, inadequate infrastructure, and an environment that is too fragile to withstand large numbers of tourists. Community-based ecotourism, in which a small number of tourists stay in a region and local people act as guides to share the local culture and special environment, offers a promising alternative to conventional forms of mass tourism.

Despite differing social and institutional contexts across small-island developing states, Palau's experience demonstrates that well-coordinated action at the national, state, and community levels can reconcile economic growth with ecological stewardship. Building on this success, the Sasakawa Peace Foundation will continue to refine and scale its Community-Based Ecotourism Model—anchored in a four-step introduction process—so that it can be adopted throughout the wider Pacific. In parallel, TaiwanICDF will extend its capacity-building programs, equipping local stakeholders with the skills and resources required to develop visitor experiences that place people, culture, and habitat at the center of a sustainable tourism economy.

Going forward, the two organizations are committed to deepening their collaboration: co-designing community workshops, aligning technical assistance with grassroots needs, and jointly championing initiatives that harness their complementary strengths. Together, they offer Palau—and other island nations—a practical roadmap toward resilient, community-driven prosperity rooted in the protection of the very natural and cultural assets on which that prosperity depends.

References

1. World Bank. (2021). *Palau overview*. Retrieved from https://www.worldbank.org/en/country/palau/overview
2. Palau Visitor's Authority. (2021). *Visitor arrivals*. Retrieved from https://www.pristineparadisepalau.com/stats
3. Tsai Bai-hui. (2021). *Palau's fishery protection and fight against climate change — A different imagination of a marine country*. https://www.twreporter.org/a/climate-change-marine-reserve-palau
4. Cheng, Y., Tseng, Y., Iwaki, Y., & Huang, M. (2021). Sustainable food security in Small Island Developing States (SIDS): A case of Horticulture project in Marshall Islands. *Marine Policy, 128*, 104378. https://doi.org/10.1016/j.marpol.2020.104378
5. Brian Holmes. (1958). *Comparative Education Review, 2*(1), 3–8. The University of Chicago Press.
6. Visiting Palau with Ol'au Palau: The World's First Ecotourism Rewards Program. (2022). Accessed October 30, 2022, from https:/ecotourism-world.com/visiting-palau-with-olau-palau-the-worlds-firstecotourism-rewards-program/

Chapter 8
Dynamic Material Culture and Digital Preservation: A Case Study of the Talugan Bunun Cultural Relics Museum

Ching-Ying Tung

Abstract This action research focuses on the cultural sustainability of Austronesian peoples, who are small in number and tend to be easily influenced by the times and mainstream culture. The Talugan Cultural Relics Museum of the Bunun tribe serves as a case study focused on establishing the contextual meaning of the Talugan's cultural relics from the perspective of authenticity based on the ethnography written by Chia-ch'in Ch'iu in 1966. In 2021, 146 museum items and 14 exclusions were listed and applications were made to hold physical and small-scale online special exhibitions from September to the end of December 2022. It is believed that some items in the collection are from the priest class. Due to the changing social structure and the erosion of many traditional beliefs, most items have lost their context and are difficult to maintain; it is suggested that a digital rather physical museum may offer an effective way to extend the life of such cultural relics.

Keywords Austronesian peoples · Bunun people · SDG 4.7 · Dramaturgy · Authenticity

8.1 Introduction

Since the end of the twentieth century, Taiwan, a multicultural society, has begun to rethink unequal cultural development caused by over-emphasis on a mono-culture. To improve the long-standing cultural fragmentation and identity crisis of those who speak Austronesian languages, which accounts for only 2.5% of the total population, Taiwan passed the Education Act for Indigenous Peoples in 1998. It established a traditional/local knowledge system, developed teaching materials, and cultivated teachers and talents for education.

C.-Y. Tung (✉)
National Chi Nan University, Nantou County, Taiwan
e-mail: cytung@mail.ncnu.edu.tw

M. C. Huang et al. (eds.), *Innovative Social Practice and Community-Based Approach to the Ocean*, https://doi.org/10.1007/978-981-96-9104-3_8

Twenty years later, Taiwan is deeply rethinking and improving the mutual understanding among the diverse ethnic groups, therefore, the Development of National Language Act was passed on 9 January 2019, and the Education Act for Indigenous Peoples was modified on 19 June 2019 to expand the implementation of multicultural and indigenous education from indigenous groups to all citizens as well as to promote the language and cultural development of various ethnic groups. Those revolutions could be seen as an action to achieve the requirements of cultural sustainability and ethnic equality of the United Nations SDGs Goal 4.7 (Education for Sustainable Development and Global Citizenship).

Taiwan is an island with immigrants from all over the world, and archaeological and linguistic research has identified Taiwan as a key player in the Austronesian language family. However, according to the ethnological material culture research in the past hundred years, among the 16 official indigenous groups, only the Yami/Tao (small ocean boat) and the Thao (small inland lake boat) have knowledge related to boat-building. In addition, the Amis have a coastal fishing culture, while other groups such as the Paiwan or Pingpu people have a record of using rafts in the past. Although Taiwanese indigenous peoples are classified as Austronesian languages (also called Austronesian Taiwanese), their interaction and migration relationship with Austronesian languages across oceans representing the Marine character remains to be studied. Thus, this action study not only aims to provide reference materials for the cultural learning of the Bunun people living in the mountain area but also tries to contribute to the comparative analysis of the cultures of Asia Pacific island countries.

8.1.1 Background

Austronesian languages [1] in the Pacific Rim define the most widely distributed ethnic group in the world, with speakers ranging from Taiwan in the north to New Zealand in the south, Easter Island in the east, and Madagascar in the southwest. There are more than 1200 Austronesian languages, with areas roughly divided into Micronesia, Polynesia, Melanesia in Oceania, Taiwan, Southeast Asia, Philippines, Malaysia, Indonesia, New Guinea, New Zealand, and Madagascar. While Austronesian ethnic groups may differ somewhat in language, as well as in their physical and cultural characteristics, they are all small in number, living in environments and cultures vulnerable to urbanization, industrialization, and global warming.

Taiwan is home to the northernmost Austronesian language family. It comprises a number of groups, ranging from Taiwan's mountain aborigines to plain indigenous groups. Roughly 574,106 of Taiwan's residents are included in these groups, accounting for 2.5% of Taiwan's total population [2]. The groups live in the high, cold areas of the Central Range and along the remote east coast. As with other Austronesian peoples, in addition to the inconvenience of transportation and living functions, such factors as natural disasters, urbanization, population mobility, and tourism have affected their social structure and cultural heritage.

This study explores the phenomenon of social changes in Taiwan's Bunun people as reflected in the material culture. Based on the 2021 Collection List [3] of the Talugan Museum of Bunun Cultural Relics, the study illustrates how teachers and students can provide for the cultural exposition of items and establish a primary digital exhibition database through cultural and digital programs. It is anticipated that such efforts will facilitate record keeping, provide cultural context, and digitize information that can be used to build a basic database for further study and curation in Sinyi township, so that these cultural items can be understood in the ever-changing environment in a form not limited by space and time. Simultaneously, this action research can also serve as a reminder to the government of the dynamic cultural changes of ethnic minorities/non-mainstream ethnic groups and provide relevant educational institutions with reference research and talent cultivation solutions.

8.1.2 Bunun People

According to the 2024 census conducted by the Council of Indigenous Peoples, the Bunun number 63,727 members, the fourth largest indigenous population in Taiwan, behind the Amis, Paiwan, and Atayal [4]. The Bunun live scattered on the tops of the central mountains, adjacent to the Pan-Atayal, Thao (Thau), and Tsou in the central areas, and the Puyuma, Paiwan, or Amis in the southeast (Fig. 8.1) [5]. They are concentrated in Sinyi Township in Nantou County. Sinyi is known as the original home of the Bunun. Since Sinyi Town is the only passage for those traveling from Nantou City to Yushan Mountain, there are many Han immigrants. According to population statistics from the Nantou County Government, the population of Sinyi Township was expected to reach approximately 14,054 by the end of 2024. Of this number, around 8670 were Bunun people, representing nearly 60% of the township's population and approximately 14% of the national Bunun population [4].

According to the population data from 1929 (when Taiwan was under Japanese rule) provided by Ch'iu Chia-ch'in [6], there were 18,072 Bunun at that time, with communities at altitudes as low as 150 m and as high as 2306 m. The population living at an altitude of 1000 to 2000 m accounted for 64.2% of the total population at that time, while the population living at an altitude of 500 to 1000 m accounted for 22.7% of the total. To facilitate governance and improve the lives of residents, the Governor's Office has, since 1930, moved the Bunun to middle- and low-altitude mountains, mainly at an altitude of 500 to 1000 m [6]. Relative to their numbers in 1929, the Bunun population has tripled over the past nine decades. In terms of living area, Ch'iu Chia-ch'in's 1966 survey found that most of the residential areas were at low altitudes, mainly 400 to 700 meters above sea level, in comparison to 1929, when the settlements were still dispersed in different areas with uneven land and it was difficult to make a living. Thus, the scope of population movement was wide, and the resultant changes in their modern life and material culture are deserving of attention.

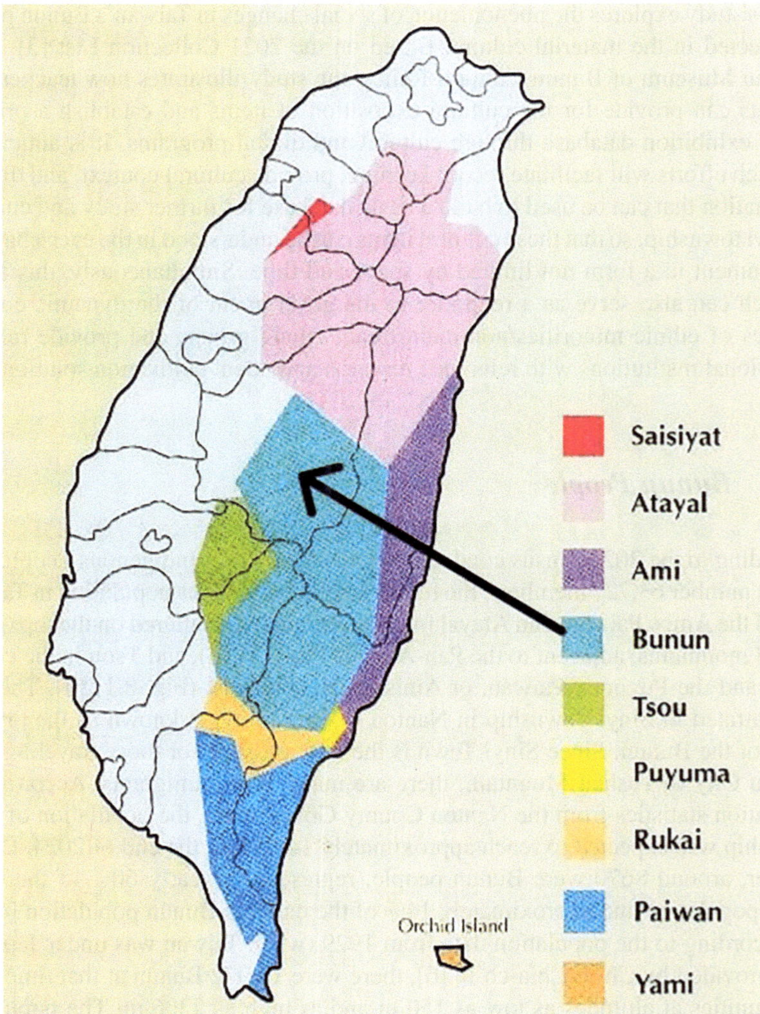

Fig. 8.1 The location of Sinyi Bunun in a map showing the distribution of Taiwan's nine indigenous tribes. Edited from ROC Yearbook (2000)

8.1.3 Talugan Museum of Bunun Cultural Relics

The Sinyi Farmers' Association is the largest operating organization in the township and has long considered the plum industry and plum scenery in winter and spring as the highlights of local leisure agriculture. In 2004, the farmer's association combined its food processing factory and brewery with Dream Works of the Mei, a cultural promoter. It began to promote agricultural products rooted in local cultural characteristics as part of the "Local Characteristics and Small Community and Business Guidance Plan", which was subsidized by the "One TownOne Product (OTOP)" policy of the Small and Medium Enterprises and Startup Administration under the Ministry of Economic Affairs. While collecting cultural relics of the Bunun to be displayed in the shopping area, the factory also developed liquor products that have won high praise in the domestic market, with names based on the Bunun culture, such as Lost Wild Boar and Elder Talk.

The establishment of the Talugan was completed in 2007, with a subsidy from the Council of Indigenous Peoples. The main Talugan building stands close to the head offices of Dream Works of the Mei. On the first floor is the tourism service & information center, along with an exhibition area for resident artists; on the second floor is the Bunun Cultural Relics Museum, where is the research field and the focus of this action research.

Simply put, Talugan is the result of government subsidies in the wake of the earthquake in central Taiwan in 1999 and the revival of aboriginal culture in 2004. It is also the first Bunun Cultural Relics Museum established in Sinyi Township. In the Bunun language, Talugan means "relay station or rest station on the hunting ground," which translates to "yi zhan" in Chinese (Fig. 8.2). The governing unit of the museum is Dream Works of the Mei, Sinyi Farmers' Association. Director Chang Chih-hsiung explained that Talugan serve as a simple rest station for hunters making their way into the mountains, providing a space in which to shelter from the wind and rain and to sit down for dinner. According to their sharing custom, Bunun hunters exchange hunting information and prey when they encounter other hunters

Fig. 8.2 Image of Talugan—a triangular shelter made from local plants for hunters' short rest—displayed in the 2022 special exhibition

there. Talugan thus provide a venue for socializing and swapping goods. In 2002, the Association established a private winery where the Talugan is located to sell its processed food and wine products to tourists visiting Yushan (Jade Mountain)[1] and the Dongpu Hot Spring.

8.1.4 The Action Plan and the Aims

Awareness of the problems at the Talugan museum as described in this action research originates from Hsieh Ching-yueh's examination of the Bunun Cultural Relics Museum in Nantou County in 2020. Based on his curatorial and museum exhibition expertise, Hsieh is not certain that the way the relics are displayed expresses the authenticity of the Bunun culture. The uncertainty arises from the unclear intent of the exhibition, the lack of display signs and explanations, and the museum's long-term failure to update the display content. For example, plastic plum flowers were used at the entrance of the exhibition hall to reflect the image of plum trees in Sinyi Township, symbolizing the core agricultural products of the Sinyi Farmers' Association. However, the relationship between plums and the indigenous peoples is not explained. Another example is the 5-m-long Bunun flagstone house. To reproduce the image of the Bunun people's habit of hanging pig bones outside their flagstone houses to demonstrate the hunting ability of their owner, the builders of the replica referred to old photos of Bunun flagstone houses, then purchased flagstones from stone merchants in Sandimen Township, Pingtung County, and bought pig bones from pork shops to hang under the eaves as a display of hunting achievements [7].

Due to the limited funds and human resources available to maintain items in the exhibition hall, as well as the poor performance of the exhibition, Dream Works of the Mei was forced to suspend operation of the museum in 2018. The absence of visitors for more than 2 years has resulted in a worsening of the preservation of the items. Seeing that the collection has become eroded, moldy, naturally weathered, and dirty, Hsieh encouraged the Bunun employees of Dream Works of the Mei to seek a subsidy from the Ministry of Culture to upgrade the Nantou County Museum and local cultural center so that they can properly maintain the items, give the items cultural content, and train staff.

We initiated an industry-university cooperative project with the grant from Ministry of Culture to conduct the 2021 exhibition inventory, presenting the cultural context and significance of the items to facilitate future maintenance, repair, elimination, and collection of relics. Based on the results of 2021, Hsieh arranged the 2022 exhibition plan according to the inventory results. After reading the literature during the first half of 2021, this action research team will curate the exhibition list

[1]Yushan (玉山), the highest point in the western Pacific region outside of the Kamchatka Peninsula, is also called Mount Jade, Jade Mountain, or Mount Yu.

and conduct digital operations from July to December with the funds provided by the Ministry of Culture and the Ministry of Education (subsidized by the University Social Responsibility project).

8.2 Viewpoint

According to Commissioner Wu Xiomei, who assisted in the inventory operation of Dream Works of the Mei, when the Talugan was built in the early twenty-first century, the GuanQuan Construction Company, operated by the Bunun people in Sinyi Township, was entrusted to oversee the project. From 2004 to 2005, the company collected display items from the Bunun people across the country. Before the museum was constructed in 2007, it was determined that there was still room in the exhibition area. Consequently, a number of cultural relics were purchased as exhibits to fill the space.

Due to the situation at that time and the fact that the personnel of the construction company participating in the collection of the cultural relics were not professionals in museum collections, it was inevitable that there would be some flaws in the exhibition. For example, although the items are represented as being from Bunun families, such families can include intermarried Bunun people, and many of the accumulated items appear to be household goods obtained from intermarried Tsou or Paiwan people in southern Taiwan. While information such as where the items were sourced and their ownership were intact, the information of family clan or tribe was not recorded during the collection of the items, so it is very difficult to compare the clan history that scholars pay attention to. Since there were no museum professionals in the farmer's association, the planning and arrangement of the exhibition space was completely entrusted to the construction company run by the Bunun leaders. Consequently, the inventory takers could only use the concept of Pan-Bunun and recorded the source information for the final collector and provider—the construction company. Finally, as Hsieh noted in his earlier survey of local museums in Sinyi, when the construction company used old photos to reproduce the traditional life scenarios, some of the display items were imitations, reproductions, or substitutes due to changes in the conditions for obtaining items. It is the absence of detailed records that has reduced trust in the authenticity of the items [7].

Since the late 1970s, anthropologists and sociologists have focused on the value and significance of cultural tourism museum items in modern society. MacCannell (1976) believed that modernization or modern society has its own standardized mode and that so-called traditional life involves the celebration of holidays, in addition to daily life. The pursuit of authentic culture through tourism can make people feel detached from current commercial life. Under such a hypothesis, tourism is seen not as an erosion of local culture by a universalizing force of commodification, but rather as a creative process that is born of combined social-cultural forces, both local and global [8]. However, in later research, Clifford (1988) broadly considered tourism and travel in different contexts. Thus, Clifford drew a clear system map to classify art and culture using the four indices of authentic, inauthentic, artifact, and masterpiece (Clifford 1988:244). Based on Clifford's classification scheme, the Talugan collection could be fit into culture (traditional or collective), not-culture (new or uncommon), and non-art (reproduced or commercial) [9].

Clifford (1997:35) also observed that authenticity might be influenced by certain ignored forces; for example, when ethnic groups need to travel, they might move about under strong cultural, political, and economic compulsions. In addition, certain travelers with these groups may be materially privileged, while others may be oppressed, including the different diasporas, borderlands, exiles, detours, and returns in the post-colonial era [10]. Because of the different analysis levels and conditions of the various ethnic groups, it is increasingly difficult to explore the meaning of authenticity in today's society. Hu (1994) summarized three principles to provide reference for analyzing the traditionality/authenticity of cultural tourism artifacts: (1) the connection between the production of artifacts and the place, (2) the evidence to show that the innovation of artifacts is connected with the past tradition, and (3) the positive significance of the artifacts to the local society [11].

Following the viewpoint of Hu (1994), this action research considers the traditionality/authenticity of the Talugan items to be established (as collected and constructed by local people with partner ethnic group's supports and creation/reproduction). The considerations behind this can be described as follows: First, in the study of the Bunun, there was originally a lack of continuous research accumulation in the material culture. Discussions surrounding the authenticity of Taiwan's Austronesian language family rely on the survey report of the aboriginal groups prior to the huge community migration during the period of Japanese rule. This research is based on the ethnography published by Ch'iu Chia-ch'in in 1966 as the main source, with other research to explain the social and cultural context of the items. The reason for this is that Japanese scholars such as Toichi Mabuchi, Yukichi Sayama, Yuzuru Okada, Okamatsu Santaro, and Masufa Fukutaro are mainly involved in research related to family organization or clan structure. After conducting field surveys in Tannan, Qingyun and Shuanglong Villages, Sinyi Township, and Nantou County from 1960 to 1962, Ch'iu believed that there were still many social and cultural contents to be supplemented. Accordingly, he wrote Social Organization of the Bunun Take Bakaha [6]. Later, the fieldwork of Bunun studies focused on a single community or a single cultural theme, regardless of kinship and clan relations. Very few Bunun items are listed in the collection of material culture published by Tsui Elaine Yi-lan and Hu Chia-yu of the Department of Anthropology of National Taiwan University [12]. Bunun elder Quan Guoxiang shared his personal views of this situation, observing that, in the past, the Bunun people lived in high mountains and moved about with the entire clan to find sufficient food. During their journey, they could not leave any smell when hunting. In addition, they adopted slash-and-burn farming and burned-up farming tracks after harvesting. To facilitate their movement, all the items they used and discarded were found in nature, until the group found a suitable place to live. Thus, most daily materials are difficult to preserve over an extended period. Ch'iu Chia-ch'in's record of the six sub-groups of the Bunun validates Quan's observation and explains that the major reason why it is difficult to establish authenticity lies in the mobility of the Bunun.

As for the branches of the Bunun, the largest Bunun community (Take Banua, 巒社群) often migrates due to food shortages or a shift in hunting grounds, then separate into other sub-groups such as the Take Bakaha, Take Todo, and Take Vantan. The Take Banua people moving to Sun Moon Lake were known as Take Bakaha (卡社群). They began to make contact with the Thao living around the Lake. Those intermingling with the Atayal became Take Todo (卓社群). To the east, the Taka Vatan (丹社群) lived in Hualien County. When the Take Banua moved to the south, they encountered the Tsou people and the Puyuma people to the southeast, whose resistance forced the Take Banua to retreat to the border area. The <u>Isbukun</u> (郡社群) Mouth har have a clear evolution history. According to Ch'iu Chia-ch'in's introduction of Japanese scholar Tōichi Mabuchi's record, the Isbukun group moved from south of the Take Todo to the Dongpu area due to drought, and began to expand to the Rukai (Drekay) after the mid-nineteenth century. Today's scholars often mention that there are five major communities of the Bunun; however, in Ch'iu's research, it is noted that the Take Pulan (蘭社群), who live near the Tsou people, have the smallest population, and that their life has almost entirely been assimilated by the Tsou (Cou) (Fig. 8.3) [5].

Understanding the material culture of neighboring ethnic groups in the process of migration can explain why the museum items are mixed with Tsou, Rukai, and Paiwan characteristics. Therefore, in addition to the modern population mobility and intermarriage mentioned by the museum staff, there has been a trajectory of cultural assimilation since the nineteenth century. As it is inevitable to avoid the blending of multi-cultural elements with Bunun cultural relics, this action research looks at the extent to which elders, experts, and scholars can identify and explain the use of the relics, so as to signify their cultural significance.

Based on the above considerations, this study regards all items as objects used or compared to the Taiwan Bunun prior to the collection in 2004 or 2007, and adopts

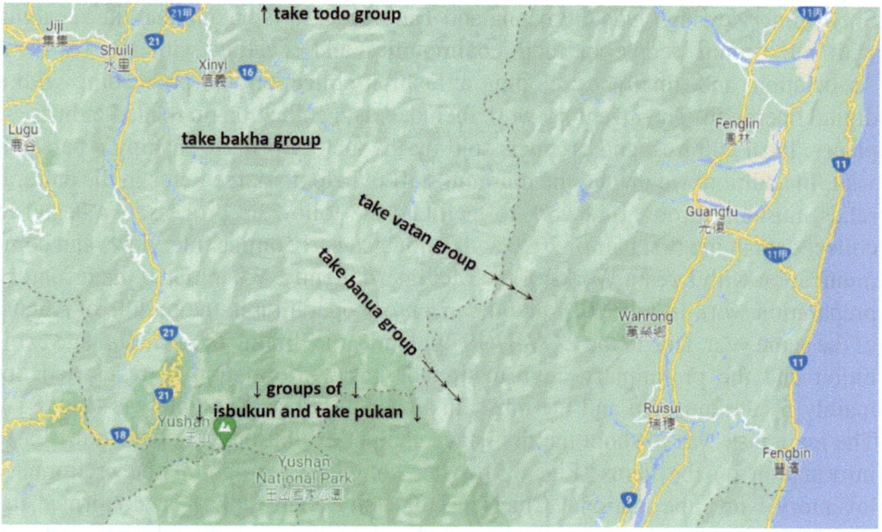

Fig. 8.3 The location and distribution of the Bunun groups

Goffman's dramaturgy to express the existence and significance of the items, exploring the relationship between the items and their cultural context [10].

Goffman's dramaturgy holds that life is a kind of human performance. It focuses on the flow and change of performance regions and their performance purposes (for tourist performance or self-identity and self-recognition), and provides descriptions of corresponding items for research purposes, which shows the front-stage manners and back-stage life needs of individuals or ethnic groups. To this end, special records should be made of the communities or regions to which the items may belong during the action. At the same time, we will, based on the concept of front stage, distinguish the material culture of performing for others and the material culture provided for ourselves by the back-stage concept.

On the other hand, due to the vicissitudes of life and the fragmentation of ethnic knowledge, the way in which some cultural relics are used has not been clearly understood. Thus, we can only attempt to extend the life of cultural relics through digital recording, as the items decline, to classify the items into no-art/no-culture categories and a cultural category, then provide primary illustrations. On this basis, with respect to the Talugan, the cultural context and information on the items can be clarified. In academia, we would hope that more detailed research can be driven in the future to demonstrate how the material culture of ethnic minorities has been evolving.

8.3 Methods and Action Design

The research methods used in this study involve reading secondary literature and conducting primary action research. The action research includes visiting and inspecting communities (Mingder, Tannan, Qingyun, Renhe, Minhe, Luluna, etc., in Sinyi), interviewing Quan Guoxiang and Tian Xue'e in Isibukun, and the speaking with the Bunun people in their communities and meeting with the Farmers' Association, and, finally, developing an exhibit collection and proceeding with a digital operation. The inventory work included data collection on related industries, places, local cultures, and products sold by the factory prior to making a personal visit. In addition, we invited the museum staff to help mark the items in the cultural relics museum through telework to facilitate the follow-up process. We began to collect data in the first half of 2020 and conducted early online interviews and communication with Dream Works of the Mei intermittently. We initiated the inventory preparation work in July 2021 and the inventory operation in the middle of August of the same year. Due to the COVID-19 epidemic, the filming of the first-stage exhibition and the preliminary confirmation of basic information were carried out mainly by the museum and the museum's resident artist, Xue Qingyao (Fig. 8.4). The main task was to shoot the first-stage cabinet exhibition and confirm the basic information on the items (Fig. 8.5). After completing a part of the preliminary inventory work, the National Chi Nan University team took over, confirmed the actual situation of the items, and carried out preliminary digital operations on September 6 and 7 (Fig. 8.6). Further, we invited the elders to identify and provide

Fig. 8.4 Setting and first attempt by Xue Qingyao

Fig. 8.5 Basic classification and coding by Wu Xiaomei

Fig. 8.6 Preliminary digitalization by Dai Zixiang and Liao Zhehan

Fig. 8.7 Elder recognition by Quan Guoxiang and Tian Xue'e

the names of the items in the Bunun language (Fig. 8.7). After the audio and video recording of the work, the Bunun students listened, typed, and reviewed, and pointed out any deficiencies. As of September 14, the digitalization of the inventory ended (Fig. 8.8). Finally, scholars and experts were invited to review and edit the inventory through the end of November (Table 8.1).

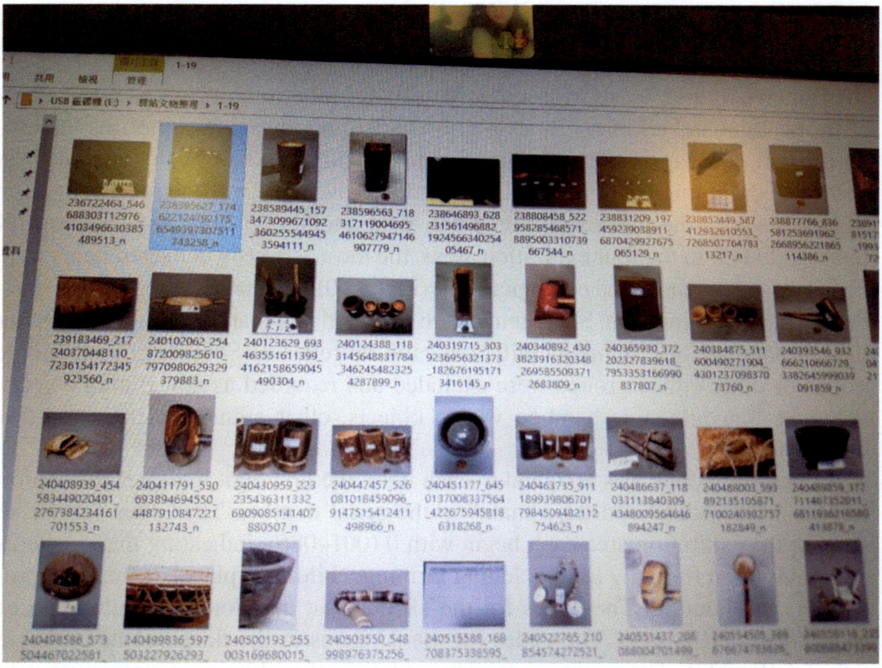

Fig. 8.8 The list of recorded items

Table 8.1 Timetable and work division of the inventory work

Phase	Task	Work project	Personnel involved
1	Literature collection	Industries and cultural information of Sinyi Township	Tung Ching-ying, Dai Zixiang, Liao Zhehan
2	Arrangement of items	Labeling, classification, and photography	Chang Chih-hsiung, Wu Xiaomei, Xue Qingyao
3	Data digitization	Clothing area label, classification confirmation, image and text digitization	Tung Cing-ying, Dai Zixiang, Liao Zhehan, Wu Xiaomei, Liu Miyun
4	Description of cultural context	Item identificatio by the Bunun elders	Quan Guoxiang, Tian Xue'e
5	Bunun language listening and typing	Video, language listening, and typing identification by the elders	Si Yao (Ciang Ispalidav) Chang Chih-hsiung (Buaq Isuz)
6	Inventory coding and filing	Compilation and compilation	Tung Ching-ying, Dai Zixiang, Liao Zhehan
7	Information supplementation	Document supplement, art editing, and proofreading	Tung Ching-ying, Dai Zixiang, Sun Shilin
8	Proofreading	Review by scholars and experts	Fang Chun-wei, Yang Chi-kai
9	Second and third proof of the inventory	Art editing and proofreading	Sun Shilin
10	Video editing	Making digital audio-visual documentaries	Tung Ching-ying, Li Yurui

8.4 Results

The Bunun Cultural Relics Museum is located upstairs from the tourist service center in the Talugan building. The exhibition area of the museum comprises the ecological hall, the flagstone house, and the main exhibition hall, which includes the clothing exhibition area (Fig. 8.9). The detailed inventory work was carried out in accordance with the four exhibition areas, with a total of 146 items listed, and 14 items excluded. In the four exhibition areas, the most seriously damaged items were the insect specimens in the ecological hall (Fig. 8.10) and the imitation plastic ornaments in the clothing area. Such items were recorded and marked as damaged. After making comparisons, items identified as cultural relics of Southeast Asian ethnic groups or other ethnic groups were excluded and recorded as non-Bunun objects, including Nanyang-style bamboo woven objects, other ethnic pottery, and other unknown objects.

A three-digit code was assigned to each item: the first digit indicates the exhibition area; the second and third make up the serial number. The codes for the 86 items in the exhibition area each begin with 0 (001–086), indicating that the items are mainly used for daily life, including farming, children's play, leisure, food production, and hunting. The codes for the 19 items in the clothing exhibition area begin with 1 (101–119). The codes for the 27 items in the flagstone house begin with 2 (201–227). These items are representative of architecture, preservation of crops, the bones of the prey, and stone pestles (Fig. 8.11). Lastly, the number 3 indicates items in the ecological hall. When proceeding from the first floor to the second floor, the ecological hall at the entrance is the first one to come into view. As this survey focuses on culture as well as ecology, the ecological hall is the last exhibition area to be inventoried. Here, 14 items (301–314) are listed, excluding the cicada specimens with serious damage. The following is a summary of the research results of the Bunun relics at the turn of the twenty-first century according to their backstage or front-stage performance, along with the usage information for the collected items.

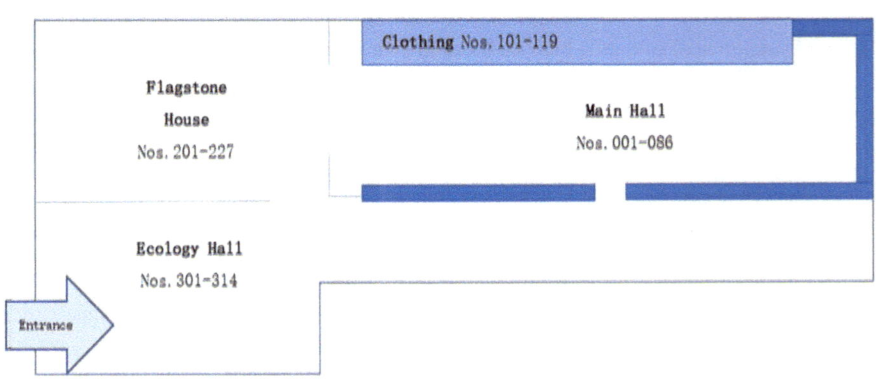

Fig. 8.9 Schematic diagram of exhibition hall and coding

Fig. 8.10 The image of entrance

Fig. 8.11 The image of flagstone house with hieroglyphic calendar board

8.4.1 Front-Stage Cultural Performance

In the clothing exhibition area, most items were produced in the late twentieth century and are worn for important ceremonies, festivals, or tourist performances; they are rarely worn in daily life. The front-stage of Goffman's dramaturgy was adopted

Fig. 8.12 The shop of the Indigenous Cultural Hall at Luluan village of Sinyi Township

Table 8.2 Title of the table

No.	Item name	Bunun name	usage information (recorded in the inventory)
102 103	Coix beads	cipula	Made of *Coix lachrymal-jobi* and *Acacia* seed, and is used as women's clothing and accessories.
104	Cattail bracelet	bistunan	Made of *Acorus tatarinowii* and hemp rope. It is a female wrist accessory.
109	Women's panel skirt	tunkilan	Women's clothing made of ramie thread and cloth, and primarily in black. The traditional pattern is mainly of a fish-like pattern, while the modern dress is often in a water ripple pattern.

to describe this kind of cultural performance, in order to identify social or ethnic status and establish aesthetics through fashion and cultural creativity that reflect the cultural elements expected by both performers and viewers. As a kind of fashion, the items and props are generally thought to be cheaply acquired and easily replaced over time. In fact, when we conducted the furfure fieldwork in Luluna village, we found many new and beautiful accessories and items of clothing waiting to be sold and worn (Fig. 8.12).

When the exhibition was held in 2022, the clothing items had been removed due to their poor preservation. However, objects embodying traditional elements could still be viewed, such as Coix Beads (Table 8.2, Nos. 102&103, Fig. 8.13) and a Cattail Bracelet (No. 104). A women's Panel Skirt (No. 109), comparable to the big fish-like wavy pattern of the Take Bakaha, was replaced by a skirt with an intricate, small, fish-like wavy pattern. The elders interviewed in July 2021 believed that the two items were of the same style.

Fig. 8.13 Coix Beads (item No. 102, cipula)

According to Yen's research, Take Todo used to eat fresh members of *Coix*. However, because it took a long time to prepare (cooking food like popcorn), they rarely used coix as their main food material. There was also wild rosary jobi (scientific name: *Coix lacryma-jobi* var. *maxima*), an inedible *Coix* variety that can only be used to make necklaces or headwear [13–15]. Clusters of fruits were hung at the door to ward off evil spirits.

As for cultural performances, the Bunun people today are best known for their intangible culture, including such features as singing eight-part harmony, a pestle sound, and the bow harp and mouth harp. Of these, the eight-part harmony is perhaps the most distinctive among the Taiwanese Austronesian peoples. When the Bunun people lived in the isolation of the high mountains, they often expressed their appreciation of nature and the joy of harvest through singing in harmony. According to the elders of the Isbukun (郡社) in the Mingder village, the songs need to be harmonious and co-created. In the past, they were a musical expression of unity and resonance in the Isbukun's sacrificial ceremonies. Today, with the movement of the Isbukun people, the eight-part harmony has expanded to become a representative cultural asset of the Bunun. Isnbukun people often practice singing with the Bunun people from other groups in their new settlement and sometimes sing for performances, apart from the sacrificial rites.

8.4.2 *Back-Stage Life Scenarios*

Goffman, the American sociologist, focuses more on personal behavior and uses the term "back-stage" to imply the "natural self" not presented in public [9]. Referring to Goffman's back-stage concept, a back-stage viewpoint of a collective ethic group can be applied to describe the items in the sections of daily life and flagstone houses on display [9, 16]. In a tourist area, the daily life performance items have less connection to outsiders/viewers and might not be immediately attractive to consumers. They require scholars to record the behaviors and articles in an objective and contextually oriented way, and in a way that is easy to read and understand.

In this section, the third chapter of Ch'iu Chia-ch'in's research related to rituals and ceremonies is taken as the main reference. The fourth chapter, Life Etiquette, and the fifth chapter, Kinship Organizations, also mention some of the articles used; however, most are herbaceous plants that need to be studied and checked, as well as pig bones, millet, chicken manure, and other biological remains. Consequently, they are not addressed in this chapter. It should be added that in Ch'iu Chia-ch'in's research on the group of Take Bakaha, the Bunun name of the items is based on the Take Bakha language. The elders identifying the items are from Isbukun, and the students responsible for language transcription are Take Banuad. As a result, the inventory report is mainly in the Take Banuad language.

The Take Bakha Bunun have maintained the practice of tying ropes to mark the day [6]. Chiu noted that the calendar divides the year into 12 months, with 30 days in each month. Ropes are knotted to mark millet production and hunting, and the reclaiming of the dry land of millet is the main activity at the beginning of the year. The Bunun people reclaim the dry land in January, sow millet in February, hold Tokokok (a celebration marking the finish of sowing) in March, plant sweet potato in April, and engage in Manato (weeding the farmland) in May. They undertake Lapakath (decontamination/plague-expelling) in June, Malaktainal (animal-ear shooting festival) in July, and Matothamoth Tolupen (bird-expelling) in August. They brew wine in September, hold a harvest festival in October, and hold Lutsanan Mulalin Tiats (storage of millet) in the days of the waning moon in November. Finally, at the full moon in December, they hold Munkailev (a ceremony for boys) with green taro in the priest's house [4]. The following content on the sacrificial rites throughout the year can be used as a reference for the descriptions in the detailed list of items in Tables 8.3, 8.4, 8.5, and 8.6.

Table 8.3 List of relics for the land reclamation in January

No.	Item name	Bunun name	Usage information (recorded in the inventory)
017	ladle	sieh	The Bunun ladles are usually made of bamboo or wood. This item is made of Makino Bamboo and is used to ladle wine when reporting war achievements. Different from those made of dried gourd in daily use.
027	spoon	tatako	Made of wood and is used to spoon millet porridge. It is convenient to cut and shovel food when eating.
075	machete	via	Made of iron, wood, hemp rope and *Calamus jenkinsianus*. It is used as a weapon or for hunting.
055/056	hoe	tannga	Made of iron, *Lagerstroemia subcostata* and *Broussonetia papyrifera*. Using the tool for farming on the slope is labor-saving. Before iron tools were introduced into the tribe, gallets or animal bones were used as hoes to plough land. Later, when other nations entered the tribe, they could obtain iron tools through trade. Only then were iron hoes introduced in the tribe.

Table 8.4 List of relics for the sowing ceremony in February

No.	Item name	Bunun name	Usage information (recorded in the inventory)
209–213	millet	maduq	Dry grain. To show how original residents deal with grains.
053	box	kalala	A box made of *Alpinia zerumbet* leaves. Reason for being excluded: the style and shape of the woven box is not Bunun style.
004	*Alpinia zerumbet* woven box	kalala	It is used for storing herbs (two pieces are combined into a group). It is made of *Alpinia zerumbet*, and is usually kept at home to contain some small items, such as herbs, spoons, and hairpins.

Table 8.5 List of relics for the weeding in May

No.	Item name	Bunun name	Usage information (recorded in the inventory)
031 033	whip for spinning top (small) (large)	duun/ ubus	Made of bamboo and the bark of *Broussonetia papyrifera* (huna/ quan). It is soft but hardens after drying. The bark can be soaked in water to soften again. Before planting millet, the Bunun people would play with the top in their house, hoping millet would grow up as fast as the spinning of the top. The longer the top spins, the better the crops will be this year.
032 034	small top large top	sulun	Made of tung tree, a toy for children. Before planting millet, the Bunun people will also whip the top in their house. The longer the top spins, the better the crops will be this year. (Note: this exhibit has an unfinished item description)

Table 8.6 List of relics for the millet harvest sacrifice and food culture

No.	Item name	Bunun name	Usage information (recorded in the inventory)
021 023 025	gourd ladle	sieh/ siiq	To scoop water. The early ancestors mainly used taro leaves or two hands to scoop water for hunting and walking. The water ladle was used in the late period.
028	pottery kettle	bozaq/ amunu	According to the displayed poster, this is a demonstration cultural relic illustrating the disappearance of the pottery craft of the Bunun in the early twentieth century. Reason for being excluded: the traditional Bunun people did not develop pottery technology, and the item made of clay is non Bunun article.
026	wooden container		Wooden. Used to store or ladle water and wine.
027	wooden spoon	tasav	Wooden. It is used to spoon millet porridge and is convenient to cut and shovel food when eating.
046	food steamer		Made of wood and cane. Used for steaming and stewing millet, rice and glutinous rice. Modern improved version has the function of cooking.
047	wooden cask	Bauzaq/ bakicu	Made of wood and *Calamus jenkinsianus* and introduced by the Japanese. The Bunun people often use this barrel for storing rice.
048	long-handle cooking spade	hainasu	Made of *Tsuga chinensis*, a hard wood. It can be used when cooking millet. It is necessary to beat millet to squeeze the starch out, making the millet sticky, so it is designed with a long handle.

For the reclamation in January, if the result of divination is an auspicious dream, the Bunun people bring sweet potatoes, wine ladles (Table 8.3, No. 017), wooden spoons (known as tatako in Take Bakha; No. 027), sabers (No. 075), igniters, and other items to the cultivated land. They first clear a circle of ground one meter in diameter, on which a fire is built for roasting the sweet potatoes. They then worship with branches stuck in the ground and use the wine ladle to scatter the wine on the floor. Later, they say a prayer before reclaiming the dry land with a hoe (Nos. 055&056) or a spade. Once the land is well dug, they begin to sow millet seeds. It is worth noting that if the spades or hoes of two people touch during their work, it is considered a sign of misfortunate or conflict, as though the two people are fighting one another with weapons. To counter this, the two must immediately drop their tools in place, surround the tools with four stones, and catch a rooster as part of a decontamination ceremony intended to ensure that there will still be a bumper harvest of millet. Following the ceremony, the tools can again be used, but the four stones must be left in place. In addition, the two whose farm tools had touched must refrain from intercourse for a month. Such a ceremony would seem to indicate that the Bunun people are cautious about and alert to the use of iron tools.

The sowing in February is practiced by the women. The "chosen millet seeds" reserved in the barn for blessing are carried during the sacrificial ceremony. Traditionally, the chosen millet seeds are the best grains collected during the previous harvest and are specially preserved in a barn (separated from the living space in the flagstone house) after the inferior-quality seeds are sifted out and the sacrificial ceremony is held. Under the eaves of the flagstone house, many millets are on display to show the way people dried them; because these are not the chosen millets, they are recorded as ordinary grain millets (Table 8.4, Nos. 209–213). The organizer of the ceremony will kill a large rooster during the blood sacrifice, bleeding it into a bowl. Retaining some of the blood, the rooster's body is moved clockwise in a circular path over the millet seeds. The blood is dropped on the seeds and the group prays for a bumper harvest. After the sacrifice, the middle and long toes of the rooster's right foot are tied to the handles of a basket made of an ethno-plant called *Alpinia zerumbet*. The rest of the rooster toes are hung on the back wall of the barn. The rooster is eaten by the entire family that night, with its head broken and eaten by the one who is to sow the seeds. The Alpinia zerumbet basket with handles was not included in the collection; the *Alpinia zerumbet* box (No. 053) that was excluded was inconvenient to use without basket handles, as it was not a common object of the Bunun. The upper and lower pieces (No. 004) made of the same *Alpinia zerumbet* can sometimes be seen in the collection of herbs; consequently, it was retained.

According to the agricultural calendar, the Bunun typically make millet wine before the weeding in May, and perform the Manato after the wine is brewed. Following the Manato, everyone dresses up and goes out to the public space, where the owner of each house whips a spinning top (Table 8.5, Nos. 031–034, Figs. 8.14 and 8.15). If the top does not fall in four spins, it is considered lucky and will be stored in the barn. After the spinning of tops, the people proceed to play on a swing

Fig. 8.14 The small spinning top (No. 032, sulun)

and pray for the millet to grow strong. The ceremonial swing is set on a flat section of ground at the center of the community. It is made of four 20-meter-long thick wooden posts, rattan ropes, and wooden boards. After the swinging, wine is sprinkled on a spinning top and the tools used for weeding as a sacrificial procedure. These are then put away. The festivities continue for 2 days.

Millet is an important food crop for the Bunun people, so the millet harvest festival in October and Lutsanan mulalin tiats in November are held in a careful and complicated manner. Only a small part of the description is presented here.

Ch'iu recorded that in the early morning on the day of the sacrificial ceremony, a priest went out to cut four one-meter-long makau (the Take Bunun-bakaha name is *Chenopodium formosanum*), a plant growing in the mountains [6]. After the makau is retrieved, it is put into the house through the right skylight (the side near the kitchen) of the house, with two pieces of makau for each family member. A prayer is said that when the millet ripens next time, the harvest will be greater than it was this year and that all the families will be protected from disaster. In contrast to Yen's research on ethnic plants of the Take-todo Bunun in Ren'ai Township, the Take-todo people put Taiwan mukun (the Take Bunun-todo name) into millet when

Fig. 8.15 The large spinning top (No. 034, sulun)

making millet wine. Mukun is planted together with millet but ripens earlier. After our contrastive study, we found that the dry red-spike plant growing in the same place with millet in the flagstone house should be Taiwan mukun rather than the fruit of Roxburgh sumac (Fig. 8.16, Nos. 226&227).

The Take Bakaha put the makau given by the priest into their newly harvested millet and cook the mix together. After cooking, they dip the new millet rice into their mouth with their forefinger. This is to ensure that they will not have stomach pain when eating millet. In addition, as the medium of millet harvest sacrifice, makau is associated with ritual tools such as the water ladle (Table 8.6, Nos. 021, 023, and 025), the pottery kettle (tapana; No. 028), and the wooden plate (kato; No. 026). Such articles are displayed in one place, but the context is not described in detail. It is speculated that the special articles for priests are not found among the common Bunun people. As most Bunun people converted to Christianity, these sacrificial tools have not been used for more than half a century, although they have been preserved into the twenty-first century. The tools for millet cooking and storage are also listed here.

Fig. 8.16 Millet in the middle and makau with millet on both sides

8.5 Discussion

In terms of academic implications, this study sorts out the cultural context related to the objects in inventory used in sacrificial agricultural ceremonies. In pursuing the process, we learned that the Bunun people often use divination (intangible), food (sharing after use), and various plants and animals (in addition to pig bones and deer bones, there are chicken feet, chicken dung, etc.) as well as a small amount of material and various plant containers. In addition to being difficult to preserve, these elements are rarely applied in their daily life and, because the priest's function has declined, they are unlikely to be inherited from an earlier generation. During the process of review, it became known that in 2021, due to a lack of plant knowledge, sacrificial knowledge, and the traditional life wisdom of the Bunun language, there are many shortcomings that still need to be addressed. Accordingly, the cultural context of more relics will be further researched in the near future.

In terms of practical implications, during the summer vacation of 2022, Hsieh Ching-yueh, an assistant professor in the Department of Cultural Resources and Leisure Studies, National Taitung University, and Su Nai, the curator from the Paiwan group, rearranged the physical exhibition (Fig. 8.17) and developed a simple online curation (https://40112thes.wixsite.com/dreamworks) to be displayed in

Fig. 8.17 Simple illustration of items in the 2022 Special exhibition

the form of a special exhibition from September to the end of December 2022. Regarding the long-term exhibition, Dream Works of the Mei, which governs the Talugan, continues to face difficulties and challenges resulting from the pandemic, and is temporarily unable to execute the operation and management of the open exhibition. Thus, plans for a long-term digital museum should be deferred until a time when all research contexts are clarified.

In terms of reflection, although there have been some notable achievements, this study underlines the need for an improvement in human resources, an expansion of in-depth research, and a bolstering of institutional quality before the Talugan Bunun Relics Museum can be operated as an authentic digital museum of scale and a first-class physical museum.

As a first priority, senior human capital needs to be nurtured, especially in the museum and curation disciplines. Practical implementation of this plan requires internal education and training, which, at this point, is constrained by a tight implementation timeline. In the future, we will need to consider reserving sufficient time and funds for education and training. Next, although we have provided preliminary findings, including a digital inventory of items and some cultural context, previous research and investigative data on the Bunun people and the plum industry are scarce, and further research will be needed in order to build on our basic investigative results. Finally, with the support of a government subsidy, this basic survey and trial curation were completed in 2021 and 2022; however, considering the issue of sustainable development, an institutional support system will be necessary. Moreover, for a cultural business to become a mission unit in an enterprise specialized in agriculture, there needs to be relevant education and a growth in internal personnel, as well as institutional support focused on sustainability. Importantly, cultural research and the training of staff are functions that could be performed in cooperation with universities working with the local museum.

Acknowledgement I would like to thank Huang Chih-huei and (late) Ho Chien-chung, the two director-generals of the Sinyi Farmers' Association, for their administrative support, and Chang Chih-hsiung (Buaq Isuz), head of Dream Works of the Mei, Wu Xiaomei (Bunun), commissioner of the Business Department, Mr. Xue Qingyao, resident artist, and Ms. Liu Miyun, a fellow worker, for their assistance in sorting out the cultural relics. In the identification of the items, I extend thanks to the two elders of the county community, Quan Guoxiang and Tian Xue'e, for providing clear cultural information. I also want to recognize the fine work of a former special class student of National Chi Nan International University, Si Yao (Ciang Ispalidav), who sorted out the Bunun language listening, typing and information supplement. For their digitalization and inventory work, I would like to thank Dai Zixiang and Liao Zhehan, the senior interns of the Department of Tourism, Leisure, and Hospitality Management. Finally, I want to thank Fang Chunwei, assistant researcher of the National Taiwan Prehistoric Museum, and Yang Chikai, assistant professor of the Department of Forestry, National Pingtung University of Science and Technology, for their professional suggestions on the revision of the contents in the inventory.

References

1. Austronesian Forum. (2020). *An introduction to the Austronesian peoples*. https://austronesianforum.org/en/menu/92C9FA5FDC5FA166E3F680777C5BB779/info.html. Accessed 22 Jan 2023.
2. Council of Indigenous Peoples. (2024). *Population census*. https://www.cip.gov.tw/zh-tw/news/data-list/FA5D874A39F5B3A4/682FB58975DE327E8058FB779C868130-info.html. Accessed 8 July 2025.
3. Tung, C. Y., Liao, Z. H., ZiX, D. (2021). *Talugan bu nong wen wu guan zhan pin qing ce bao gao shu (Collection List of Talugan Bunun Cultural Relics Museum)*, Nantou. (unpublished report).
4. Nantou County Government. (2024). *Population census*. https://ntdash.nantou.gov.tw/ntdash-web/statistical/05aboriginaltribe. Accessed 8 July 2025.
5. ROC Yearbook. (2000). *Distribution of 9 indigenous tribes*. http://www.taiwan-database.net/images/LL-M01/image159.jpg. Accessed 28 August 2023.
6. Ch'iu, C. C. (1966). *Bu nong zu ka she qun de she hui su zhi (Social Organization of the Take Bakaha Bunun)*. Institute of Ethnology. Academia Sinica.
7. Hsieh, C. Y. (2020). Nan tou xian yuan zhu min zu wen hua guan she de ding wei yu wei lai fa zhan (The Orientation and Future Development of the Native Ethnic Culture Museum in Nantou County). In: *Proceeding of Paper Presentation workshop for 2020 the 2nd Symposium on Water-Sand Interconnection-- Local Connection and Social Practice*, National Chi Nan University, 12 June 2020, 179–202。.
8. MacCannell, D. (1976). *The tourist: A new theory of the leisure class*. Schocken Books.
9. Clifford, J. (1988). *The predicament of culture: Twentieth-century ethnography, literature, and art*. Harvard University Press.
10. Clifford, J. (1997). *Routes: Travel and translations in the late twentieth-century*. Harvard University Press.
11. Hu, C. Y. (1994). Bo wu guan zhong di guan guang wen hua-- xian dai mai luo xia "chuan tong" de bian xing (Tourist Culture in Museum- The Transformation of "Tradition" in modern context). *Museology Quarterly, 8*(2), 39–45. https://doi.org/10.6686/MuseQ.199404_8(2).0007

12. Hu, C. Y., & Tsui, E. Y. L. (1998). *Tai da ren lei xue xi Ino Kanori cang pin yan jiu (Studies on INO'S Collection at Department of Anthropology of National Taiwan University)*. National Taiwan University Press.
13. Yen, H. F. (2021). Nan tou xian ren ai xiang bu nong zu wu jie bu luo shi yong zhi wu duo yang xing (Edible plant diversity of Bunong Wujie tribe in Renai Township, Nantou County). *Special Issue on Taichung District Agricultural Improvement Farm, 144*, 52–77.
14. Haivangang, B., & Tung, G. S. (2009). Bu nong zu sheng qun min zu zhi wu yong zhi chu bu diao cha (A preliminary investigation on the application of ethnic plants in Bunun society). *Taiwan Journal of Indigenous Studies, 2*(2), 69–95. https://doi.org/10.29910/TJIS.200906.0003
15. Haivangang, B. (2016). Bu nong zu de min zu zhi wu yu sheng huo (Ethnic plants and life of the Bunun). *Eco Everything, 50*, 54–58.
16. Goffman, E. (1959). *The presentation of self in everyday life, 1st*. Anchor Books. (first published in Scotland in 1956).

Part IV
Evaluating Blue Impact from Social and Environmental Perspective

Chapter 9
Application of the Sustainable Livelihoods Framework to Analyze the Effect of the USR Program: A Case Study of the Badouzi Fishing Village

Hui-Chiao Wang

Abstract Following the Sustainable Livelihoods Framework (SLF), this research discusses the livelihood changes in the Badouzi Fishing Village under the University Social Responsibility Program (USR Program) conducted by the National Taiwan Ocean University (NTOU). These livelihood changes are assessed according to the interaction of vulnerability contexts, livelihood resources, transforming structures and processes, livelihood strategies, and livelihood outcomes. Based on the SLF, appropriate evaluation indicators are developed and applied to the sustainable livelihood of fishing villages. From interviews with stakeholders, it was found that the NTOU USR Program produced higher incomes, with reduced vulnerability and better sustainable use of the natural resource base of the village. In addition to increasing the popularity and profitability of local fishing and fisheries, the USR program also identified ways to develop local tourism, as well as leisure and recreation activities. The insights provided in this study should enable local authorities and city governments to devise feasible strategies to further improve livelihoods.

Keywords USR Program · Sustainable livelihoods framework · Badouzi fishing village · Stakeholders · SDG 11

9.1 Introduction

In Taiwan, 114 institutions of higher education conducted 220 projects in 239 areas during the first phase of Taiwan's University Social Responsibility (USR) Program (2018–2019). In addition, 97 institutions of higher education conducted 217 projects during the second phase (2020–2022).[1] One USR Program, the Prosperity for

[1] Center for University Social Responsibility Ministry of Education https://usr.moe.gov.tw/

H.-C. Wang (✉)
National Taiwan Ocean University, Keelung, Taiwan
e-mail: joan@mail.ntou.edu.tw

M. C. Huang et al. (eds.), *Innovative Social Practice and Community-Based Approach to the Ocean*, https://doi.org/10.1007/978-981-96-9104-3_9

Fisherman, Fishing Village, and Fishery-International Blue Economy Pilot Zones was launched by the Ministry of Education and conducted by the National Taiwan Ocean University (NTOU) in the Badouzi fishing village over a 5-year period. In pursuit of Sustainable Development Goals 11 (Sustainable Cities and Communities) and 14 (Life Below Water), the project focused on improving the society, ecology, and economy of the village, where commercial fishers have suffered a number of predicaments.

The Badouzi fishing village, located in northeast Taiwan, is in an important fishery zone (Fig. 9.1). The industry structure and the livelihood of residents are inseparable from the fishery. However, as in the case of fishing villages generally, Badouzi has been seriously affected by climate change, overfishing, marine pollution, and other global factors [1]. The total catch and resources of the fisheries have declined year by year and prices have been unstable. Adding to this predicament, the manpower and community structure of the Badouzi fishing village has had to deal with aging, grandparenting, and a decline in the fishing population. Despite the multiple long-term efforts conducted under the USR Program, little or no research has been undertaken to evaluate the practical effects of the project. The present study is intended to help fill this gap by exploring the effects of the USR project on the livelihoods of residents of the Badouzi fishing village.

The study applies the Sustainable Livelihoods Framework (SLF) to estimate the effects of the NTOU-led projects on the village and to assess the livelihood changes. SLF is a people-centered, actor-oriented, evidence-based approach to rural development that strives to understand the complicated reality of villager livelihoods and, according to its proponents, overcome difficult rural development challenges [2–6]. This research uses a qualitative approach in which library and field studies are conducted, along with a questionnaire survey and focus group discussions by stakeholders. It is argued that the SLF offers a practical and effective basis for

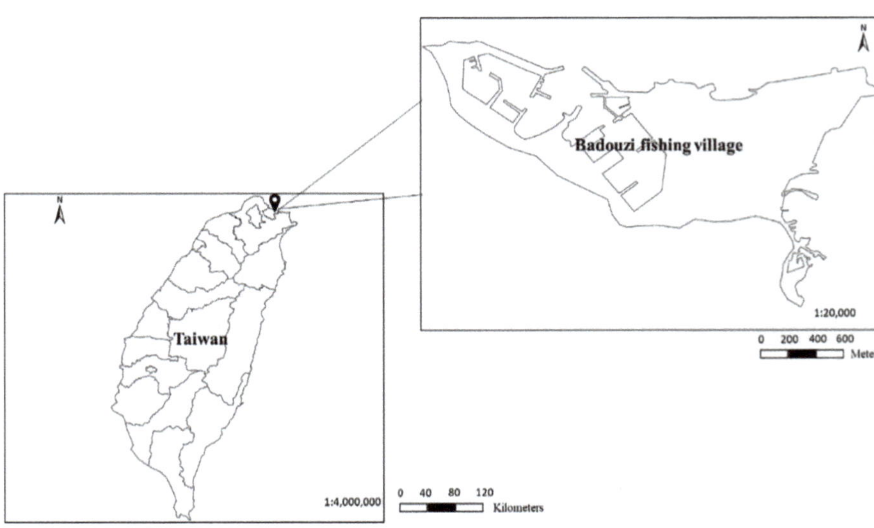

Fig. 9.1 Location and layout of Badouzi fishing village, Keelung, Taiwan

analyzing the complex livelihoods of a community, using five key components: vulnerability context, livelihood resources, transforming structures and processes, livelihood strategies, and livelihood outcomes [4, 7–10]. According to the SLF, the five dimensions of livelihood capital are financial capital, natural capital, human capital, physical capital, and social capital [7, 11, 12]. Additionally, the SLF offers a sound qualitative approach to assessing livelihood changes [10, 11] and facilitating our understanding of stakeholder opinions. For these reasons, the SLF was adopted in this study to compare USR Program-induced changes in livelihoods in the fishing village and assess whether these changes have enhanced the sustainability of these livelihoods.

The present research sought to determine whether the livelihood of the Badouzi fishing village changed during the 5-year efforts of the USR project conducted by NTOU and to establish which of the livelihood capital categories was most affected. This chapter first provides a general introduction to the SLF and the USR Program. Next, the current situation of the Badouzi fishing village is described, along with the research approach used in the study. The progress of the applied qualitative analysis is then reported, after which the opinions of stakeholders are summarized, the study's results are presented, and the implications of the study's findings are discussed. The chapter concludes by identifying the study's main limitations and offering recommendations for future research.

9.2 Literature Review

9.2.1 Sustainable Livelihoods Framework

The SLF is derived from the livelihoods perspective that first gained favor the 1990s, when it was used by the UK government and aid agencies to help poor and vulnerable people make ends meet in a more effective manner [2, 3, 5, 13]. Over the ensuing 20 years, the concept was refined and widely applied with more rigor and a more sophisticated understanding of its limitations, and came to be used by developing countries [14, 15] to improve the efficiency and productivity of their agricultural practices. However, the basic framework leaned more towards political economy analysis, largely failing to address the diversity and complexity of people's livelihoods. Today, the SLF developed by DFID (Department for International Development) has become the main research tool of development institutions, research institutions, and countries looking to improve the livelihoods of the poor and strengthen the sustainability of these livelihoods [3] . Because the SLF takes into account the complexity of people's livelihoods and focuses on the interests of communities in the development process, and due to it being used to assess livelihood sustainability in both developing countries and developed countries [9, 15–17], the sustainable livelihood framework has proven to be a useful analytical tool for evaluating the livelihood sustainability of primary industrial communities.

The SLF is composed of five key components: vulnerability contexts, livelihood assets, transforming structures and processes, livelihood strategies, and livelihood outcomes [7, 11, 12, 16]. The framework begins with a discussion of the vulnerability context, including the impact, trend, and seasonality encountered in the external environment where people live. Importantly, these factors are not necessarily negative; on the contrary, some may be positive. Vulnerability contexts are often affected by the domains of economics, politics (local, national, and regional), information power dynamics, demographic trends, formal and information institutions, and often conflict(s) in transforming structures and processes, especially those levels of government and the private sector that affect poor people in transforming structures. In terms of lifestyle assets, there are five categories of lifestyle capital: natural capital, physical capital, economic/financial capital, human capital, and social/cultural capital. In this study, we identify the changes attributable to the USR Program in the five classes of livelihood capital, illustrating the effectiveness of the SLF. Transforming organizations and structures influence whether and how a diversity of livelihood assets is accessed and transformed into livelihood strategies. A diversity of macro conditions and social trends constitute the broad context for people's livelihoods. Livelihood resources are inputs to a livelihood system and are used to generate livelihood outcomes [11, 13].

9.2.2 *Regional Revitalization*

In 2012, the cabinet of Japanese Prime Minister Shinzo Abe introduced the concept of Regional Revitalization and set the Educational Function and Social Mechanism to guide the creation of educational programs to meet the needs of local economic and social development [18, 19]. In view of the situation in Japan, the Taiwan government set regional revitalization as a national policy at the strategic level of national security. By following the principle of putting people first and through the combination of regional revitalization and innovation, Taiwan seeks to revitalize local industries, create employment, promote the return of local populations, and achieve the goal of "balancing" Taiwan (from a briefing on the National Strategic Plan for Regional Revitalization as approved by Executive Yuan 1,080,103). Based on this, university teachers are urged to adjust their curricula to adapt to changes in the current environment and help the young generations acquire the ability to overcome future problems and shoulder the responsibility of local development. In terms of the overall planning of regional revitalization, education is an important topic for discussion—it can be transformed into a mode in which college teachers and students provide assistance within communities. Accordingly, the Ministry of Education plans to implement the USR Program in the higher education system as a way to encourage university teachers and students to enter local communities through their courses. This has the potential to not only help residents deal with the difficulties they face in their communities, but also foster the professional competence of students and develop the abilities needed to cope with the world of the future.

Xu (2019) [20] pointed out that regional revitalization is closely related to the characteristics of the local cultural industry, resident awareness, and government policies. The core strategy of promoting regional revitalization through field activation is to stimulate local consciousness and promote regional revitalization from bottom to top, to ensure that industries, government, education, and research can integrate with each other to bring the comprehensive effect of resources into play, and to use examples from various countries to revive space and promote local communication. Zheng [21] pointed out that Taiwan Regional Revitalization should explore five core issues: the internal or the external, tradition or innovation, life or livelihood, sightseeing or other, and how to build local confidence. Based on the concept of Regional Revitalization, the USR Program is seen as a key livelihood opportunity to enhance the income of local community residents and raise living standards while at the same time reducing pressure on environment resources.

9.2.3 USR Program

In response to globalization and the advent of the era of the knowledge-driven economy, the educational system in many countries has set the goal of cultivating diverse abilities in students. Since 2018, Taiwan has adopted the Higher Education Sprout Project as a major policy instrument, with the improvement of teaching quality and learning effectiveness as a core component [22]. In pursuit of its goal, Taiwan's Ministry of Education has in recent years promoted the USR Program and the Teaching Practice Research Program to accelerate changes in Taiwan's higher education and ensure its responsiveness to global changes. The main purpose of the USR Program is to guide university teachers and students to form crossover teams that serve as a local core think tank in regional development, actively exploring local demands and solving problems through cooperation and by leveraging local advantages. This is used to drive the innovative development of local enterprises and community cultures. Moreover, through their learning and participation, engaged college students are instilled with a sense of being needed by their communities and building an identity there [23].

In reviewing the national strategic plan for regional revitalization in Taiwan, Zhang [24] found that only the USR Program was listed by the Ministry of Education. The goal of the program is described as cultivating college students who can create value for local development and foster their ability to learn by doing to address problems [25–27]. Through the interaction of schools and industry and by further meeting the needs of industry, the program is aimed at nurturing the ability of students to practice and act, thus promoting local recognition of students and opening opportunities for entrepreneurship [25, 26, 28]. The goals of the USR Program also include connecting junior colleges and local communities, guiding the integration of teaching innovation with social practice, and developing student abilities to solve future world problems [28, 29]. Given the achievements and implementation outcomes of the USR Program conducted in the Badouzi fishing village over

5 years, the USR Program is seen as a key potential livelihood opportunity for islands and coastal regions, with the ability to raise living standards and reduce pressure on fishing resources.

From 2018 to 2022, NTOU used a USR Program subsidy from the Ministry of Education to implement the "Prospect for Fisherman, Fishing Village, and Fishery International Blue Economy Pilot Zones" in the Badouzi Fishing Village. In order to put the spirit of the USR into practice and effectively improve the livelihoods of local fishermen in the village, the NTOU USR Program conducted social practices through multiple courses, with many teachers and students working in the field. By observing the status quo of the fishing village, the university assessed the difficulties facing local fishermen and encouraged students to use their professional knowledge and skills acquired through various courses to address the problems that were adversely affecting the livelihoods of the fishermen in Badouzi Village. With its nearly 5 years of effort, NTOU has earned the confidence and trust of the local residents and has, through its active cooperation with the Keelung Municipal Government, the National Marine Science and Technology Museum, the Keelung District Fishery Association, and the Local Development Association, clearly helped to improve the livelihood of the fishermen in the village.

9.3 The Status Quo of Badouzi Fishing Village

A fishing port is one of the principal symbols of Taiwan fisheries. Marine fishery resources, fishermen livelihoods, and fishery culture are closely related to fishing ports. Fishing ports function as places for vessel berthing, loading and unloading, replenishment, facility maintenance, and more. With the emergence of Taiwan's fishing ports and the development of its fishing industry, the 1970s can be said to be the heyday of Taiwan fisheries, driving the robust development of its fishing villages. There are six fishing ports in Keelung, from east to west, the Wanghaixiang Fishing Port, Changtanli Fishing Port, Badouzi Fishing Port, Zhengbin Fishing Port, Waimushan Fishing Port, and the Dawulun Fishing Port. The Badouzi Fishing Port and the Zhengbin Fishing Port are Class-I; the remainder are Class-II [30].

The NTOU USR Program extends over the six fishing villages adjacent to the Badouzi Fishing Port: Badou Village, Changtan Village, Bisha Village, Shazi Village, Xinfeng Village, and Xinfu Village. Taiwan has a total of only nine Class-I fishing ports; two are nearby the Badouzi Fishing Village: the Badouzi Fishing Port and the Zhengbin Fishing Port. In the 1970s, owing to the capacity of the Badouzi Fishing Port, there were hundreds of steel fishing boats berthing there, providing most of the catch for northern Taiwan. As such, the value and quantity of the catch from inshore- and offshore-fishing boats in Badouzi became evident. Residents in such occupations as fisher, fishmonger, ship repairer, aquatic product processing plant worker, and haenyo (female diver) earned their livelihood from the fishing industry. During this period, residents of the Badouzi Fishing Village depended on fishery activities to support themselves and their families and were engaged in fishery-related employment. Not surprisingly, when the glory days of Badouzi fisheries ended, the village residents faced severe vulnerabilities and their assets declined.

The following describes the status quo and dilemma of the Badouzi Fishing Village that gave rise to the NTOU's USR Program there.

9.3.1 *Fishing Villages Have Faded and the Prosperity of Fisheries Has Disappeared*

Currently, most of the fishing villages along the North Keelung Coast depend on offshore fishery. However, the greenhouse effect and overfishing have led to the depletion of fishery resources, and the past glory of Keelung, with its booming fisheries, has disappeared. The coastal catch has decreased sharply: in 2011, the catch of coastal fishery was 2210 metric tons; by 2021, it had fallen to only 7.3 metric tons. Affected by environmental changes, the utilization rate of the fishing ports has dropped significantly. Not only is the fishery population aging, but the number of fishermen engaging in traditional fishing activities is decreasing. Fishing villages are in decline and are witnessing the exodus of young people.

9.3.2 *The Number of Fishermen Keeps Changing*

According to statistics published by the Taiwan Fisheries Agency, the number of people registered in pelagic fisheries in 2011 was 1022; by 2011, that number had fallen to 440. In recent years, the population of pelagic fishermen has dropped by 56.9%. In addition, the number of fishermen in offshore fisheries decreased from 3486 to 2622, down 24.8%. However, the number of coastal fisheries began to rise in 2015; by 2020, that number had increased from 600 to 1278, an increase of 113%. Table 9.1 shows the relevant statistics in greater detail.

9.3.3 *More Coastal Fishing Vessels than Offshore and Oceangoing Vessels*

There are currently 685 fishing vessels and sampans registered in Keelung, including 82 vessels with a gross tonnage of over 50 tons, 101 vessels with a gross tonnage of 20–50 tons, and 502 vessels with a gross tonnage of less than 20 tons. Fishing vessels weighing less than 20 tons are typically owned by fishermen living in permanent coastal areas, while those weighing more than 20 tons are owned by fishermen who engage in offshore and pelagic fishery.

Table 9.1 Statistics of fisherman population in Keelung City

Number of fishermen	Category		
Year	Pelagic fishery	Offshore fishery	Coastal fishery
2011	1022	3486	0
2012	1090	3532	0
2013	1405	3819	0
2014	1190	3805	0
2015	900	2850	600
2016	885	2787	597
2017	860	2760	590
2018	860	2760	590
2019	576	2820	588
2020	456	2584	1003
2021	440	2622	1278

Data source: The website of Taiwan Fisheries Agency

9.3.4 Destruction of Marine Ecological Habitat

Most of the fishing villages along Taiwan's north coast rely on offshore fishing for their livelihoods; however, the greenhouse effect and overfishing have depleted fishery resources. Although the overall catch has increased (the catch of coastal fisheries increased from 42,000 metric tons in 2020 to 47,000 metric tons in 2021; the catch of offshore fisheries increased from 4.9 metric tons in 2020 to 7.2 metric tons in 2021), the main fishing methods used by the fishermen are lampara net and trawling—harmful methods that are generally associated with bycatch (unwanted or unsellable catch that is simply discarded by the fishermen) and will wreak havoc on the marine ecology in the short term and negatively affect livelihoods in the long term.

9.4 Research Design

The sustainable livelihood approach has proved to be a valuable research tool for identifying matters of concern for local communities regarding their source of livelihoods and barriers to small-scale aquaculture [31–33]. A recent study found that the introduction of tourism into traditional fishing villages has improved the livelihood of their primary industry. Yujiale tourism uses existing fishery and marine culture resources to create employment opportunities and income for local residents, and to supplement the livelihood of traditional fisheries [17]. In seeking to understand the reasons behind the choice of livelihood strategies in the Badouzi Fishing Village and assess the benefits of the NTOU USR Program, the SLF developed by DFID was adopted as this study's primary research method.

9.4.1 *Stakeholders*

To ensure the correctness and professionalism of the evaluation indicators (vulnerability contexts, livelihood assets, transforming structures and processes, livelihood strategies and livelihood outcomes) in the Badouzi Fishing Village SLF, relevant research results presented in the reference literature were used, along with stakeholder interviews. The stakeholders included the Curator of the National Museum of Marine Science and Technology (NMMST), a city government official, a teachers at NTOU, the village chief, leaders of the fishermen, the fisherman's association and Community Promotion Association, and representatives of the recreation industry (see Table 9.2 for details). The researchers invited stakeholders connected to the sustainability of the Badouzi Fishing Village and repeatedly consulted the evaluation indicators that had been preliminarily constructed according to the SLF. In addition, references to Apine et al. (2019) [31] and Su et al. (2016) [12] were used, and the opinions of all the stakeholders were collected and sorted in order to determine the final evaluation indicators.

9.4.2 *Construction of the Evaluation Indicators for Sustainable Livelihood in the Badouzi Fishing Village*

9.4.2.1 The Evaluation Index of Vulnerability Contexts

Vulnerability is a key to livelihood sustainability. It includes shocks, trends, and seasonality [7, 15, 34]. It can adversely affect the assets of the poor as well as their choice of livelihoods, although not all the vulnerabilities are negative. The vulnerability context includes shocks, e.g., conflict, illness, floods, storms, droughts, pests, diseases, seasonality (e.g., prices and employment opportunities), and critical trends (e.g., demographic, environmental, economic, governance, and technological trends) [35].

Based on the sustainable livelihood framework, the opinions of stakeholders, and references to prior research [14, 17, 31, 35, 36], the evaluation indicators of the vulnerability context in the Badouzi Fishing Village are summarized in Table 9.3.

9.4.2.2 The Evaluation Index of Livelihood Assets

Livelihood assets consist of Natural, Physical, Social, Human, and Financial forms of capital [7, 34], which are portrayed as follows:

- Natural capital: natural resources, such as land and forests, on which people depend for their livelihoods.
- Financial capital: monetary income, such as cash, savings and wages, to build confidence in pursuing livelihoods.

Table 9.2 Data from stakeholders

	1	2	3	4	5	6	7	8
Service unit	National Marine Science and Technology Museum	Traditional fishing boat	Keelung Government	Recreational fishing boat	NTOU	Local tourism association	Keelung district fishery association	Badouzi fishing village
Role	Chief	Skipper	Section chief	skipper	Associate professor	Chairman	Executive Secretary	Village head
Function	Caring for the livelihoods of fishermen and recording the coastal marine ecology.	Representative of skippers in the nearshore fishing industry.	Promoting regional revitalization and activities related to the fishing industry.	Operating leisure fishing and tourism on Keelung Islet.	Preserving the local fishing industry culture	Operating local fishing village tourism and designing tour packages.	Caring for the livelihoods of fishermen and promoting the education on fish consumption	Caring for the livelihoods of local fishermen and safeguarding fishing villages.
Work experience	5–10 Years	Over 20 Years	10–15 Years	10–15 Years	5–10 Years	Over 20 Years	Over 20 Years	10–15 Years
Age	41–50	51–60	41–50	61 or above	41–50	61 or above	51–60	51–60

Table 9.3 The evaluation index of vulnerability contexts

Type	Evaluation indicators
Shocks	Lower catches, depleted fishery resources, climate change
Demographic trend	Population migration, population aging
Educational trend	Education on fish consumption, marine resources conservation, marine environment protection
Technological changes	Sustainable fishing methods,[a] scientific and technological fishing methods
Seasonality	Northeast monsoon, typhoon

[a]The main characteristics of a sustainable fishery should be that the fishing gear and the method used to catch fish are highly selective, with no bycatch or at most a minimum level of bycatch, no sweeping of populations, no catching of juvenile or undersized fish, no over-effort and over-exploitation, and no or minimal impact on the marine environment and other fauna. Traditional artisanal fisheries generally fulfill all or most of these conditions, as they have evolved over thousands of years, during which a vast knowledge of the marine environment, ecology, biology, and the behavior and life history of most marine animals has been acquired and applied. In addition, traditional artisanal fishers fish for their livelihood, not for the making of large profits, as is the case with current industrial marine fisheries (Dammannagoda, 2018) [37]

Table 9.4 The evaluation index of livelihood assets

Type	Evaluation indicators
Natural capital	Overall household labor force, education level of adult labor force
Physical capital	Marine environment, marine ecology, fishery resources
Economic/Financial capital	Number and type of fishing boats
Human capital	Household cash income, credit opportunities
Social/cultural capital	Participate in community organizations

- Physical capital: basic infrastructure, such as roads, and equipment, such as machines, which people use to generate income.
- Human capital: labor capacity or the capacity to work in terms of education, health, skills and knowledge.
- Social capital: relations and networks that support coordination and cooperation [35].

Assets are fundamental to the poor. Based on the sustainable livelihood framework, the opinions of shareholders, and several references [34, 36, 38], the evaluation indicators of livelihood assets in the Badouzi Fishing Village are summarized in Table 9.4.

9.4.2.3 The Evaluation Index of Transforming Structures and Processes

Structures are hardware in the public and private sectors that develop and carry out laws and policy, provide services, and carry out a wide range of other tasks that have an impact on people's livelihoods. The public sector includes the various levels of government that formulate policies, grant subsidies, and develop strategies to

Table 9.5 The evaluation index of transforming structures and processes

Type	Evaluation indicators
International policy	EU Yellow Card Fishery IUU,[a] the U.S. C29 Forced Labour Convention[b]
National policy	Transformation of traditional fishery into recreational fishery, fishing off season, fishing-ban season, regional revitalization, USR Program
Institution	Fishermen's union, captains' organizations (Fisherman's Representative)
Local government development strategy	Inshore squid season, protected area

[a]Illegal, unreported, and unregulated (IUU) fishing is a broad term that captures a wide variety of fishing activity. IUU fishing is found in all types and dimensions of fisheries; it occurs both on the high seas and in areas within national jurisdiction. It concerns all aspects and stages of the capture and utilization of fish, and it may sometimes be associated with organized crime. Reference to broad activities classified as illegal, unreported, and unregulated fishing (FAO)

[b]The Forced Labour Convention, the full title of which is the Convention Concerning Forced or Compulsory Labour, 1930 (No.29), is one of eight ILO fundamental conventions of the International Labour Organization. Its object and purpose is to suppress the use of forced labor in all its forms irrespective of the nature of the work or the sector of activity in which it may be performed. The Convention defines forced labor as "all work or service which is exacted from any person under the menace of any penalty and for which the said person has not offered himself voluntarily" (P19), with few exceptions, such as compulsory military service [40]

influence local development. Organizations in the public and commercial sectors are considered structures in the SLF. A process is made up of policy, laws, culture, and institutions, and can be considered software [7, 34]. The lives of stakeholders are affected by structures and institutions, and the varied ways in which development interventions may strengthen or weaken these livelihood activities. Transforming structures and processes plays an important role in shaping livelihood assets and outcomes. The environment of structures and processes also influences livelihood strategies and results. The laws, rules, policies, operational plans, agreements, cultural norms, and practices that govern processes, in turn, define how structures function [35].

Based on the sustainable livelihood framework, the opinions of stakeholders, government policy, and reference to previous research [15, 35, 39], the evaluation indicators of transforming structures and processes in the Badouzi Fishing Village are summarized in Table 9.5.

9.4.2.4 The Evaluation Index of Livelihood Outcomes

Livelihood outcomes are a reflection of the successes and objectives that livelihood strategies aim to achieve. Outcomes are always the pathway to assessing livelihood sustainability, and the scale of analysis is of paramount importance [13, 34]. Based on the sustainable livelihood framework, the evaluation indicators of livelihood outcomes in the Badouzi Fishing Village, as in other impoverished villages, consist of more income, increased well-being, reduced vulnerability, improved food security, and more sustainable use of the natural resource base.

9.4.2.5 The Evaluation Index of Livelihood Strategies

Using a compilation of the in-depth interviews conducted with stakeholders, Badouzi's livelihood strategies can be analyzed and discussed. The results derived from this are crucial and constitute the most significant contribution of this study.

9.5 Research Findings

9.5.1 Main Sources of Livelihood for the Residents in Badouzi Fishing Village and the Underlying Reasons

To understand the livelihood strategies of Badouzi Fishing Village residents, we first need to understand their main sources of livelihood and the reasons why these sources predominate. In this study, the two questions proposed in [14] were used to explore and research this topic. Specifically, each of the eight stakeholders was asked about the evaluation indicators of sustainable livelihoods in the Badouzi Fishing Village; the two questions were discussed in an open-ended manner.

The eight stakeholders shared the view that the main sources are industries or jobs related to fishery, such as fishing, selling fish, dealing with fish catch, fish processing, cooking fish products, making bait, fishing nets, repairing fishing boats, carrying passengers along with fishing, and promoting fishery culture. However, the residents are engaged in these fishery-related industries or jobs mainly because of their geographical location, living environment, family or family influence, and property inheritance. The Badouzi Fishing Village stands next to the Wanghaixiang Fishing Port, Changtanli Fishing Port, Badouzi Fishing Port, and the Zhengbin Fishing Port. It is not surprising, then, that fishery-related jobs are part of the residents' daily life. Family elders are often engaged in related jobs, with fishing boats and fishery processing factories owned by their families. Most residents in the village live off fishing, under the combined influence of such factors as high accessibility and convenience for residents to engage in fishing, long-term contact with this sector, existing wealth-making tools at home, direct inheritance of techniques from seniors, direct cash income from fish sales, preferential loans, and fishery subsidies.

Below is an explanation of why the residents of the Badouzi Fishing Village take fishery as their main source of livelihood in terms of vulnerability contexts (Table 9.6), lifestyle assets (Table 9.7), and transformation structures and processes (Table 9.8) in the SLF.

9.5.1.1 Vulnerability Contexts

Vulnerabilities have both a positive and a negative effect on the assets and livelihoods of residents. In the Badouzi Fishing Village, the evaluation indicators of shocks include smaller catches, depleted fishery resources, and climate change, all of which have an extreme effect on the livelihood of commercial fishers. Table 9.6

Table 9.6 Indicators of vulnerability contexts

Type	Evaluation indicators	Explanation
Shocks	Lower catches	In recent years, fishing boat skippers have found that the catches are smaller, and it has become more difficult to catch fish. It often takes much more time to do so. In some cases, fishing income cannot cover the cost fuel and labor.
	Depleted fishery resources	Fish, agar, and flying fish eggs have decreased. In earlier times, there were plentiful fishery resources along the coast; now, there are fewer such resources in the coastal waters; the fishery resources that fishermen can obtain continue to decrease.
	Climate change	Climate change is a global issue. Rising sea water temperatures impact the growth of coral and the ecosystem as a whole.
Demographic trend	Population migration	Because their household economy has improved, and because the next generation has been better educated, the older captains do not want their children to engage in such tiring work as fishing. Therefore, they encourage their children to move to neighboring metropolitan cities to make a living.
	Population aging	Because members of the younger generation are migrating to larger cities, the population left in the villages is aging; the ages of the fishing boat skippers those captains who go fishing are also on the rise.
Educational trend	Education on fish consumption	Consumers and students need fish-based diet education that encourages them to consume nutritious fish products at reasonable prices and in season.
	Marine resources conservation	Marine resources are exhaustible. Only by conserving and enhancing the value of marine resources can we ensure the sustainability of marine resources without harming the livelihood of fishermen.
	Marine environment protection	By educating the public in terms of beach cleaning, sea cleaning, and marine waste management, the marine environment and marine ecology could be protected, and fishermen can gain the opportunity to utilize abundant marine resources and improve the livelihood.
Technological changes	Sustainable fishing methods	Fishing by lampara net and trawling produces bycatch, harms the marine ecology, and injures fish, resulting in lower market prices. Sustainable fishing methods can effectively solve these problems and increase the value of fish.
	Scientific and technological fishing methods	New tools like the fish detector, GPS, and the LED fish collecting lamp are increasingly used on fishing boats. As such tools are widely applied, they have become indispensable tools for fishermen.
Seasonality	Northeast monsoon	Keelung is located in the northeast of Taiwan. Winter is the season of the northeast monsoon. Fishermen are often unable to go to sea due to the monsoon's impact, which severely impacts their livelihood.
	Typhoon	When a typhoon hits, fishing boats must return to harbor. From the arrival of the typhoon to its departure, the boats cannot go to sea, sometimes for 7–10 days, which reduces fishing income.

details the predicaments of Badouzi residents in terms of shocks, demographic trends, educational trends, technological changes, and seasonality.

9.5.1.2 Livelihood Assets

Based on the SLF's livelihood assets and the views of the eight stakeholders, Table 9.7 summarizes the reasons that residents in the Badouzi Fishing Village choose fishery-related industries or jobs as their main source of livelihood.

Table 9.7 Indicators of livelihood assets

Type	Evaluation indicators	Explanation
Natural capital	Overall household labor force	To make a living, families living in fishing villages own fishing boats or fishing tools for earning money. Considering the labor force of the entire family and the prospect of more income, most residents will choose fishery as their source of livelihood.
	Education level of adult labor force	In the early days, residents of fishing villages were ill-educated, so they chose jobs within the family or in industries they often contacted in their daily living environment. Thus, the industries or jobs related to fishery were typically their first choice.
Physical capital	Marine environment	Badouzi Fishing Village is adjacent to an important fishing ground in the north. Such environmental conditions encourage residents to make a living by fishing.
	Marine ecology	The fishing grounds near Badouzi feature diverse ecological conditions. In addition to fishing in all seasons, the stunning scenery of the underwater coral reef serves as a driving force to attract residents to live on the sea.
	Fishery resources	The offshore fishery resources available to fishing villages are a source of livelihood for fishermen. Therefore, accessibility, convenience, and the difficulties of fishery resources (the source of livelihood) are taken into account; this is one of the factors residents consider.
Economic/financial capital	Number and type of fishing boats	To earn more income, fishermen would rather use the money they earn to buy boats and use the boats to catch more fish than invest in real estate or stocks.
	Type of fishing boats	Because the catch is seasonal, fishermen can use a variety of fishing tools and methods to catch fish, including various types of fishing gear, fishing nets and cages—all in an effort to reduce the vulnerability caused by seasonal factors; that is, they use multifunctional fishing boats as their fishing choice.

(continued)

Table 9.7 (continued)

Type	Evaluation indicators	Explanation
Human capital	Household cash income	Selling fish is the major income source of a fishery, and all transactions are cash based, whether fishermen sell fish in the market or sell their catches directly to affluent businessmen. The cash income from such sales is the source of livelihood for the fishermen.
	Credit opportunities	Fishermen obtain funds by means of credit. Both low-interest loans and interest subsidies are important factors that encourage fishermen to buy boats.
Social/cultural capital	Participate in community organizations	The community organizations of fishermen include fishermen unions and captains' organizations. Classes in production and marketing are offered. Such community organizations provide and share the latest information to reduce the impact of external environmental vulnerability and help increase income.

9.5.1.3 Transforming Structures and Processes

Table 9.8 summarizes the reasons why Badouzi residents rely on fishery-related industries or jobs as their main source of livelihood from the perspective of the SLF's transformation structures and processes, based on the views of the eight stakeholders.

9.5.2 Contribution of the USR Program to Badouzi Fishing Village

The USR Program conducted by NTOU extended over the 5-year period from 2018 to 2022, with four teachers devoting themselves to the Badouzi Fishing Village. The program has achieved remarkable results in terms of talent cultivation and local employment. A total of five graduates have passed the recruitment examination of the Keelung District Fishery Association and become formal employees: one graduate has passed the civil service examination and become a government employee in the Keelung City Government, two graduates work as contracted employees, one graduate serves as a yacht steward at the Badouzi Yacht Harbor, and another 11 graduates have become professional guides for Keelung Islet.

To enhance the local tour experience, the program has assisted the local tourism association in undertaking educational programs sponsored by the Ministry of Education, developing a new DIY activity (dyeing with *Dioscorea matsudai*), leading elementary school students in outdoor marine education activities, and organizing Keelung City teacher training camps.

Table 9.8 Indicators of transforming structures and processes

Type	Evaluation indicators	Explanation
International policy	EU Yellow Card Fishery IUU, the U.S. C29 Forced Labor Convention	The fishery in Badouzi is exemplified by coastal and offshore fisheries, while pelagic fisheries are gradually declining; international policies thus have little impact on fishery in the Badouzi Fishing Village.
National policy	Transformation of traditional fishery into recreational fishery	Impacted by climate change, overfishing,[a] marine pollution, and other factors, Taiwan's Fisheries Agency encourages the transformation of traditional fisheries into exclusive or part-time recreational businesses to ease pressure on fishery resources, while also helping to balance the livelihood of fishermen.
	Fishing off season	Observing a fishing off season during which the operation of fishing vessels is prohibited is used to restore and sustain marine resources. Taiwan introduced a voluntary fishing moratorium and fishermen receive rewards through application. Fishermen consider the moratorium as a way to adjust their livelihood when measuring labor force, catch, and weather conditions.
	Fishing-ban season	Fishing-ban season is an important measure for protecting fishery resources and a strategy for maintaining the sustainability of such resources. However, it directly affects fishermen's catch and income.
	Regional revitalization	The launch of regional revitalization has prompted many young people to return to their hometowns and consider how to use the characteristics of their hometowns to start their own businesses. The unique culture and history of fisheries in local fishing villages is also one of the factors that promote the regional revitalization of fishing villages.
	USR Program	The USR Program is part of regional revitalization. Through education, university teachers and students engage in field work to help solve local/regional problems and drive development. With the help of the USR Program, many fishing villages have gradually created alternative types and sources of livelihood.
Institution	Fishermen's union	The local fishermen unions provide fishermen with preferential deposits, low-interest loans, and interest subsidies, which are timely and concrete help for the sustainable livelihood of fishermen.
	Captains' organizations	Members of various captains' organizations provide each other with useful information on fishing, fisheries, and sea conditions. They also offer technical support through information transmission.
Local government development strategy	Inshore squid season	Inshore squid season is a well-known fishing activity in Keelung. The promotion of the activity has improved the sales volume and popularity of Keelung's fishing catch.
	Protected area	The establishment of Wanghaixiang's Chaojing Bay Marine Protected Area, which is adjacent to the Badouzi Fishing Village, has greatly improved the surrounding marine environment and marine ecology, which will certainly help fishermen's livelihood.

[a]Comprehensive definitions of overfishing, incorporating multiple organizational scales (management stock, species, assemblage, community, ecosystem), could help to identify ecosystem attributes that are not adequately addressed under single-species management [41]

The program has also assisted the Keelung District Fishery Association in promoting its online fishery e-commerce platform, resulting in a multi-fold increase in annual sales revenue. To promote local tourism, the program surveyed the human, cultural, geographical, industrial, and tourism resources of Badouzi and published a book on Badouzi's ecological tourism, allowing more people to gain an understanding of Badouzi and attracting potential tourists to the area [42].

In the area of industry counseling, the program has assisted recreational fishing boat operators by increasing the diversity of tour offerings, adding education on fish consumption and beach-cleaning activities, and incorporating ESG and SDG concepts to expand the enterprise client base and attract family tourists.

9.5.3 The Opinions of Stakeholders Regarding the USR Program

According to the observations and views of the eight stakeholders interviewed for the study, and in terms of the connotation of the SLF, the contributions of the USR program to the sustainability of local livelihoods include more income, reduced vulnerability, and more sustainable use of the natural resource base. Since their arrival in Badouzi, the NTOU teachers and students have contributed a wide range of fresh ideas and practices to the marketing of local fishing, not only improving the popularity of local fishing, but also directly increasing the income of the fishermen. Through the subtle influence and information exchange between captains, some of the fishermen are now handling their catch and selling it themselves at a desirable price, even marketing it through community platforms. In this way, it is not necessary to transfer the catch to the market for sale, nor rely on the amount of catch to determine household income; rather, the fishermen can make a living with a smaller catch and higher prices, which tends to stabilize use of the ocean's natural resources. The stakeholders believe that the NTOU teachers and students have been very successful in utilizing fishery culture and creativity to develop new approaches to marketing local catch. Thanks to continuous efforts in marketing and publicity, the sales volume of local catch has significantly improved. This plan has been extremely helpful in ensuring a sustainable livelihood for Badouzi residents.

In addition to helping improve the sales of the local fishing catch, the teachers and students from NTOU have also aided local professionals who concurrently run recreational fishing boats and the Association in an effort to optimize the travel situation and enhance community network marketing. Through activities featuring industry and school exchanges and travel experiences, the students recorded and marketed local travel from the perspective of young people and brought new tourists for local sightseeing, leisure, and recreation. Because the USR Program facilitates the marketing of local tourism, it not only increases the revenue of the local tourism industry, but also urges other traditional fisheries to transform into part-time leisure fisheries, which aligns with the national policies exemplified by the SLF transformation structures and processes—the transformation of traditional fisheries into leisure fisheries [43]. This has relieved pressure on fishery resources and, moreover, reduced vulnerability and rendered the use of natural resources more stable.

While the program has contributed to higher incomes and reduced vulnerability, it is imperative to ensure that these gains are sustainable in the long term. This involves not only maintaining the economic benefits but also preserving the natural resource base that the village depends on. Future evaluations of the USR Program should include rigorous assessments of the ecological impact of increased fishing and tourism activities. Additionally, the program could explore innovative strategies for resource management, such as the development of marine protected areas or the promotion of sustainable fishing practices. By integrating these elements, the USR Program could serve as a model for other coastal communities seeking to balance economic development with environmental stewardship.

9.5.4 Livelihood Strategies of Residents in the Badouzi Fishing Village

According to the views of the eight stakeholders, Badouzi residents rely on fishery-related work as a source of livelihood, and most are engaged in fishing and selling fish. This is mainly because the fishing grounds near Badouzi are characterized by a rich and diverse fish catch; the area has earned a favorable reputation thanks to the inshore squid season, the USR Program, and regional revitalization. However, due to the lack of marketing, branding, sales channels, and the fishermen's habit of selling their entire batches of catch to large traders, the fishermen of Badouzi are unwilling to sell processed and refined fish products.

With reference to the evaluation indicators of vulnerability contexts, livelihood assets, and transforming the structures and processes of the SLF, the eight stakeholders interviewed for this study made a number of suggestions for improvement. Firstly, the Badouzi Fishing Village should aim to establish local fishing brands, organize local fishermen to catch fish, develop direct sales centers to deal with the catch, and sell catches in small quantities, at higher prices; furthermore, the marketing work should be publicized in combination with the inshore squid season, the USR Program, and regional revitalization. In this way, because of the increased value of the catch, not only will the income of the fishermen increase, but their living standards will improve. With the cooperation of local fishermen, consumers will know the source of the catch, and food safety will be assured. By handing over their catch to direct sales centers for processing and selling, the fishermen would no longer determine their income based on the amount of catch, preferring instead to increase their income based on a smaller catch of high-quality and high-priced fish. This would not only ease the pressure on fishery resources, but also stabilize the use of natural resources and reduce the vulnerability of the external environment. This livelihood strategy echoes the goal of livelihood outcomes in the SLF, including more income, increased well-being, reduced vulnerability, improved food security, and the more sustainable use of the natural resource base. In this way, the ultimate goal of sustainable marine resources, sustainable fishing villages, and sustainable livelihoods of fishermen can be realized.

9.6 Conclusions and Suggestions

Based on the SLF, this study applies the evaluation indicators of vulnerability contexts, livelihood assets, and transforming structures and processes to the sustainable livelihood of fishing villages. Through stakeholder interviews related to these indicators, it was found that the USR Program conducted by NTOU has made significant contributions to local sustainable livelihoods, including higher income, reduced vulnerability, and more sustainable use of the natural resource base. All eight of the participating stakeholders agreed that the contribution of NTOU to the sustainable livelihood of the Badouzi Fishing Village has been significant. In addition to effectively improving the popularity and sales of local fishing, it has helped in the positive development of local tourism and the expansion of leisure and recreation activities. The USR Program is one of the five key components of the SLF, the national policy focused on transforming structures and processes, and plays a part in regional revitalization. Its target is to enable university teachers and students to enter the field through education, constructively address issues on site, and promote the development of the field.

It was also found that Badouzi residents live on fishery-related jobs, with most engaging in catching and selling fish, and that they rely on natural capital and physical capital. They use their fishing boats to catch fish and earn cash income for their families, typically using their cash income and preferential credit to buy more fishing boats to earn more money. However, due to the lack of marketing, branding, sales channels, and the fishermen's habit of selling entire batches of catch to large traders, they are unwilling to sell processed and refined fish products. As a result, they earn money based only on the amount of catch, which leads to pressure on fishery resources and inevitably increases the impact of vulnerability contexts. To address this, this study recommends that the Badouzi Fishing Village integrate the benefits of livelihood capital and utilize the benefits of vulnerability contexts while transforming structures and processes to increase the value of local catches in order to achieve the goal of livelihood outcomes.

Based on this study's research findings, it is recommended that the next phase of the USR Program at NTOU focus on developing tourism itineraries, improving tourism quality, and designing DIY activities with local characteristics, as most stakeholders agree that local tourism and leisure activities foster the positive development of sustainable livelihoods. In addition, given that the age of most tour guides in fishing villages is relatively high, future USR programs should focus on attracting young people to return to their hometowns, encouraging them to settle in fishing villages, and cultivating local tourism talent.

With respect to fishery sales, although Badouzi is known for its fresh and abundant catches, the lack of creative sales methods, outdated fish processing techniques, and exploitation by middlemen prevent the village fishermen from obtaining good profits through selling their catches. Therefore, it is recommended that the USR Program organize workshops for the fishermen to introduce them to creative marketing models for fish products, new fish processing techniques, and e-commerce channels to increase their income.

Although the SLF has published several articles internationally, and it has been verified that the SLF is effective in formulating sustainable livelihood strategies for impoverished or highly vulnerable areas, this is the first time that research on the topic has focused on Taiwan and the livelihood of fishing village residents. It should be noted that the acquisition of relevant indicators and the conversion of stakeholder views do not fully echo the entire SLF and that the depth and scope of this research were somewhat constrained by the limited resources and time available. It is suggested that future scholars visit a larger number of stakeholders of different types when conducting similar research in order to construct more effective livelihood strategies for achieving sustainable goals. While this research was designed to explore the topic in a qualitative way, it is suggested that future researchers conduct their investigation using quantitative measures and analyses.

While the USR Program has successfully diversified the roles of stakeholders in the Badouzi Fishing Village, the integration of trans-disciplinarity remains underdeveloped. Trans-disciplinarity, which involves the collaboration of various academic disciplines and local knowledge, is crucial for addressing complex, real-world problems. In the context of sustainable livelihoods, a trans-disciplinary approach could facilitate a more holistic understanding of the interconnections between economic, environmental, and social factors, thereby enriching the program's impact. To this end, future iterations of the USR Program should prioritize the incorporation of diverse academic perspectives, including those from environmental science, economics, and sociology, alongside local expertise. This could be achieved through interdisciplinary workshops, collaborative research projects, and the inclusion of broader stakeholder groups, such as environmental NGOs and local entrepreneurs.

Acknowledgement This work was financially supported by the National Science and Technology Council, Taiwan (grant numbers 112-2621-M-019 -006-) and Taiwan's USR Program of Ministry of Education—Prosperity for Fisherman, Fishing Village and Fishery—International Blue Economy Pilot Zones.

References

1. Borras, S. M., Jr. (2009). Agrarian change and peasant studies: Changes, continuities and challenges – An introduction. *The Journal of Peasant Studies, 36*(1), 5–31. https://doi.org/10.1080/03066150902820297
2. Chambers, R., & Conway, G. (1992). *Sustainable rural livelihoods: Practical concepts for the 21st century*. IDS Discussion Paper 296. https://opendocs.ids.ac.uk/opendocs/handle/20.500.12413/775
3. Scoones, I. (2009). Livelihoods perspectives and rural development. *The Journal of Peasant Studies, 36*(1), 171–196. https://doi.org/10.1080/03066150902820503
4. Scoones, I. (2015). *Sustainable livelihoods and rural development*. Practical Action Publishing. https://practicalactionpublishing.com/book/2123/sustainable-livelihoods-and-rural-development
5. De Haan, L. J. (2012). The livelihood approach: A critical exploration. *Erdkunde*, 345–357. https://www.jstor.org/stable/41759104

6. Duojie, C. (2022). Beyond sustainable livelihoods: A diverse economies approach to rural peasant livelihoods in China's Qinghai Province. *Asia Pacific Viewpoint, 63*(1), 12–24. https://doi.org/10.1111/apv.12331
7. DFID U K. (1999). *Sustainable livelihoods guidance sheets* (p. 445). DFID.
8. Carney, D., Drinkwater, M., Rusinow, T., Neefjes, K., Wanmali, S., & Singh, N. (1999). *A brief comparison of the livelihoods approaches of the UK Department for International Development (DFID), CARE, Oxfam and the United Nations Development Programme (UNDP).* Department for International Development.
9. Hussein, K. (2002). *Livelihoods approaches compared.* Department for International Development.
10. Adato, M., & Meinzen-Dick, R. S. (2002). *Assessing the impact of agricultural research on poverty using the sustainable livelihoods framework* (No. 581-2016-39396). https://doi.org/10.22004/ag.econ.16074
11. Natarajan, N., Newsham, A., Rigg, J., & Suhardiman, D. (2022). A sustainable livelihoods framework for the 21st century. *World Development, 155*, 105898. https://doi.org/10.1016/j.worlddev.2022.105898
12. Su, M. M., Wall, G., & Jin, M. (2016). Island livelihoods: Tourism and fishing at long islands, Shandong Province, China. *Ocean & Coastal Management, 122*, 20–29. https://doi.org/10.1016/j.ocecoaman.2015.11.014
13. Scoones, I. (1998). *Sustainable rural livelihoods: A framework for analysis.* https://opendocs.ids.ac.uk/opendocs/handle/20.500.12413/3390
14. Levine, S. (2014). How to study livelihoods: Bringing a sustainable livelihoods framework to life. *Researching livelihoods and services affected by conflict* 22. https://securelivelihoods.org/wp-content/uploads/How-to-study-livelihoods-Bringing-a-sustainable-livelihoods-framework-to-life.pdf
15. Clarke, J. (1997). A framework of approaches to sustainable tourism. *Journal of Sustainable Tourism, 5*(3), 224–233. https://doi.org/10.1080/09669589708667287
16. Carney, D. (2003). *Sustainable livelihoods approaches: progress and possibilities for change* (p. 64). Department for International Development.
17. Tao, T. C., & Wall, G. (2009). Tourism as a sustainable livelihood strategy. *Tourism Management, 30*(1), 90–98. https://doi.org/10.1016/j.tourman.2008.03.009
18. Liang, Z. M. (2019). Analysis of Japanese education policy on regional revitalization. *Journal of Education Research, 304*, 112–125.
19. Liang, Z. M. (2019). Research on important policies of Japanese regional revitalization education in recent years. *Chung Cheng Educational Studies, 18*(2), 85–107.
20. Xu, Y. T. (2019). The road from field activation to regional revitalization in Taiwan. *Taiwan Economic Research Monthly, 42*(5), 104–111.
21. Zheng, Z. K. (2019). Five thoughts on regional revitalization. *CommonWealth Magazine.* https://opinion.cw.com.tw/blog/profile/60/article/8669
22. Ministry of Education. *The Phase II University Social Responsibility Program (2020–2022).* https://www.edu.tw/News_Plan_Content.aspx?n=D33B55D537402BAA&sms=954974C68391B710&s=333F49BA4480CC5B
23. Center for University Social Responsibility Ministry of Education. https://usr.moe.gov.tw/tw
24. Zhang, S. C. (2022). Research on the integration of regional revitalization into citizenship education in rural high schools. *Taiwan Educational Review Monthly, 11*(9), 100–106. http://www.ater.org.tw/journal/article/11-9/free/05.pdf
25. Liu, W. H. (2022). University social responsibility to promote coastal partnership: Introducing Taiwan coastal communities. *Marine Policy, 146*, 105303. https://doi.org/10.1016/j.marpol.2022.105303
26. Liu, W. H., Lee, H. C., Sung, W. Y., & Yang, T. Y. (2022). The roles of Taiwanese universities in coastal revitalization: A study of two case projects. *Marine Policy, 139*, 105050. https://doi.org/10.1016/j.marpol.2022.105050

27. Ting, K. H., Cheng, C. T., & Ting, H. Y. (2021). Introducing the problem/project based learning as a learning strategy in University Social Responsibility Program-A study of local revitalization of Coastal Area, Yong-An District of Kaohsiung City. *Marine Policy, 131*, 104546. https://doi.org/10.1016/j.marpol.2021.104546
28. Wu, M. Q. (2018). The practice of university social responsibility. *Public Governance Quarterly, 6*(1), 62–67.
29. Lin, C. F., & Yu, P. J. (2018). Practice and promotion of university social responsibility. *New Taipei Journal of Nursing, 20*(2), 1–7. https://doi.org/10.6540/NTJN.201809_20(2).0001
30. Keelung District Fishery Association. http://klfish.naffic.org.tw/WebPad/WebPad.aspx?EpfJdId9UuBd9cRTJuhikWgSZBzBephxIji8elPPGMY%3d
31. Apine, E., Turner, L. M., Rodwell, L. D., & Bhatta, R. (2019). The application of the sustainable livelihood approach to small scale-fisheries: The case of mud crab Scylla serrata in South west India. *Ocean and Coastal Management, 170*, 17–28. https://www.sciencedirect.com/science/article/abs/pii/S0964569118306963
32. Chen, H., Shivakoti, G., Zhu, T., & Maddox, D. (2012). Livelihood sustainability and community based co-management of forest resources in China: Changes and improvement. *Environmental Management, 49*(1), 219–228. https://link.springer.com/article/10.1007/s00267-011-9775-4
33. Mbaiwa, J. E., & Stronza, A. L. (2010). The effects of tourism development on rural livelyhoods in the Okavango Delta, Botswana. *Journal of Sustainable Tourism, 18*(5), 635–656. https://doi.org/10.1080/09669581003653500
34. Shen, F., Hughey, K. F., & Simmons, D. G. (2008). Connecting the sustainable livelihoods approach and tourism: A review of the literature. *Journal of Hospitality and Tourism Management, 15*(1), 19–31. https://doi.org/10.1375/jhtm.15.19
35. Serrat, O. (2017). *Knowledge solutions: Tools, methods, and approaches to drive organizational performance* (p. 1140). Springer Nature.
36. Ye, D. H., & Liu, Y. C. (2022). Application designing poverty alleviation based on the evaluation of Yao Nationality's Livelihood Framework. *Packaging Engineering, 43*(6), 157–165. https://doi.org/10.19554/j.cnki.1001-3563.2022.06.021
37. Dammannagoda, S. T. (2018). Sustainable fishing methods in Asia Pacific Region. *Sustainable Aquaculture*, 95–122. https://link.springer.com/chapter/10.1007/978-3-319-73257-2_3
38. Aazami, M., & Shanazi, K. (2020). Tourism wetlands and rural sustainable livelihood: The case from Iran. *Journal of Outdoor Recreation and Tourism, 30*, 100284. https://doi.org/10.1016/j.jort.2020.100284
39. Melles, G. B. (2022). Designing social innovation for sustainable livelihoods. In *Designing social innovation for sustainable livelihoods* (pp. 1–11). Singapore.
40. ILO. (2007). *General Survey Concerning the Forced Labour Convention, 1930 (no. 29), and the Abolition of Forced Labour Convention, 1957 (no. 105).*
41. Murawski, S. A. (2000). Definitions of overfishing from an ecosystem perspective. *ICES Journal of Marine Science, 57*(3), 649–658. https://doi.org/10.1006/jmsc.2000.0738
42. Wang, H. C. (2019). *The ecological tourism of Badouzi Village*. Wu-Nan Book Inc. https://www.wunan.com.tw/bookdetail?NO=14611
43. Chen, C. L. & Chang, Y. C. (2017). A transition beyond traditional fisheries: Taiwan's experience with developing fishing tourism (P. 85). *Marine Policy, 79*, 84–91. https://doi.org/10.1016/j.marpol.2017.02.011

Chapter 10
University–Community Engagement in Advancing Sustainable Fishing Village Development: A Case Study of Excellent Fishing Neighbourhood Build-Up Project

Ching-Yu Yang, Wen-Hong Liu, Hsiao-Chien Lee, and Chih-Cheng Lin

Abstract This case study elaborates on how the National Kaohsiung University of Science and Technology (NKUST) facilitate sustainable development of the aquaculture industry through its community engagement. This study identifies five major outcomes derived from the performance evaluation: (1) eco-friendly technology and concepts improve aquaculture operational practices; (2) transformation of fishery by-products into local-featured products based on circular economy concepts and university expertise; (3) online and offline shops as the cornerstones of habitat direct selling mode; (4) establishment of experiential tourism based on fishing village culture and fish-based diet education; (5) construct international collaborations with universities from Japan, local small-scale fishers, and green energy enterprises. The outcomes of this study could help the local government, policymakers, community stakeholders, and industry experts gain insights into the overall indicators that underpin sustainable fishing village development.

Keywords Fishing Village Revitalization · University Social Responsibility (USR) · Sustainable Production and Consumption, Blue Economy

10.1 Introduction

Taiwanese fishing villages are primarily located in remote or rural areas. These communities encounter problems such as the persistent outflow of young adults, an increasing aging population in the fishery industry, and a shortage of employment opportunities [1]. According to recent observations and investigations, traditional fishing villages in Taiwan, such as Linbian Town and Jiadong Town, have faced several issues in recent years. These issues include the high demand for electricity and water in aquaculture farming; however, most fish farmers lack responsible

C.-Y. Yang · W.-H. Liu · H.-C. Lee · C.-C. Lin (✉)
National Kaohsiung University of Science and Technology, Kaohsiung, Taiwan
e-mail: cclin108@nkust.edu.tw

M. C. Huang et al. (eds.), *Innovative Social Practice and Community-Based Approach to the Ocean*, https://doi.org/10.1007/978-981-96-9104-3_10

production technology in green and intelligent aquaculture, which results in their inability to deal with extreme climate change and environmental pollution problems. A further issue is that many fish farmers lack knowledge or try to save costs and end up misusing aquaculture drugs. Therefore, providing guidance and training workshops to aquaculture fish farmers is becoming increasingly important to improve their knowledge and maintain food safety.

Further to the above, the main focus of traditional fishing villages is on primary production, which lacks value-added products. This limits the potential to increase the value of aquaculture products and, more importantly, fails to stimulate the economic development of fishing villages. Finally, marketing and distribution are difficult for small-scale aquaculture farmers because they lack enough marketing resources, and their prices are determined by intermediaries, undermining the value of these fishing villages as brands.

Institutions of higher education are now integrating social responsibility principles into their teaching and research activities and their management and community engagement activities [2, 3]. Taiwan's Ministry of Education has also started the University Social Responsibility (USR) Program since 2017 [4]. This chapter takes National Kaohsiung University of Science and Technology (NKUST) as a case to discuss the USR Program's Excellent Fishing Neighbourhood Build-Up Project (EFNBUP), which might serve as a reference point for the universities interested in promoting the regional revitalization of fishing villages.

By utilizing the educational system of the university, EFNBUP has involved students and incorporates innovative proposals into the community. The project team has established an innovation service centre in the local community, focusing on local issues, connecting with local sentiments, and building a mechanism of mutual trust. Additionally, EFNBUP has integrated these proposals into the school's curriculum to encourage students to participate in community innovation projects. This approach has fostered a sense of community engagement and civic responsibility among students while addressing local needs and concerns. Moreover, NKUST not only actively utilizes internal resources to implement EFNBUP but also strives to enhance the links between regional industry, government, academia, and research institutions. NKUST has integrated resources from various government departments and local authorities, as well as local schools. Furthermore, it links expertise in green energy and information technology to introduce professional technologies to help address the needs of talent and development in Pingtung's fishing villages. The collaboration and communication between university students, teachers, local residents, and the aquaculture industry is aimed at promoting mutual learning and growth within the community. By working together, it is hoped that cultural and industrial resources of fishing villages will be cherished, and local regional revitalization will be facilitated.

10.2 Literature Review

10.2.1 USR: Definition and Importance

The concept of USR has its roots in the early twentieth century when universities began to acknowledge their role beyond traditional academic pursuits. The "social contract" between universities and society gained prominence in the mid-twentieth century, as universities started to emphasize their responsibilities beyond education and research [5]. The definitions of University Social Responsibility (USR) vary in the literature, with the primary point of divergence being the clarification of responsibility. Specifically, there is debate over whether the university should be responsible towards its internal stakeholders, such as students and staff, or towards external stakeholders, such as partners and the community [6]. For instance, as stated by Giuffré and Ratto [7], the concept of USR can be characterized as the capacity of a university to promulgate and apply a defined set of overarching principles and distinct values. This is achieved through four fundamental processes: management, teaching, research, and extension. These processes involve delivering educational services and disseminating knowledge while upholding ethical standards, practicing effective governance, demonstrating environmental consideration, engaging with society, and advancing core values. On the other hand, Vasilescu et al. [8] elucidate the concept of USR from a citizenship perspective, portraying it as the imperative to enhance dedication to civic responsibilities and dynamic engagement in citizenship activities. This entails volunteerism and an ethical orientation, fostering the cultivation of a civil citizenship ethos by motivating students and academic personnel to offer societal benefits to their immediate locale. Additionally, it involves advocating ecological and environmental devotion to foster local and global sustainability.

Despite the varying definitions of University Social Responsibility (USR), the fundamental principle is that universities should assume a more critical and significant role as local think tanks. Universities should focus their efforts on addressing the development issues of local industries, community culture, cities, and rural areas. By doing so, universities can fully realize their value, promote regional development, and facilitate value creation [1]. USR holds promise in addressing the multifaceted requirements of society, as universities possess the inherent capability to foster the welfare and engagement of various stakeholders, encompassing students, alumni, parents, faculty, and the immediate community [9]. By embracing the principles of USR, universities can play an active role in tackling complex economic, social, and environmental challenges, ranging from poverty and inequality to climate change and sustainable development [10]. Such active involvement holds the potential to catalyze constructive social transformation and play a pivotal role in advancing the collective betterment of society [11]. Moreover, USR serves as a means for universities to meet their moral and ethical commitments. As integral social entities, universities bear a responsibility to society, and USR affords them the opportunity to actively engage in resolving pressing societal challenges. By seamlessly integrating social responsibility into their foundational objectives, universities can harmonize their endeavours with the prevailing values and requisites of society. Acknowledging social responsibility as a pivotal facet of their role is paramount in safeguarding universities against a singular focus on pedagogy and research, instead ensuring their active and meaningful participation in enhancing societal well-being [11]. Furthermore, the adoption of USR concepts in university operations can facilitate the implementation of sustainable policies, thereby reducing their environmental impact, promoting responsible consumption and production, and contributing to the achievement of the United Nations Sustainable Development Goals (SDGs [10]). Specifically, the actions of universities in relation to USR primarily contribute to the achievement of the SDG4—quality education. Additionally, they also contribute to the SDG 6—clean water and sanitation, and SDG 7—affordable and clean energy [12].

10.2.2 The Key Successful Factors of USR

As outlined by The University Meets Social Responsibility (UNIBILITY) [13], the optimal strategies to practice the USR model encompass several important factors and processes as follows:

1. Top-Down Implementation: The USR model should be integrated from the highest level of university management and should pervade all aspects, ranging from strategic decision-making to human resource management.
2. Organizational Awareness: All levels of the university should be aware of and aligned with the USR concept.
3. Avoiding Administrative Limitation: USR should not be confined to a mere administrative unit but rather be integrated into the core fabric of the university.
4. Understanding Impact: It serves as a tool to comprehend, track, and assess the university's societal impact.
5. Stakeholder Dialogue: Engaging in dialogues with stakeholders is imperative, as it influences daily operations and interactions with them.
6. Prioritization through Internal and External Dimensions: Focus on specific aspects of USR while prioritizing activities through both internal and external lenses.
7. Cultivating Engagement Culture: Cultivating a culture of engagement with USR is crucial for its success.
8. Transparency and Evaluation: The university should be transparent and evaluate outcomes arising from dialogues with stakeholders.
9. Clear Vision for Outreach: The university should have a clear vision for the significance of community outreach and stakeholder engagement. This vision should be aligned with the institution's identity, resources, context, and missions.

10. Academia-Business Interaction: Recognize the potential synergy between academia and business as a driving force to address societal needs and offer solutions to pressing challenges.

Rababah et al. [14] suggest that a coherent and precisely outlined USR strategy which should align with the needs and interests of all stakeholders, and implementing effective management practices facilitates the communication among stakeholders, thereby ensuring the pursuit of a shared goal. Moreover, regular evaluation and assessment of USR initiatives are important to measure their effectiveness and impact, and evaluation indicators can include the level of stakeholder engagement, the quality of educational processes, and the development of scientific activities.

Based on the suggestions mentioned above, the NKUST's USR project team has formulated implementation strategies and evaluation indicators to realize the performance of the project.

10.3 Method

10.3.1 Methodology

The present article adopts an instrumental case study approach [15], which uses a particular case to gain insight into an issue or theory. The instrumental case study method positions the researcher as seeking greater insight into an issue in a particular place and time to generate an information-rich case. Instrumental case studies are appropriate for developing theories that facilitate understanding of issues, and it is often used when researchers aim to understand something specific or unique about a case that can contribute to broader knowledge or understanding [15]. The instrumental case study approach is suitable as the methodology for this study, which aims to understand how universities can assist in the regional revitalization of fishing villages through the USR practice of NKUST.

10.3.2 Setting

According to task attributes, the NKUST's USR project team divided ten departments and institutions into different sub-teams. These sub-teams comprise the Department of Aquatic Food Science, the Department of Aquaculture, the Department of Business Information Application, the Department of Industrial Design, the Institute of Ocean Affairs and Industry Management, the Department of Tourism Management, the Department of Applied Japanese, the Department of Shipping Management, the Teaching Development Center, and the Basic Education Center. They also work with different stakeholders and groups, including regional fishing associations, fish farmers, government departments, community associations, and social enterprises, to create a new model of responsible production and marketing. The plan aims to reduce the use of aquacultural water and drugs, improve the added value of products through the innovative R&D and design of circular and economical processing, and promote the concept of sustainable seafood through food and fishery education. Furthermore, it can spur public consumption of local aquatic products, improve the competitiveness of fishing villages, and ultimately boost the regional revitalization and development of fishing villages.

Linbian Town and Jiadong Town in Pingtung County are the target areas for carrying out this plan. The coastal towns in the southwest of Pingtung country are major aquaculture towns in Taiwan. These townships' fishers are mostly small-scale fish farm owners. They mainly breed fish species of high economic value, such as grouper and noon larvae. However, due to the information asymmetry and opaque channels in the production and marketing processes, the fisheries have encountered problems such as imbalance in production and sales and unstable profitability. This has in turn led the aquaculture industry chain to become increasingly fragile. Consequently, the aquaculture industry in Linbian is gradually dying. Therefore, the neighbouring university, NKUST, has thus implemented the USR project in these townships to facilitate regional revitalization.

10.3.3 Criteria for Selecting Indicators

To achieve the desired results of the EFNBUP, we have selected the indicators through a series of procedures: First, members of each sub-team conducted interviews with stakeholders and proposed initial performance indicators based on their expertise and the results of these interviews. Second, we convened an expert panel to gather advice from industrial and academic experts. Lastly, after several rounds of discussion between project team members, a consensus was reached on the final set of indicators. Meanwhile, our selection of indicators adopts the standards of Dale et al. [16], as elucidated below:

1. Practical (easy, timely, and cost-effective to measure);
2. Sensitive and responsive to both natural and anthropogenic stresses to the system;
3. Unambiguous with respect to what is measured, how measurements are made, and how response is measured;
4. Anticipatory of impending changes;
5. Predictive of changes that can be averted with management action;
6. Estimable with known variability in response to changes;
7. Sufficient when considered collectively [16].

Based on the aforementioned procedures and standards, NKUST has established evaluation indicators and cooperated with stakeholders in the target areas to implement the EFNBUP.

10.3.4 Categories of Indicators

EFNBUP, includes 30 indicators in five categories, as shown in Fig. 10.1, The descriptions are as follows.

10.3.4.1 Indicators of Common Performance

This category is a common performance indicator of the USR Program proposed by the Ministry of Education, encompassing the participation of teachers, students, and off-campus personnel, as well as the professional development of teachers. It also encompasses the USR incentive mechanism, and integrating cross-field curriculums. For the participations of teachers and students, it is about the outcomes of teacher and student participation in project-related work promotion, field practice, curriculum development and teaching, course enrolment, and other related activities. For example, the project report of community revitalization or the proposal of local industry development. The participation of off-campus personnel refers to the outcomes achieved by domestic and international individuals from various fields when participating in the EFNBUP. For instance, local primary school teachers collaborated with the project team to develop place-based instructional materials on fish-eating for their students. The professional development of teachers mainly involves USR case studies or course development sharing and observation, teacher workshops, and other collaborative learning activities. The USR incentive mechanism is to enhance the motivation of teachers in NKUST to participate in EFNBUP. Some teachers who have implemented the USR program have been promoted, thereby increasing their willingness to participate in social practices. And the integrating cross-field curriculums is to establish the USR-related "I-Turn Regional Revitalization Credit Program," which consists of 21 courses and 38 credits in total. Students are encouraged to enroll in this program.

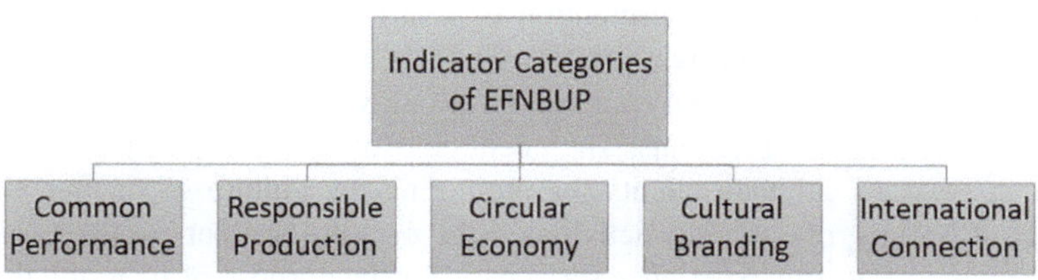

Fig. 10.1 Categories of indicators applying in EFNBUP

10.3.4.2 Indicators of Responsible Production

This category comprises the indicators of the cultivation of aquaculture talents, technical guidance on friendly aquaculture management and industry care activities. The cultivation of aquaculture talents focuses on nurturing professional aquaculture management talents with an international perspective. And the technical guidance on friendly aquaculture management and industry care activities is to enhance the aquaculture industry's know-how of eco-friendly aquaculture management techniques and improve operational efficiency and effectiveness by providing industry guidance.

10.3.4.3 Indicators of Circular Economy

This category comprises the indicators of providing courses related to aquatic product processing technology, holding competitions for the development and innovation of local aquatic products, organizing exhibitions of innovative products. The courses related to aquatic product processing technology is to strengthen the aquaculture processing skills of local aquaculture personnel to improve their capability and increase the efficiency and effectiveness of aquaculture processing. The competitions for the development and innovation of local aquatic products are to encourage fishermen to innovate in the aquaculture industry. And the exhibitions of innovative products are to exhibit innovative and research-based products to increase the visibility of innovative products.

10.3.4.4 Indicators of Cultural Branding

This category comprises the indicators of the establishment and promotion of smart platforms, student-oriented project-based learning courses, the talent cultivation for promoting fishing village culture, and the improvement of on-site experience services. The establishment and promotion of smart platforms is to constructing a smart information platform by university students to promote community marketing. The project-based learning courses aim to cultivate university students' ability to solve local practical problems. The talent cultivation for promoting fishing village culture is to cultivate talents for promoting the culture of fishing villages through a variety of learning activities with a multi-age perspective. And the improvement of on-site experience services is for the purpose of fostering the care and sense for the community and the fishery industry among local residents and students.

10.3.4.5 Indicators of International Connection

This category comprises the indicators of the cooperation on talent cultivation and technology R&D. The talent cultivation is about collaborating with international enterprises to cultivate aquaculture talents, enhance students' and fishermen's competitiveness. The technology R&D is to enhance aquaculture technologies and effectively promote industry upgrading by collaborating with international partners.

10.4 Results

10.4.1 Strategies and Implementation

The NKUST USR team has adopted four strategies to achieve the planned objectives. The strategies and specific actions are described as follows.

10.4.1.1 Eco-friendly Aquaculture Technology Application

Since the introduction of science and technology is essential to the sustainable development of the aquaculture industry [17], we utilized advanced technology to facilitate local aquaculture production based on a responsibility system. Here are specific measures:

First, set up characteristic courses combining aquaculture and fishing villages, cultivate aquaculture management professionals with independent learning and teaching mode, and strengthen students' learning interest and teaching efficiency through on-site communication and observation. Second, inspire students to devote themselves to local aquaculture services through service-oriented practice, and help with industrial transformation. Third, develop key technologies for friendly aquaculture management (the application technology of probiotics and water quality improver), guide local fishermen to reduce consumption of aquaculture water and drugs, and take the responsibility for producing high-quality aquatic products. Fourth, assist fishermen to enhance the viability of aquatic animals and increase their industrial income through on-site survey and online/offline consulting services.

10.4.1.2 Circular Aquaculture Economy Innovation

The circular economy emphasizes the strategy or principle of recovery and regeneration, which is quite conducive to the sustainability of the aquaculture industry and the environment [18]. The project team has developed innovative products based on the concept of the circular economy. Specific measures consist of practicing the on-site innovation and the workshops for R&D of aquaculture products according to courses, using fishery product wastes for processing and R&D to increase the added value of products, and assisting in the commercialization and quantification of innovative products to foster local features.

10.4.1.3 Community Branding of Fishing Village

Cultural branding highlights the idea of regional revitalization, and is designed to activate communities and create a brand culture through planning, marketing, evaluation and other ways [19]. The team has shaped and promoted the culture of fishing villages based on this idea. Specific measures consist of using strategies (10.4.1.1 and 10.4.1.2) to produce and process aquatic products, and work with the fishermen' unions, production & marketing classes and communities in Linbian and Jiadong Towns to create their own products and visual images of fishing grounds, design packaging and marketing with local characteristics, create new marketing channels, promote local production and marketing, stabilize the value and price of the products for consumers, and create a win-win result for production and consumption. Moreover, the project team has incorporated fishing village culture such as fishing village tours and fish-eating education into the smart tour guide system and marketing strategy to build a sense of identity and increase the popularity of fishing villages.

10.4.1.4 Slow Fish Education Plus Experiential Tourism

The idea of "slow fish" has been promoted to encourage the public to eat the local aquatic products as well as seafood obtained via sustainable means of fishing. Educational activities such as having a field trip to the fish ponds, experiencing one day fisherman, preparing a meal by using the local aquatic products, and etc. have been held. Such activities enhance the students 'understandings of local aquaculture [20]. Meanwhile, the concept of experiential tourism promotes the sustainable economic development with minimal impact on the environment of local community [21]. Tourists coming to the fishing village not only admire the natural scenes, but also experience the aquaculture industry and, following that, purchase the local aquatic products as souvenir. Based on these ideas, the project team has developed strategies with specific measures comprising the construction of a curriculum module focused on fish-eating education in primary schools located in fishing villages, the development of a series of picture books about the culture of fishing villages as part of the "Hands Together Project," the hosting of training activities for experts in fresh food, the regular organization of fish-eating education forums, and the establishment of fish-eating experience classrooms in collaboration with local fishermen.

10.4.2 *Indicators of Performance.*

10.4.2.1 Indicators of Common Performance

The indicator of the participation of teachers and students focuses on improving the understanding of USR among teachers and students, facilitating the study of USR-related courses, and supporting communication and collaboration among core members of the USR project team. The quantitative results show that 24 teachers and 2563 students participated in the program, and 20 activities were launched to facilitate communication among teachers. These efforts aim to promote the active participation of teachers and students in the USR project and to enhance their understanding and engagement with the subject matter.

The indicator of the participation of off-campus personnel focuses on strengthening the connection between stakeholders on site, cooperative communities and teams, and enhancing the sense of identity and trust in the project team among locals. The quantitative results show that 19 cooperative groups and 7 cooperative schools were involved in the project, and 134 people participated in community practice activities. These efforts aim to promote active participation and collaboration among off-campus personnel, and to foster strong connections between the project team and local communities.

The indicator of the professional development of teachers helps teachers understand the methods for USR on-site operation and promotion, and learn about the USR promotion means and experiences of various countries. It also aims to bolster the connection between teachers from the school and those from other schools, and encourage participating teachers to use PBL and on-site subjects to conduct courses in curriculum planning. The quantitative results show that ten meetings for USR case sharing were held, 6 USR lectures were given, and 11 activities for teacher study and co-learning across schools were launched. These efforts aim to promote the professional development of teachers and enhance their ability to effectively implement USR in their teaching practices.

The indicator of the USR incentive mechanism focuses on reducing the burden on teachers, providing opportunities for the promotion of participating teachers, and stimulating teacher participation in the USR program. The quantitative results show that 13 courses were offered by 22 teachers, three teachers were promoted, and one post-doctoral researcher was transferred to the position of assistant researcher. These efforts aim to provide incentives for teachers to actively participate in the USR program and to support their professional development.

As to the indicator of integrating cross-field, by offering the "I-Turn Regional Revitalization-Based Credit & Course," teachers and students are enabled to break away from traditional learning frameworks and approaches, and to better think about on-site problems and solutions from the perspective of different fields. The introduction of this course has led to the emergence of informal learning communities among students, increasing their willingness to choose USR-related courses. The quantitative results show that one course was constructed and four class groups were established. These efforts aim to promote cross-disciplinary learning and collaboration among teachers and students, and to foster a deeper understanding of USR-related issues.

10.4.2.2 Indicators of Responsible Production

The indicator of the cultivation of aquaculture talents focuses on cultivating high-quality domestic aquaculture talents. The quantitative results show that 12 courses were offered, combining practical aquaculture technology with the international community, and 706 aquaculture management personnel with an international outlook were cultivated. Additionally, four local youth training workshops were held and a demonstration team of innovative aquaculture technology was established with the engagement of local youth. Furthermore, the technical guidance on friendly aquaculture management and industry care activities is another important indicator. This indicator aims to improve friendly aquaculture management technology through industrial guidance. The quantitative result shows that 110 activities were held to achieve this goal. In sum, these efforts aim to promote the development of the aquaculture industry and to support the cultivation of high-quality domestic talents in the target areas..

10.4.2.3 Indicators of Circular Economy

The indicator of opening the workshops for the R&D of aquatic product processing technology aims to strengthen the aquatic product processing technology of local aquaculture and fishery personnel. The quantitative result shows that nine courses were opened to achieve this goal. These efforts aim to promote the development of the aquatic product processing industry and to support the professional development of local aquaculture and fishery personnel.

The indicator of the competitions for the development and innovation of local aquatic products encourages fishermen to invest in aquatic product innovation through the hosting of competitions. The quantitative result shows that four competitions were hosted to achieve this goal. These efforts aim to promote the development of the local aquatic product industry and to support the innovation and creativity of local fishermen.

The indicator of exhibition for the development and innovation of products aims to exhibit innovative products through the hosting of exhibitions. The quantitative result shows that two exhibitions were held to achieve this goal. These efforts aim to promote the development of innovative products and to showcase their potential to a wider audience.

10.4.2.4 Indicators of Cultural Branding

The indicator of the establishment and promotion of smart platforms aims to build an intelligent information platform in collaboration with university students, in order to promote community marketing. The smart tour guide system and the platform system for aquaculture production were both promoted by students for three sessions. Additionally, EFNBUP offered a total of 18 courses in the module of Technology Application and Cultural Formation.

The indicator of the project-based courses for students emphasizes the cultivation of college students' ability to solve practical problems. The quantitative results show that one contest for publishing practical achievements based on the practice in the fishing villages was held, and 10 off-campus contests for student achievements based on subjects were also held. These efforts aim to promote the development of practical problem-solving skills among college students and to support their engagement with real-world issues.

The indicator of the talent cultivation for the promotion of fishing village culture conducts various activities from a multi-dimensional perspective and cultivates talents of different ages for the promotion of fishing village culture. The results show that 40 students engaged in on-site social services, four workshops were held for creative development and training of student teams from senior high schools in the fields, nine workshops were set for creative development and training of student teams from senior high schools in the fields, 13 courses on fish-eating culture and fishing village tourism were opened, six workshops were organized on basic fish-eating training for local primary school teachers, and six cross-field lectures and sightseeing tours were provided with the help of local young fishermen.

The indicator of improving local experience-oriented services emphasizes taking root in the community and inspiring community residents and school children to love their hometown and fish. The quantitative results show that five care services in fishing villages or promotion activities of fish-eating education were launched, and five activities for the interaction among primary school children were held. These efforts aim to promote the development of local experience-oriented services and to support the engagement of community residents and school children with their hometown and its culture..

10.4.2.5 Indicators of International Connection

The indicator of cooperation in talent cultivation emphasizes the cooperation between NKUST and international enterprises. The results show that three lectures and exchange meetings for international aquaculture enterprises were held, and two workshops were organized for international enterprise internships of university. These efforts aim to promote the development of talent cultivation through cooperation among international enterprises and to support the professional development of university students.

Moreover, the indicator of cooperation in technological R&D aims to improve aquaculture technology through international cooperation. The quantitative results show that one platform for the technological exchanges of international aquaculture was established to promote the industrial upgrading of both sides, and one product R&D workshop was organized for the Japanese alliance universities to exchange experience in product R&D, design, and marketing in Taiwan. These efforts aim to promote the development of aquaculture technology through international cooperation and to support the exchange of knowledge and expertise among participating institutions..

10.5 Discussion

The four strategies and five indicators implemented in this program have scored remarkable achievements. The specific impacts are described as follows.

10.5.1 Aquaculture Technologies and Concepts Improve the Local Aquaculture Industry

The project team has improved the water quality by introducing probiotic culture technology, enhanced local fish catch of small-scale fisheries, and improved fishermen's behavior of drug-use aquaculture, in order to achieve the goal of saving water and electricity, and gradually change the operation pattern and industrial development of local small-scale fisheries.

10.5.2 The Concept of Circular Economy Helps to Develop Fish By-products Into Innovative Fish Specialties

The project team has properly used fish wastes and fish by-products to improve the production value of local small-scale fisheries. Guided by the concept of circular economy, the team has developed and processed the remaining fish scales after selling into collagen drink and collagen ice-cream. It has also produced instant packed food of various flavors from the fish bred with friendly technologies of cooperative small-scale fisheries.

10.5.3 Establish the Business Model of Direct Sales from the Place of Origin

The project team has assisted local small-scale fishery personnel in establishing online and offline sales mechanisms, signed a contract with i3 Fresh—the largest domestic e-commerce platform of agricultural and fishery goods, and continued to assist many small-scale fishermen in selling fish on the shelves. The physical stores have also been opened.

10.5.4 Create a Five-Sense Experience Journey

In combination with fishing village culture, local fishing products, local small fishing grounds, fish-eating education, water activities and theme homestays, the team has established a sightseeing tour of Ryukyu ecology and culture in Linbian Town. Winner Travel Co., Ltd established by alumni has transformed the experience tour into a business-style tour which is one of few sightseeing tours of fishing village culture researched, planned, and experimented by college student teams from southern Taiwan and finally transforming into a business style.

10.5.5 Cooperate with Japanese Universities, Local Small-Scale Fisheries and Green-Energy Industries to Organize a Practice Competition

In addition to the sponsorship and response of domestic green-energy industries, this competition has also established a mechanism for revenue increase and feedback through the project, and encouraged domestic consumers to support friendly small-scale fishery products by consuming "NKUST" products. This has increased the revenue by 5% through the platforms, and the additional profit has been allocated to the sustainable growth of rural communities, and helped create a sound business environment for young people returning to their hometown. The National Kaohsiung University of Science and Technology and "NKUST" group are also vigorously appealing enterprises, institutions and groups to consolidate the sales channels and sales volume of friendly fishery products by means of co-branding, endorsements, and designated feedback objects, in a bid to help the small fishery economy in Linbian and Jiadong grow steadily in the new business model.

10.6 Conclusion

The achievements accumulated since the pilot project started have received recognition, as seen in the awards presented since 2020, such as the 2022 TSAA Taiwan Sustainable Action Gold Award for the "'NKUST' Shape Plan"; the 13th TCSA Gold Award (2020) for "USR & Plan for the Sustainable Development of Fishing Villages in Pindong"; the 2020 CSR Academic Paper Award for the "Strategy and Practice of USR&CSR Cooperation to Create Value for Fishing Villages - Taking Linbian Fishing Village in Pingtung as an Example."

For instance, in 2020, the NKUST team won the golden award in the 13th TCSA (Taiwan Cooperate Sustainability Awards) as one of the Distinguished Sustainable Industry Cases: Sustainable USR Plans. The team was particularly awarded the Best Academic Essay, in which the team shared its experience of co-creating fishing village values by promoting regional revitalization with the Linbian community at Pingtung. Moreover, the outcomes of EFNBUP have been published in the journal of Marine Policy [20, 22], which is a highly regarded publication in the social science citation index. These publications have the potential to significantly increase the international visibility and impact of EFNBUP.

In the future, the project will introduce the management technology of fish-electricity symbiotic aquaculture, combine with intelligent aquaculture, strengthen the education of aquatic food safety, and guide the local industries to abide by the certification system and specifications related to food safety, in a bid to enhance the competitiveness of the project. It is expected to facilitate the upgrading of traditional aquaculture industry, and the responsible production and sustainable development of energy transformation. It is hoped that the team's experience can contributively add to the discovery on the sustainable development of fishing villages, especially in East Asia. The outcomes of this study could help the local government, policymakers, city stakeholders, and industry expertise to gain insights of the overall indicators that underpin sustainable fishing village development, which could motivate other coastal countries to build their own blue economy of fishing villages.

References

1. Liu, W. H., Lee, H. C., Sung, W. Y., & Yang, T. Y. (2022). The roles of Taiwanese universities in coastal revitalization: A study of two case projects. *Marine Policy, 139*, 105050. https://doi.org/10.1016/j.marpol.2022.105050
2. Garde Sánchez, R., Rodríguez Bolívar, M. P., & López-Hernández, A. M. (2013). Online disclosure of university social responsibility: A comparative study of public and private US universities. *Environmental Education Research, 19*(6), 709–746. https://doi.org/10.1080/13504622.2012.749976
3. Ralph, M., & Stubbs, W. (2014). Integrating environmental sustainability into universities. *Higher Education, 67*(1), 71–90. https://doi.org/10.1007/s10734-013-9641-9

4. Center for University Social Responsibility, Ministry of Education. (2020a). *About USR* (in Chinese). Web of Center for USR, Ministry of Education. https://usr.moe.gov.tw/about-1
5. Barnett, R., & Guzmán-Valenzuela, C. (2022). The socially responsible European university: A challenging project. *International Journal of Sustainability in Higher Education, 23*(4), 752–766.
6. Parsons, A (2014). *Literature Review on Social Responsibility in Higher Education*, Occasional Paper Number 2, UNESCO Chair for Community Based Research and Social Responsibility in Higher Education.
7. Giuffré, L., & Ratto, S. E. (2014). A new paradigm in higher education: University social responsibility (USR). *Journal of Education and Human Development, 3*(1), 231–238.
8. Vasilescu, R., Barna, C., Epure, M., & Baicu, C. (2010). Developing university social responsibility: A model for the challenges of the new civil society. *Procedia-Social and Behavioral Sciences, 2*(2), 4177–4182.
9. Sharma, D., & Sharma, R. (2021). University social responsibility initiatives: An empirical study of private and state universities of Rajasthan. *Psychology and Education Journal, 58*(1), 5480–5491.
10. Resch, K., & Dima, G. I. (2022). Guest editorial: European perspectives on the socially responsible and engaged university. *International Journal of Sustainability in Higher Education, 23*(4), 749–751.
11. Tilak, J. B. G. (2022). Social responsibility of higher education. *Social Change, 52*(4), 478–490.
12. Castro, A. J., Zanello, L., Lizcano, J., & Daza, A. (2022). USR as a tool for meeting the SDGs: A systematic review. *IEEE Revista Iberoamericana de Tecnologias del Aprendizaje, 17*(1), 48–55.
13. University Meets Social Responsibility (UNIBILITY). (2017). *Guidelines for Universities Engaging in Social Responsibility. The UNIBILITY Consortium.* Edited by Mark Wallace (Dublin City University, Higher Education Research Centre) and Katharina Resch (University of Vienna, Austria, Postgraduate Center).
14. Rababah, A., Nikitina, N. I., Grebennikova, V. M., Gardanova, Z. R., Zekiy, A. O., Ponkratov, V. V., et al. (2021). University social responsibility during the COVID-19 pandemic: Universities' case in the BRICS countries. *Sustainability, 13*(13), 7035.
15. Stake, R. E. (1995). *The art of case study research.* Sage.
16. Dale, V. H., Efroymson, R. A., Kline, K. L., Langholtz, M. H., Leiby, P. N., Oladosu, G. A., et al. (2013). Indicators for assessing socioeconomic sustainability of bioenergy systems: A short list of practical measures. *Ecological Indicators, 26*, 87–102.
17. Lieke, T., Meinelt, T., Hoseinifar, S. H., Pan, B., Straus, D. L., & Steinberg, C. E. (2020). Sustainable aquaculture requires environmental-friendly treatment strategies for fish diseases. *Reviews in Aquaculture, 12*(2), 943–965. https://doi.org/10.1111/raq.12365
18. Regueiro, L., Newton, R., Soula, M., Mendez, D., Kok, B., Little, D. C., et al. (2021). Opportunities and limitations for the introduction of circular economy principles in EU aquaculture based on the regulatory framework. *Journal of Industrial Ecology*. https://doi.org/10.1111/jiec.13188
19. Daldanise, G. (2020). From place-branding to community-branding: A collaborative decision-making process for cultural heritage enhancement. *Sustainability, 12*(24), 10399. https://doi.org/10.3390/su122410399
20. Lee, H. C. (2022). Promoting slow fish education in southern Taiwan coastal areas: An empirical case study of five elementary schools. *Marine Policy, 138*, 104995. https://doi.org/10.1016/j.marpol.2022.104995
21. Smith, W. L. (2006). Experiential tourism around the world and at home: Definitions and standards. *International Journal of Services and Standards, 2*(1), 1–14.
22. Liu, W. H. (2022). University social responsibility to promote coastal partnership: Introducing Taiwan coastal communities. *Marine Policy, 146*, 105303.

Chapter 11
Sustainable Financing for Marine Protected Areas (MPAs): A Case Study of the Shiretoko Natural World Heritage Site

Miko Maekawa, Junko Toyoshima, and Mitsutaku Makino

Abstract This chapter examines the financial sustainability and relevant mechanisms of the Shiretoko marine protected area (MPA), part of the Natural World Heritage Site in Hokkaido, Japan, designated in 2005. Given the loss of marine biodiversity globally and the renewed commitment to the conservation of biodiversity under the Kunming-Montreal Global Biodiversity Framework (GBF), analyzing a concrete case of a relatively successful conservation efforts and examining the critical issue of sustainable financing and the potential of innovative funding are of significant value. This chapter is expected to provide useful lessons for other MPAs and conservation activities in Japan and beyond.

Keywords Marine protected area · *Satoumi* · Shiretoko · Financing · SDG14

11.1 Introduction

According to the Global Assessment Report on Biodiversity and Ecosystem Services, over one-third of marine mammals and nearly one-third of sharks, shark relatives, and reef-forming corals are threatened with extinction [1]. The loss of biodiversity in both terrestrial and marine areas is of grave concern worldwide, and the importance of site-specific, tailor-made conservation activities cannot be overemphasized. Shiretoko, in Hokkaido, Japan, has a long history of co-management

M. Maekawa (✉)
Sasakawa Peace Foundation, Tokyo, Japan
e-mail: maekawa@spf.or.jp

J. Toyoshima
Institute of Global Environmental Strategies, Hayama, Kanagawa, Japan

M. Makino
Ocean Policy Research Institute (OPRI), The Sasakawa Peace Foundation, Tokyo, Japan

The University of Tokyo, Tokyo, Japan

M. C. Huang et al. (eds.), *Innovative Social Practice and Community-Based Approach to the Ocean*, https://doi.org/10.1007/978-981-96-9104-3_11

systems led by local fishers that can be considered as effective *satoumi* activities. These management systems were formalized and cross-sectoral coordination was enhanced during application for UNESCO World Heritage Site status, with an eye on maintaining this status once obtained. The main financial source for the Shiretoko site is public funding; however, private sector funding also plays a critical role in providing supplementary funds to maintain operation of the site. Shiretoko was one of the earliest sites to introduce the system of national trust in Japan. The Shiretoko Foundation, a private entity, also plays an important role in carrying out conservation activities and research work at the site.

In December 2022, after years of negotiation and interruptions due to COVID-19, the Kunming-Montreal Global Biodiversity Framework (GBF) was finally agreed to at the 15th meeting of the Conference of Parties to the UN Convention on Biological Diversity, presided over by China, in Montreal, Canada. The GBF includes four goals and 23 targets to be achieved by 2030, as well as four long-term goals for 2050 related to the 2050 Vision for Biodiversity, which is a global vision of a world living in harmony with nature [2]. These sets of targets aim to motivate concrete actions to reduce threats to biodiversity as well as meeting people's needs through sustainable use and benefit-sharing. Among the multiple targets, Target 2 and Target 3 make specific reference to area-based management. GBF Target 2 reads: "Ensure that by 2030 at least 30 per cent of areas of degraded terrestrial, inland water, and coastal and marine ecosystems are under effective restoration, in order to enhance biodiversity and ecosystem functions and services, ecological integrity, and connectivity." GBF Target 3 highlights the goal of providing protected areas around the world:

> [A] TARGET 3: Ensure and enable that by 2030 at least 30 per cent of terrestrial, inland water, and of coastal and marine areas, especially areas of particular importance for biodiversity and ecosystem functions and services, are effectively conserved and managed through ecologically representative, well-connected and equitably governed systems of protected areas and other effective area-based conservation measures, recognizing indigenous and traditional territories, where applicable, and integrated into wider landscapes, seascapes and the ocean, while ensuring that any sustainable use, where appropriate in such areas, is fully consistent with conservation outcomes, recognizing and respecting the rights of indigenous peoples and local communities including over their traditional territories.
>
> CBD [2]

Target 3 includes the so-called 30 by 30 initiative, designating 30% of areas under national jurisdiction as protected areas or other effective area-based conservation measures <OECMs> by the year 2030, previously expressed in agreements such as the Nature Compact signed at the G7 Summit in 2022, preceding the 15th Conference of Parties (COP15) of the CBD. Under the previous long-term conservation goals, the Aichi Targets, the level of achievement was not high and off track to reach the 2050 Vision for Biodiversity. The Global Biodiversity Outlook 5 provided a comprehensive analysis of the progress of the Aichi Targets, and it indicated that at the global level none of the 20 targets have been fully achieved, though six targets have been partially achieved. The Target 11 on the proportion of the planet's land and oceans designated as protected areas was also among the six targets, which were partially achieved. More specifically, about15% of the world's terrestrial and freshwater environments were covered by protected areas. About 7.5% of the marine area was covered, including 17.2% of marine areas within national jurisdiction, and 1.2% of marine areas beyond national jurisdiction, in August 2020, according to the World Database on Protected Area [3]. The newly agreed upon global framework should provide significantly strengthened efforts to accomplish those goals.

In Japan, as a follow-up to CBD COP15, in 2023, a Roadmap for the realization of Nature Positive was approved by the Japanese Cabinet. Under the overarching mission of realizing Nature Positive and Reinvigorating Nature, Japan's most recent National Biodiversity Strategies and Action Plans (NBSAPs) identifies five Basic Strategies and related Action Goals. Under Action Objective 1-1—to conserve at least 30% of terrestrial and marine areas through protected areas and OECMs, and to strengthen the effectiveness of management of these areas—Goal: 1-1-11 targets the "Expansion of natural seaside conservation areas, and Promotion of satoumi that create a virtuous cycle of environmental preservation and regeneration of coastal areas and utilization of local resources" [4].

Marine protected areas (MPAs) are considered one of the effective tools for marine biodiversity conservation and sustainable use globally. As of January, 2023, the global coverage of MPAs has expanded to 8.16%, which includes 18,444 protected areas, with a total area of 29,581,563 km^2 [5]. Adding 195 other effective area-based conservation measures (OECMs) to the database increases the coverage of marine areas to 8.26%. However, it has been pointed out that the financial shortfall for MPAs is large, and recent reports estimate that roughly \$300–\$967 billion US dollars needs to be invested in biodiversity conservation each year in order to reach and maintain the current global targets. MPAs are primarily supported by domestic government spending, which comprises 57–80% of the total annual investment in biodiversity conservation; other major sources of finance include official development aid (ODA), and private finance that includes philanthropic support [6]. Staff and budget capacity have been identified as the most important factors correlated with MPA performance. It is estimated that as much as 65% of the MPAs do not have an adequate level of funding [7]. An estimated 24.3 billion US dollars is being spent on the global protected area network annually (with 282 million US dollars being spent on MPAs), well short of the 68 billion US dollars deemed necessary for adequate management of protected areas [8].

According to existing reviews and guidelines published on sustainable financing measures, there are a number of different funding types. Grants, where the money given to conservation efforts does not have to be returned, are one of the major types. Grants can be either public (provided by the government or multilateral organizations) or private (donations from philanthropies, foundations, or businesses). Market-based tools constitute another type; these include a wide variety of measures such as user/access fees, payment for ecosystem services, and biodiversity/carbon offsets [9]. In recent years, conservation finance is perceived more holistically than as the sheer input of budgets. The Conservation Finance Alliance (CFA) proposes a definition for such an encompassing notion in which conservation finance is described as "mechanisms and strategies that generate, manage, and deploy financial resources and align incentives to achieve nature conservation outcomes" [10].

This paper examines the case of the Shiretoko marine protected area, part of the Natural World Heritage Site in Hokkaido, with a focus on the sustainability of its financial resources and mechanisms. The Shiretoko World Natural Heritage Site is distinctive among the 25 World Heritage Sites registered in Japan as of June 2023. Of the five Natural Heritage Sites in Japan, only two sites, Shiretoko and the Ogasawara Islands, include sea areas as part of their Heritage Sites. Shiretoko has a long history of conservation and innovative financing for conservation, which makes it an excellent candidate for further analysis.

The heritage site consists of a part of the Shiretoko Peninsula, located at the northeastern tip of Hokkaido and flanked by the Sea of Okhotsk and the Nemuro Strait, and its surrounding marine areas within three kilometers of the coastline [11], as indicated in Fig. 11.1. The municipalities located in the site are Shari town (population size: 4392) in Shari-gun, and Rausu town (population size: 4392), in

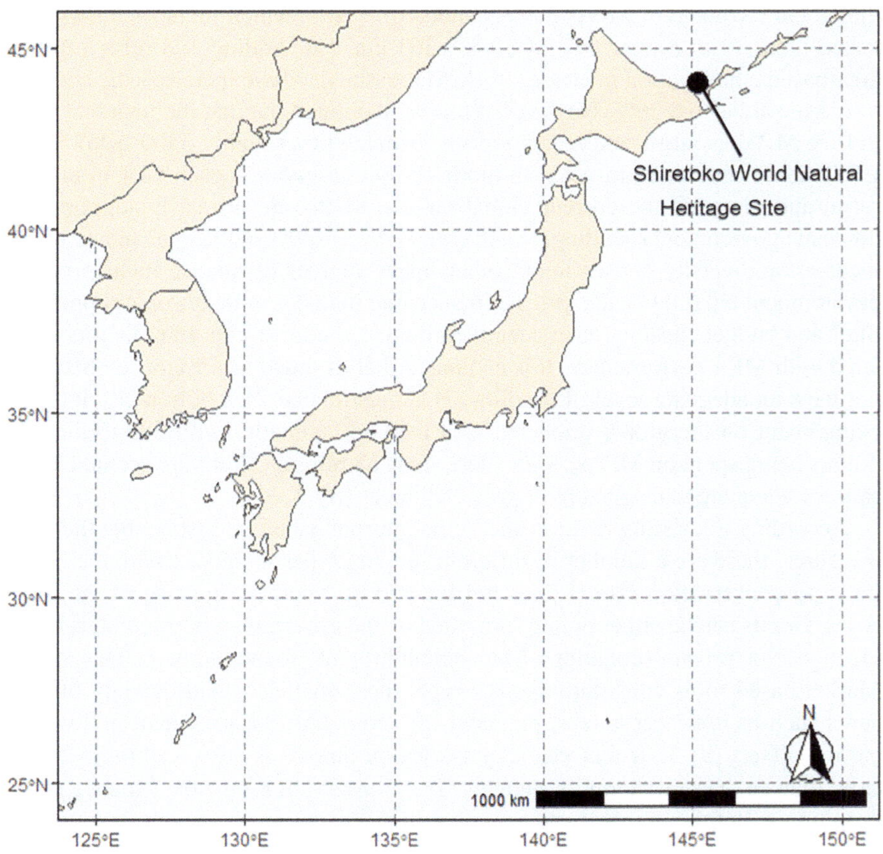

Fig. 11.1 Map of Japan and the location of Shiretoko World Natural Heritage Site [12]

Menashi-gun, Hokkaido prefecture. The heritage site is approximately 71,100 hectares in area (including approx. 22,400 ha of marine area) [11].

The Shiretoko area is an example of the interactions between marine and terrestrial ecosystems and extraordinary ecosystem productivity, largely influenced by the formation of seasonal sea ice at the lowest latitude in the northern hemisphere. Shiretoko has a long history of voluntary co-management systems led by local fishers, which can be considered as effective satoumi activities. ("Satoumi" is a combination of "village" (sato) and "sea" (umi) in Japanese, essentially indicating "a sea where high productivity and conservation of biodiversity are achieved through human intervention in harmony with natural ecosystems" [13]) These management systems were formalized and cross-sectoral coordination was enhanced during the application process seeking UNESCO World Heritage site status, with a focus on maintaining this status, once granted.

The main source of financing for the Shiretoko site is public funding; however, private sector funding plays a critical role in providing supplementary funds to cover the costs of maintaining the site's operation. Shiretoko is one of the earliest sites to introduce the system of national trust in Japan. The Shiretoko Foundation, a private entity, also plays a crucial financial role. Insofar as the importance of new types of private funding such as blue bonds and the blue carbon credit scheme has increased markedly in recent years globally [14], this paper also examines the potential of sustainable financing for the Shiretoko site and the necessary incentives for fund providers. Such an investigation can offer useful lessons for other MPAs and *satoumi* sites in Japan and beyond.

11.2 Method

The research method used in this case study comprises a literature review, fieldwork, and semi-structured interviews with experts. The literature review and desk study were conducted by collecting literature that was available online, including scientific journals, reports, and related statistics on fishery and the budgets of both the central government and local governments of Japan. In order to understand and interpret the data and give context to the specific information gathered, semi-structured interviews were conducted with local experts. The interviewees were asked to provide their thoughts on 5 questions: 1) What are the public budget and financial expenditures related to conservation and management activities in Shiretoko, especially in the marine area?; 2) What are the private contributions and expenditures related to conservation and management activities in Shiretoko?; 3) Are there any non-budgetary types of contributions, such as in-kind contributions and volunteering? 4) Are there any innovative or new types of funding for conservation?; and 5) What are the challenges and concerns? The study was conducted from April 2022 to March 2023. Five experts were interviewed; four of the interviews were carried out in person and one was conducted online.

11.3 Results of the Shiretoko Case Study

11.3.1 Background of the Shiretoko Site

11.3.1.1 Ecological Background

Its name, derived from the Ainu language, Shiretoko means "the end of the land," reflecting its remote and untouched natural beauty. The area is renowned for its rich biodiversity, unique ecosystems, and stunning landscapes, which include mountains, forests, rivers, and coastal areas. The Shiretoko Peninsula and its surrounding waters are situated at the lowest latitude of the world's seasonal sea ice zone in the Northern Hemisphere. Its high primary productivity, including the blooming of phytoplankton due to vertical mixing after the melting of sea ice, supports a wide variety of species, such as fish, marine mammals, and seabirds [15]. In the Shiretoko Peninsula, 36 species of terrestrial mammals and 22 species of marine mammals have been identified and its coastal sea areas, including the Steller sea lion (*Eumetopias jubatus*) and sperm whale (*Physeter macrocephalus*), large mammals such as the brown bear (*Ursus arctos*) and sika deer (*Cervus nippon yesoensis*). It serves as a habitat for species such as the endangered Blakiston's fish owl (*Ketupa blakistoni*) and various migratory birds [11].

Shiretoko is unique for its connection between the sea and land through a food chain that begins with phytoplankton. Forty-two species of freshwater fish and 261 species of marine species have been identified on and around the Shiretoko Peninsula, where the area is mostly populated by northern fish. One of the key characteristics of the heritage site is the dominance of salmonids in its rivers [11]. Figure 11.2 identifies the areas and zones within the national park boundary. The marine area is categorized as national park ordinary zones. In such ordinary zones, the large-scale establishment of facilities, extraction of minerals, or setting up advertising displays requires notification of the Minister of the Environment. In areas categorized as special zones, stricter regulations apply. Establishing facilities, cutting trees, land formation, or vehicle use in certain of these areas requires permission from the Minister of the Environment [16].

The Shiretoko National Park represents approximately 86% of the World Natural Heritage Site. There are also the Wilderness Area, the National Wildlife Protection Area, and the Forest Ecosystem Reserve within the World Heritage site (WHS) to legally ensure conservation [11]. Overall, 95% of the heritage site (terrestrial) is the National Forest, administered by the Forestry Agency, and the remainder of the lands are owned by the national government, Hokkaido Government, Shari town, Rausu town, and some private landowners [11]. Overlapping these areas, within the WHS, there are Zone A: the area where strict management is pursued into the future, and Zone B: the area where both conservation of the natural environment and use for sustainable tourism and fisheries that do not diminish the value of the area of the heritage site. The marine area of WHS extends up to 3 km from the coastline and is designated within Zone B.

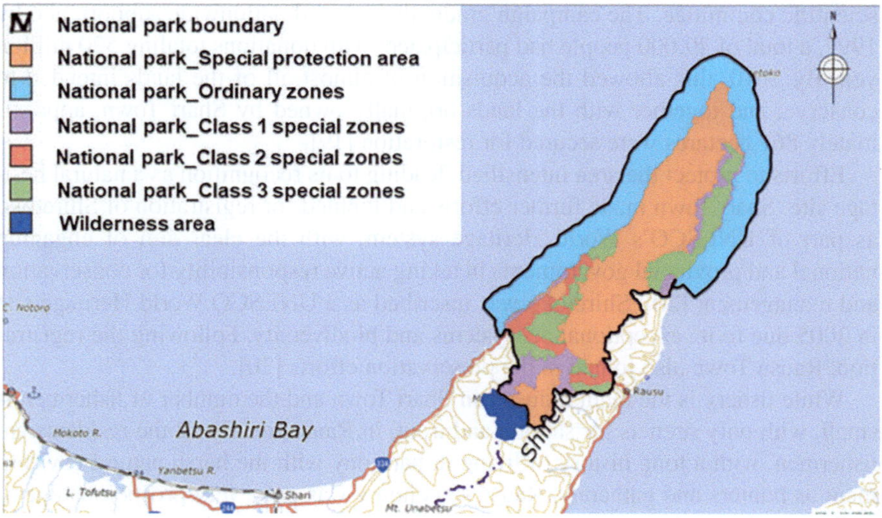

Fig. 11.2 Map of Shiretoko National Park area. Source: [17]

11.3.1.2 Socio-economic Background

The Shiretoko area has been inhabited for thousands of years, with the indigenous Ainu people having a deep cultural and spiritual connection to the land. In the late 19th and early 20th centuries, incoming settlers began to explore and develop the region. This period saw the construction of roads and settlements, but the harsh climate and challenging terrain limited extensive development. Throughout the twentieth century, awareness of Shiretoko's ecological significance grew. In 1964, Shiretoko National Park was established, encompassing much of the peninsula. Although Shiretoko had been designated as a national park, the involvement of the national government has historically been minimal. During the period of rapid economic growth, a wave of overexploitation swept over Shari Town on the Shiretoko Peninsula. At that time, despite requests from the town, the Environment Agency and Hokkaido Government were not keen on nationalizing the privately owned lands for the purpose of conservation. The Forestry Agency owned the lands, which were mostly designated as Class 3 Special Zones under National Park Law and thus vulnerable to further exploitation. In order to save reclamation sites within the national park from overdevelopment, Shari Town launched the "100 Square Meter Forest Planting Movement" in 1977, ahead of the Japan National Trust movement [18]. The action was initiated by town mayor Yutaka Fujiya, who had previously learned about the British National Trust movement. Prior to the movement, the hit song "Shiretoko Sentimental Journey," recorded in 1971 by Tokiko Kato, made Shiretoko a popular northern destination for tourists. The land purchased through the Trust Movement was farmlands developed in the Iwaobetsu area, and attempts to restore the forests were first unsuccessful, which led those involved to seek advice from experts and establishing a reforestation committee, a forerunner of the current scientific committee. The campaign gradually received nationwide support, and by 1997, a total of 49,000 people had participated, with donations totaling 520 million yen. By 2010, this allowed the acquisition of almost all of the lands intended to conserve, and together with the lands originally owned by Shari Town, approximately 861 hectares were secured for restoration [19].

Efforts to protect the area intensified, leading to its recognition as a natural heritage site. Shari Town made further efforts and lobbied for registration of Shiretoko as part of UNESCO's World Heritage system, with the clear aim of engaging national and provincial governments in taking active responsibility for conservation and management [20]. Shiretoko was inscribed as a UNESCO World Heritage site in 2005 due to its exceptional ecosystems and biodiversity. Following the registration, Rausu Town also joined in the preservation efforts [20].

While fishery is the main industry in Shari Town and the number of fishermen is small, with only set nets for salmon and trout, in Rausu, nearly all the residents are fishermen, with a long history of living in harmony with the harsh natural environment as hunters and gatherers. Rausu's economy was once very prosperous due to walleye pollock (*Gadus chalcogrammus*) fishing; however, in the 1980s, when pollock were no longer being caught, the incomes of Rausu's fishermen plummeted. The fishermen switched to kelp fishing and aquaculture and have continued efforts to add value to other fish species to sell. In WHS, the majority of forests are designated as the Shiretoko Forest Ecosystem Reserve, and there are no forestry operations.

According to the Management Plan for the Shiretoko World Natural Heritage Site developed in 2009, in Shiretoko, "the management of the heritage site aims to conserve the state of the natural environment and its diverse wildlife for future generations," and the following viewpoints are required for management: 1. Collaboration and cooperation with the local communities, 2. Adaptive management, 3. Comprehensive management of the terrestrial and marine areas, 4. Management by area classification, and 5. Coexistence with primary industries such as the fishery industry [11]. Since designation as a UNESCO World Heritage site, under these principles, a new coordination system among departments and ministries has been established, composed of three organizations: the World Natural Heritage Site Liaison Committee, the Appropriate Use and Ecotourism Committee, and the Scientific Council [21]. Within the overall framework of the Management Plan for the Shiretoko World Natural Heritage Site, the "Multiple Use Integrated Marine Management Plan," specific to marine areas, was developed through discussions conducted by the Marine Working Group (WG) under the Scientific Council [23], in the following years: the Multiple Use Integrated Marine Management Plans for First Term in 2007, Second Term in 2013, Third Term in 2018, and Fourth Term in 2023 were formulated respectively. Under this arrangement, the Marine WG is managed by the Hokkaido Government, while the Riverine Structures WG and the management of the national forests are the responsibility of the Forestry Agency, as indicated in Fig. 11.3. The Ecotourism WG is managed by the Ministry of the Environment. Figure 11.3 shows the results of the Working Groups are presented to the Scientific Committee twice a year. The Ministry of the Environment serves as the secretariat, but it has only a very limited budget for marine areas. Surveys on

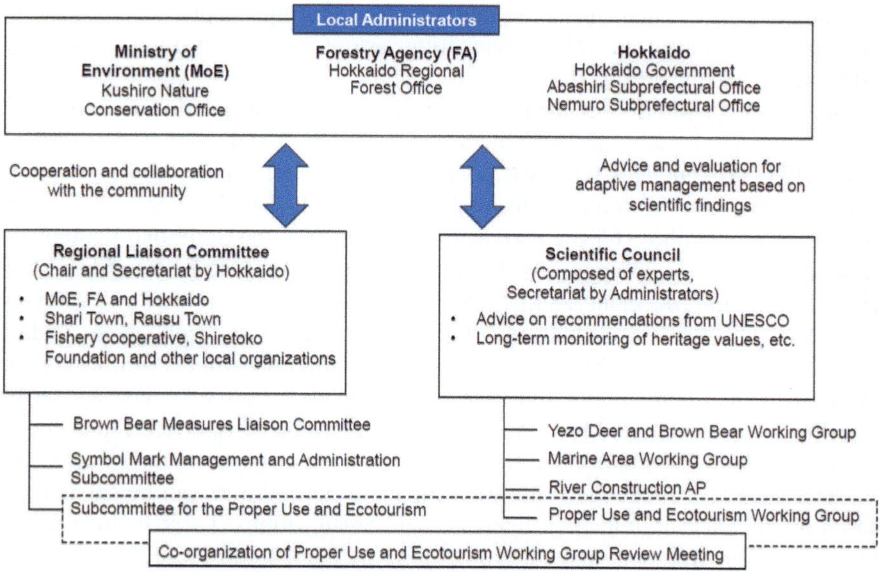

Fig. 11.3 Shiretoko World Natural Heritage Management System. Source: Adapted and translated by authors based on the material provided by the Kushiro Nature Conservation Office

benthic species are conducted once every few years. The Fishery and Forestry Department of Hokkaido Prefecture is not an official member of the WG but participates as an observer in the WG meetings.

A feature of marine area management is the adoption of the "Shiretoko approach," which places no restrictions on the voluntary management already carried out by fishermen, and coordinates laws and regulations related to marine ecosystem conservation and fishing, voluntary management by fishermen, and voluntary rules for marine tourism under the management plan [22]. Efforts are ongoing to balance conservation with sustainable tourism and local development, ensuring the protection of its unique environment and species. Overall, Shiretoko's history reflects a journey from indigenous stewardship and isolated wilderness to global recognition as a site of outstanding natural value.

11.3.1.3 History and Mechanism of Sustainable Financing in Shiretoko and Future Challenges

In the early years of conservation, specific funds were allocated within the Shari Town budget, which was later separated out as the Shiretokopia Management Foundation (later established as the Shiretoko Foundation). Against the wave of economic growth and exploitation, the cutting down of forests was controlled through the 100 Square Meter Forest Planting Movement, based on the share born by the Shari Town budget and donations made, and this period could be considered as "restriction of development" phase. This was followed by the second phase, the "maintenance and management" of Shiretoko area. During this phase, the Shiretoko Foundation was entrusted with implementing various government-funded conservation activities in the area [23].

According to Makino et al. (2009), right after the designation as UNESCO WNH, the administrative costs for the Shiretoko WNH area in 2006 were estimated at 473,474,000 yen. This total was composed of five principal costs: 1) Running costs for the scientific council and working groups (17,548,000 yen), 2) Running costs for the committee for the review of proper use and the Shiretoko Ecotourism Association (15,120,000 yen), 3) Research and monitoring activities (54,731,000 yen), 4) River improvement (284,927,000 yen), and 5) Personnel (101,778,000 yen) [22]. The personnel costs budgeted for supported personnel who were mainly engaged in Shiretoko affairs: five full-time and four part-time positions in the Ministry of Environment, one full-time position in the Forestry Agency, and seven full-time positions in Hokkaido Prefecture. The personnel costs were calculated as the number of officers multiplied by the average wage of government officers.

More recently, the budgets allocated for the protected area can be categorized based on the relevant ministries, agencies, and organizations. These include: 1) the Ministry of Environment and Forestry Agency, 2) Hokkaido Prefecture, 3) Shari Town and Rausu Town, 4) the Shiretoko Foundation, 5) Personnel, 6) Independent Research, and 7) Other. This included contracts and activities to maintain and restore ecosystems in Shiretoko through improvements in infrastructure and park facilities, dissemination of essential information to tourists to protect the environment, and research, among others. For 5) Personnel, according to the Shiretoko White Paper 2021, the patrols were conducted by the staff members of the Ministry of Environment (16 staff), the Forestry Agency (17 staff) and Hokkaido Government (7 staff) in the Japanese fiscal year 2021. This could provide a rough estimate of personnel costs at 266,800,000 yen, which was multiplied by the annual average wage of government officers. Although it was not possible to conclude the overall administrative budgets for the allocations of 1) to 7) mentioned above, as the Shiretoko Foundation is the primary sub-contractor commissioned by the Government entities, the following section will illustrate the projects conducted by the Foundation to highlight the microcosm of the activities implemented in Shiretoko WNH. Within these budgets are various innovative types of income, such as national trust, crowdfunding, and a hometown tax (Furusato Nozei). In Shari Town, thanks to hometown tax income, in 2024, 24,963,000 yen and 5,263,000 yen were spent, respectively, on projects under Hometown Support Green Fund and Hometown Support Work Fund. Those projects supported mostly terrestrial activities, but they also included projects such as "Optimization of use in national parks", "Protection and management of natural environment" and "Conservation and expansion of salmon and trout natural spawning environment", which could have had marine-related components [24]. There appears to be room to increase income through raising the user fees in the form of entry authorization fees and other means also.

Based on the "Multiple Use Integrated Marine Management Plan," a variety of marine related projects and research efforts are implemented and reported. Under the budget of the Ministry of Environment, the Shiretoko Foundation has been contracted to hold scientific committee meetings. The Nature Center is also run by the Foundation as one of the major conservation activities commissioned by the Ministry of Environment. The Rusha River is undergoing dam modification work scheduled for completion in 2024, led by the Hokkaido Government. On completion, its effects will be evaluated by monitoring the upstream migration of fish, and improvement measures will be instituted as necessary.

In this context, the Shiretoko Foundation is the primary organization and the service provider for conservation-related activities in Shiretoko. The Foundation receives funding from various sources, including government ministries. The purpose of the Foundation is "to conduct surveys and research on the natural environment of the Shiretoko Peninsula and its surrounding areas, as well as to spread awareness of nature conservation, and thereby contribute to the conservation and proper use of the natural environment" [25]. In fiscal year 2021, the Foundation's revenues were 392.98 million yen, 80% of which was revenue mostly from projects commissioned by government agencies such as the Ministry of the Environment, which was the top contractor, followed by the Forestry Agency. The Foundation sought other types of funding in the form of corporate donations, membership fees, the sale of goods, giving lectures, and accepting trainees [26]. Figure 11.4 shows the breakdown of ordinary revenues for fiscal year 2021. Among the 41 primary projects implemented by the Shiretoko Foundation in 2021, the activities were mostly land-based, yet they included prominent marine-related projects such as "Hokkaido salmonid fish monitoring survey", "Environment research and technology

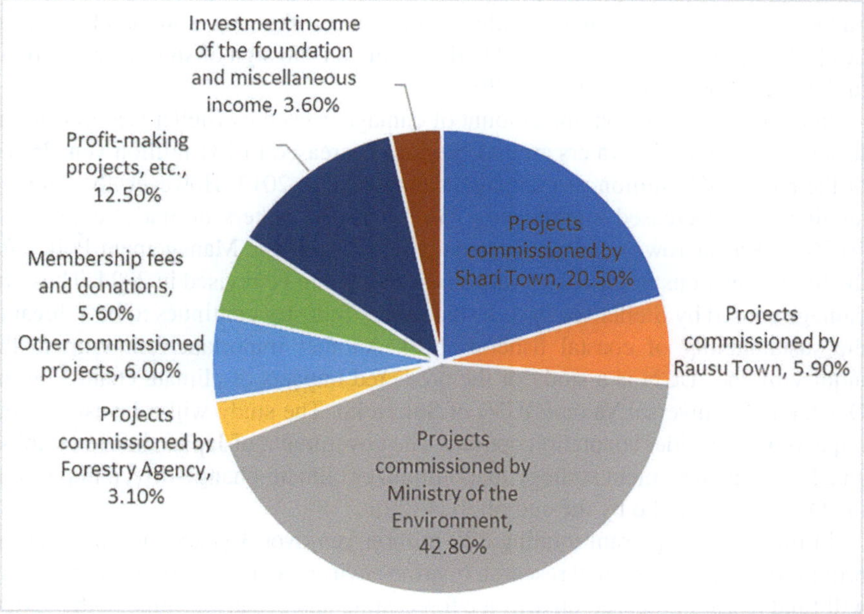

Fig. 11.4 Breakdown of ordinary revenues of Shiretoko Foundation for FY 2021. Source: [27]

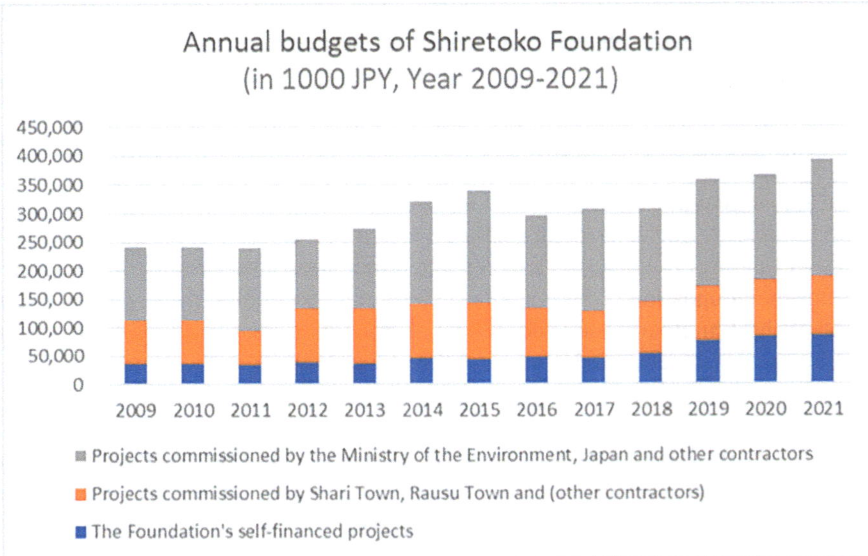

Fig. 11.5 Annual project budgets of Shiretoko Foundation. Source: [27]

development fund (ERTDF) joint project" with the Hokkaido University and "Rausu river juvenile fish survey".

Figure 11.5 shows the annual project budgets of the Shiretoko Foundation from 2009 to 2021. As indicated, there has been a rather steady increase in the overall budget, with the three major budget components showing similar characteristics [28]. Despite the impacts by COVID-19, there is no sign of significant decrease in the overall budgets in 2020 and 2021.

In the current situation, the amount of damage caused by Steller sea lions to the fishery industry in the waters around Nemuro decreased to 131 million yen, 36.8% of the record 357 million yen damage experienced in 2013. However, the value of landing also decreased significantly (58.0% in the waters around Nemuro and 40.7% in Rausu Town) during the same period. The Basic Management Policy for the Steller sea lions in Japanese waters is scheduled to be revised in 2024. Thus, the damage caused by Steller sea lions to the fishery industry continues to be a threat to the sustainability of coastal fisheries [26]. Another important follow-up to the inquiry by the IUCN is a study of the predicted impacts of climate change on the Outstanding Universal Value (OUV) of Shiretoko. The study will reinvestigate the impacts and consider adaptation options. The government of Japan aims to establish an adaptive management strategy that minimizes climate-change-driven impacts on the OUV of Shiretoko by the end of 2024 [29].

In this context, a grant totaling 120 million yen over 3 years and aimed at the promotion of environmental research (marine environment) was approved; the grant will fund research focused on drift ice forecasting and ocean warming. Other external research activities mostly involve research on marine mammals, whose estimated population in the region is approximately two million. A research team from the Tokyo University of Agriculture and others is conducting a survey of seals on a regular basis. The Ministry of the Environment conducts a survey of shallow water areas once every five years. Fish are looked at in terms of catches. An ecological survey of the shellfish population in the rocky area has been conducted; however, further investigation is necessary due to an oil leak and the potential impact of changes in the flows of the drift ice. These research projects are mostly initiated and led by non-resident researchers mobilizing competitive external research funds on a voluntary basis and provide important scientific input to the understanding and monitoring of the site and subsequent follow-up activities.

Regarding entrance fee income, the tourist association is concerned about a possible decline in the number of visitors due to the charging of an admission fee. In 2021, an estimated 163,500 tourists visited Shiretoko, roughly half the annual number of tourist visits in the years from 2012 to 2016, pre-COVID-19. Currently, tourists are charged for walking on the ground pathways at Shiretoko Goko Lakes (250 yen for adults, 100 yen for children up to 11 years old) and 132,000 tourists visited the Shiretoko Goko Lakes in 2021. Walking on the elevated wooden path is free. Since there are few roads into the backcountry, bus days were established as a regulation on private cars, and a fee was charged. Several of the experts in Shiretoko raised the possibility of expanding and raising this type of fee-based entrance charge or income for conservation activities in the area.

Traditionally, Japanese national parks apply the "regional system," a system that designates areas regardless of land ownership and provides protection by regulating activities [30]. This enables protections with less budgets not requiring large-scale purchases of lands. Although a large proportion resources for nature conservation administration is allocated to national parks in Japan, the budget designated for national parks has decreased after peaking in early 2000s. It is at only about 80 JPY per capita and about 30 JPY per national park user [30]. To meet the increasing needs of national park management, operational reliance on visitor-based revenue is on the rise globally [32]. The benefits of cost-sharing are to raise funds for management and operational costs and to restrict the number of users [33]. According to a survey conducted in 2013, 87.8% of respondents are willingness to pay up to 1000 yen as entry fee for national parks in Japan [31]. A study by Shoji et al. in 2021 conducted in Japan indicates that pricing policies imposed on park visitors were preferred over taxes, among the seven major pricing policies: general entrance fee: fees for use; concession fees; a royalties and profit shares; licenses and permits; voluntary donations and taxes [34].

In addition to the 100 Square Meter Forest Planning Movement, new funding mechanisms such as hometown taxes (Furusato Nozei) and crowdfunding have evolved, which is on the rise. Earmarked funding is more transparent; however, the downside is that after several years of a purpose-oriented campaign, there is a tendency for financial contributions through crowdfunding to decrease. Another important element has been the in-kind contributions by researchers, citizen volunteers, and other stakeholders, which are vital, but not necessarily systematically documented in monetary terms. For instance, the contribution by the fisher folks in

Shiretoko, particularly with respect to the co-management and monitoring of fishery resources, is an important basis for the sustainable use of natural resources in the area. In addition, the Marine Area Working Group compiles data twice a year, carried out with external inputs. Both resident and non-resident researchers and professors provide data, research outputs, and comments, mostly on a voluntary basis and as a show of "goodwill." Their contributed time and effort should also be considered important factors. It is also important to conduct a needs assessment to identify the need for the use of additional funding. Based on the updated needs assessment, taking into account the impacts of climate change and other environmental stresses, periodic monitoring, adaptive measures, and striking balance between the sustainable use and conservation efforts are necessary. Shiretoko could be considered as a best practice, and a model for additional funding will could serve as a useful reference for other PAs in Japan. After the tour boat accident off the Shiretoko Peninsula in April 2022, which took the lives of 20 passengers and crew, and six still missing, the number of tourists decreased. This terrible incident calls for strict implementation of safety standards and proper inspections by the authorities. The foreseen pressure from luxury hotels and sea activities needs to be regulated also. The increase in budgets should contribute to the benefits of controlling overuse.

11.4 Discussion

As indicated, the budgets allocated for the protected area in Shiretoko are executed by the Ministry of Environment and Forestry Agency, Hokkaido Prefecture, Shari Town and Rausu Town, and the Shiretoko Foundation. Funds were budgeted to cover personnel costs, support research, and provide for various other activities related to maintaining and restoring ecosystems in Shiretoko, including improvements in infrastructure and park facilities and the dissemination of essential information to tourists to protect the environment. Following the designation of Shiretoko as a UNESCO Natural World Heritage site, the allocation of budgets by the central government, specifically the Ministry of Environment and Forestry Agency, has increased significantly. Coupled with continued leadership and commitment by Shari Town, along with the contributions of Rausu Town, local conservation efforts and the level of financial inputs have increased gradually. As mentioned, these budgets feature various innovative types of income, such as the national trust, crowdfunding, and hometown taxes (Furusato Nozei). There have been cases of successful fundraising such as for the protection of endangered Japanese grouse in Myoko Togakurenzan National Park and a trail maintenance and vegetation restoration project in Daisetsuzan National Park. For the hometown taxes, recently, crowdfunding is also used as a method for collection. The benefits of crowdfunding are the clarity, target-based approach, and the accountability of donations, as donated funds are used for earmarked activities. On the other hand, this type of fundraising may not be suitable for securing flexible operational budgets in the long run. There remains room to increase income through raising the user fee in the form of an entry authorization fee and by other means. Stable incomes from both fisheries and tourism in the area contribute to the foundation of economic activities and tax base in Shiretoko. As described previously, in the "restriction of development" phase in Shiretoko, forest conservation was successful (stopping the mass cutting down of trees) through the 100 Square Meter Forest Planting Movement, which mobilized nationwide attention and support for the area, with ordinary citizens making donations. This was followed by the "maintenance and management" phase of the Shiretoko World Heritage Site, which established the Shiretoko model management structure. In this context, the Shiretoko Foundation played an essential role in implementing the various government-funded conservation activities in the area. The experience of Shiretoko suggests that, given the new threat of climate change and its predicted impacts on the ecosystems in the area, a third phase of "active conservation" will be necessary, and new and innovative kinds of funding will need to be explored and tested. Shiretoko as UNESCO NWH has an advantage of its globally acknowledged Outstanding Universal Value (OUV) and the branding associated with it. Establishing a model for long-term government funding was key. Sheretoko was successful in mobilizing private funding also through the 100 Square Meter Forest Planting Movement, and more recently through crowdfunding and hometown taxes. In-kind contribution by local stakeholders especially co-management with fisherfolks is the foundation of monitoring and conservation activities in the marine areas in Shiretoko. It is a good example to learn from for other sites, although unique local needs have to be met by tailor-made approaches.

11.5 Conclusion

This chapter examined the case of the Shiretoko marine protected area (MPA), a part of the Natural World Heritage Site in Hokkaido, Japan, focusing on financial sustainability and its relevant mechanisms. As explained, following the designation of Shiretoko as a UNESCO Natural World Heritage site, the allocation of budgets by the central government, specifically the Ministry of Environment and Forestry Agency, increased significantly. Combined with continued leadership and commitment by Shari Town and Rausu Town, conservation efforts and the level of financial inputs have increased gradually and been maintained. The case of Shiretoko suggests that adequate public financial support is the foundation of sustainable financing. The branding of Shiretoko and the recognition of Shiretoko's OUV and its designation as a Natural World Heritage site were critical. Not all conservation sites enjoy similar status in terms of UNESCO registration; nevertheless, the model of the Shiretoko approach in terms of co-management and multi-sector collaboration can be seen as a highly effective and generalizable conservation management model. Establishing the Shiretoko Foundation as a dedicated entity for conservation efforts is another example of good practice. In the context of increasing threats from climate change and its impacts on the ecosystems in the area, following the previous phases of "restriction of development" and then to "maintenance and management", a new phase of "active conservation" appears necessary, and new and innovative kinds of funding need to be explored and tested. This type of continued endeavor should inform other MPAs and conservation activities in Japan and beyond.

Acknowledgments The authors are grateful to the Ocean Policy Research Institute of the Sasakawa Peace Foundation and the Nippon Foundation for their support for this research. We would also like to express our sincere appreciation to the experts and stakeholders who provided their observations and insights during the interviews.

References

1. IPBES. (2019). *Global assessment report on biodiversity and ecosystem services of the Intergovernmental Science-Policy Platform on Biodiversity and Ecosystem Services* (E. S. Brondizio, J. Settele, S. Díaz, and H. T. Ngo Editors.). IPBES secretariat, Bonn. 1148 pages. https://doi.org/10.5281/zenodo.3831673.
2. Convention on Biological Diversity (2022) Kunming-Montreal global biodiversity framework Draft decision submitted by the President, Canada, Montreal. Accessed January 10, 2023, from https://www.cbd.int/doc/c/e6d3/cd1d/daf663719a03902a9b116c34/cop-15-l-25-en.pdf
3. Secretariat of the Convention on Biological Diversity (2020) *Global biodiversity outlook 5 – Summary for policy makers.*
4. Ministry of the Environment, Japan. (2023). *Seibutsu Tayousei Kokka Senryaku 2023–2030: neicha pojitibu jitsugen ni muketa roudo mappu* [*National biodiversity strategies and action plans (NBSAPs) 2023–2030: Roadmap for the realization of nature positive*] (in Japanese). Accessed May 22, 2023, from https://www.biodic.go.jp/biodiversity/about/initiatives6/files/1_2023-2030text.pdf
5. UNEP-WCMC, Protected planet. Marine protected areas. Accessed January 10, 2023, from https://www.protectedplanet.net/en/thematic-areas/marine-protected-areas
6. Brander, L. M., van Beukering, P., Nijsten, L., McVittie, A., Baulcomb, C., Eppink, F. V., et al. (2020). The global costs and benefits of expanding marine protected areas. *Marine Policy, 116*, 103953. https://doi.org/10.1016/j.marpol.2020.10395
7. Gill, D. A., Mascia, M. B., Ahmadia, G. N., Glew, L., Lester, S. E., Barnes, M., et al. (2017). Capacity shortfalls hinder the performance of marine protected areas globally. *Nature, 543*(7647), 665–669.
8. Waldron, A., Adams, V., Allan, J., Arnell, A., Asner, G., Atkinson, S., … & Zhang, Y. (2020). *Protecting 30% of the planet for nature: costs, benefits and economic implications.*
9. Bos, M., Pressey, R. L., & Stoeckl, N. (2015). Marine conservation finance: The need for and scope of an emerging field. *Ocean & Coastal Management, 114*, 116–128.
10. Meyers, D., Bohorquez, J., Cumming, T., Emerton, L., Heuvel, O.V.D., Riva, M., & Victurine, R. (2020). Conservation finance: A framework, *Conservation Finance Alliance*. Accessed May 22, 2023, from www.cfalliance.org. https://doi.org/10.13140/RG.2.2.14186.88000.
11. Ministry of Environment, Forestry Agency, Agency for Culture Affairs, Hokkaido Government. Management plan for the Shiretoko World Natural Heritage Site. Accessed May 22, 2023, from https://shiretokodata-center.env.go.jp/data/management/kanri/chiki_kanrikeikaku_eng.pdf
12. Developed by the authors.
13. Yanagi, T. (2012). *Japanese commons in the coastal seas: How the satoumi concept harmonizes human activity in coastal seas with high productivity and diversity*. Springer Science & Business Media.

14. Shiiba, N., Wu, H., Huang, M. C., & Tanaka, H. (2022). How blue financing can sustain ocean conservation and development: A proposed conceptual framework for blue financing mechanism. *Marine Policy, 139*. https://doi.org/10.1016/j.marpol.2021.104575
15. Government of Japan. (2004). *2004 World Heritage Nomination List Japan*. Accessed May 5, 2021, from http://shiretoko-whc.com/data/process/200401/english_01/E02.pdf
16. Ministry of the Environment, Japan. (2023). Natural park systems in Japan Accessed August 1, 2023, from https://www.env.go.jp/en/nature/nps/park/doc/files/parksystem.pdf
17. Biodiversity Center of Japan, Ministry of the Environment. Retrieved June 4, 2021, from http://gis.biodic.go.jp/webgis/
18. Ministry of the Environment, Japan. (2023). *National parks of Japan, Shiretoko National Park, the 100 square meter movement, efforts*. https://www.env.go.jp/en/nature/nps/park/shiretoko/effort.html#:~:text=In%20order%20to%20save%20reclamation,that%20has%20been%20acquired%20is
19. Shari Town. (2022). *Homepage of The 100 square-meter forest movement trust*. Accessed November 1, 2022, from https://100m2.shiretoko.or.jp/
20. Interview with Dr. Takahiro Nobetsu, on 15 November, 2022 in Shari Town.
21. Toyoshima, J., Fujii, I., Maekawa, M., Tsunoda, T., Kamada, N., Hidaka, H., et al. (2022). Assessing effectiveness of satoumi activities in Japanese coastal areas from ecological and socioeconomic perspectives. *Ocean & Coastal Management, 230*, 106354.
22. Makino, M., Matsuda, H., & Sakurai, Y. (2009). Expanding fisheries co-management to ecosystem-based management: A case in the Shiretoko world natural heritage area, Japan. *Marine Policy, 33*, 207–214.
23. Fujiya, T., Fujii, K., & Yamakawa, T. (2014). Shizen hogo mondai ni okeru hiyou to sonofutan – Shiretoko Shari-cho no torikumi wo jireini (Costs and burdens in nature conservation issues -a case study of Shari Town, Shiretoko). (in Japanese). *Hitotsubashi Keizaigaku (Hitotsubashi Economics), 7*(2), 113–259.
24. Shari Town Hokkaido. (2025). *Furusato ouen kifu no tsukaimichi (Reiwa rokunendo jisshi jigyou) (Usage of Hometown Support Donations <Projects implemented in FY2024>)*. (in Japanese). Accessed August 1, 2025, from https://www.town.shari.hokkaido.jp/material/files/group/33/R6zissizigyou2.pdf
25. Shiretoko Natural World Heritage Site Scientific Council. (2022). Long-term monitoring plan for the Shiretoko World Natural Heritage Site (JFY2012–2021) comprehensive evaluation report March 2022. Accessed May 1, 2023, from https://shiretokodata-center.env.go.jp/data/process/202211/longrange_monitoring_r04_en.pdf
26. Shiretoko Foundation. (2023). *Homepage of Shiretoko Foundation*. https://www.shiretoko.or.jp/#.
27. Shiretoko Foundation. (2021). Nenji houkoku 2021 (Annual report 2021). (in Japanese). Accessed August 1, 2023, from https://www.shiretoko.or.jp/wps/wp-content/uploads/2022/08/AnnualReport2021.pdf
28. Shiretoko Foundation (2009–2021) Developed based on Nenji houkoku 2009 to 2021 (Annual report 2009 to 2021). (in Japanese). Accessed August 1, 2023, from https://www.shiretoko.or.jp/annual/
29. Government of Japan. (2022). State of conservation report of Shiretoko (Japan) (N1193) in Response to the World Heritage Committee Decision 44 COM 7B.186. Accessed August 1, 2023, from https://shiretokodata-center.env.go.jp/data/process/202211/hozen_report_44_en.pdf
30. Ministry of the Environment, Japan. (2008). *National park system: Beautiful Japanese nature and its inheritance in Japan*. Accessed January 10, 2022, from http://www.env.go.jp/nature/np/pamph5/
31. Cabinet Office, Government of Japan. (2013). *Kokuritsu koen nikansuru seron chousa* (*Public Opinion Survey on National Parks*). Accessed January 10, 2023, from https://survey.gov-online.go.jp/h25/h25-kouen/

32. Weaver, D. B., & Lawton, L. J. (2017). A new visitation paradigm for protected areas. *Tourism Management, 60*, 140–146.
33. Tamura, T. (1956, Reprinted in 2006). Kokuritsu koen no nyuuenryou ni tsuite: (Entree fees for national parks). National Parks, 19, 84.
34. Shoji, Y., Kim, H., Kubo, T., Tsuge, T., Aikoh, T., & Kuriyama, K. (2021). Understanding preferences for pricing policies in Japan's national parks using the best–worst scaling method. *Journal for Nature Conservation, 60*, 125954, ISSN 1617-1381. https://doi.org/10.1016/j.jnc.2021.125954

Chapter 12
Digital Narratives of the Matsu Islands: A Case Study of Theme-Based Travel Planning by University Students in Taiwan

Cheng-Yi Eric Lin and Sheng-Wen Tseng

Abstract Using digital narrative assignments, images of the Matsu Islands, a significant Taiwanese military forefront with abundant ecological and cultural resources that attract tourists, are explored by students in a liberal arts course at a public university in Northern Taiwan, with the aim of promoting theme-based travel. The action research conducted here employs the narrative inquiry approach to design a course and analyze research data. Six short films on theme-based travel planning produced by forty-four study participants were carefully examined. Three iconic images representing the history of the Matsu Islands were identified: military post, beaches, and liquor. It was found that the participating students performed well on Lambert's (2010. *The digital storytelling cookbook*) narrative elements "point of view" and "dramatic question," as well as on "soundtrack." However, improvements in emotional content and the narration voice are needed. Recommendations for improving the liberal arts curriculum based on these results are presented.

Keywords Digital narratives · Short film · Liberal arts curriculum · Matsu Islands · Taiwan

12.1 Introduction

It is often a criticism of college students in Taiwan that they much prefer devoting their time to professional studies rather than pursuing a liberal arts education [1–3]. Taiwanese students often consider liberal arts courses boring and unimportant [4, 5]. In an earlier study, Li [5] reported that 44.7% of questionnaire respondents skipped their liberal arts classes more than once. Furthermore, in answering a question on learning initiative in liberal arts education, the respondents tended to

C.-Y. E. Lin
National Dong Hwa University, Hualien, Taiwan

S.-W. Tseng (✉)
National Taiwan Ocean University, Keelung, Taiwan
e-mail: swtsengtw@email.ntou.edu.tw

M. C. Huang et al. (eds.), *Innovative Social Practice and Community-Based Approach to the Ocean*, https://doi.org/10.1007/978-981-96-9104-3_12

evaluate themselves as passive learners. In response to this lack of motivation, some liberal arts course instructors use participatory approaches to interact with students in class, employing such measures as class discussion [6], game-based activities [3], theme-based learning [7, 8], and experiential learning [9].

Since 2017, the Ministry of Education in Taiwan has encouraged universities to cooperate with local communities to fulfill University Social Responsibilities (USR). Universities are urged to analyze community problems, ascertain needs, and develop plans to solve the problems in cooperation with community leaders and local residents [10]. In an effort to make the liberal arts curriculum more meaningful for students, the authors integrated a liberal arts course with a USR project focused on the Matsu Islands, the site of one of the campuses of the National Taiwan Ocean University (NTOU).

The Matsu Islands make up Taiwan's Lianjiang County and are located in the estuary of the Minjiang River in Fujian Province, China. In all, Matsu comprises four townships and five islands: Nangan Township (Nangan Island), Beigan Township (Beigan Island), Dongyin Township (Dongyin Island), and Juguang Township (including Dongju Island and Xiju Island) (Fig. 12.1). The main languages spoken in Matsu are Mandarin Chinese and the Matsu dialect, a dialect of Hokkien [11]. Since 1949, due to the military confrontation between the two sides of the Taiwan Strait, Matsu has become the front line of the Republic of China (Taiwan) facing off against the mainland's military threat; 1949 thus began the period of military control in Matsu. To integrate all the various resources needed to support military operations, the Matsu Battlefield Political Affairs Committee was established in July 1956, with the aim of unifying the military and political governance of the islands [12].

During the period of military control from 1949 to 1992, the Nationalist Army of the Republic of China built large-scale military facilities in Matsu, including underground tunnels, strongholds, turrets, ports, training bases, and military hospitals, adding a rich military color to the islands [11]. In November 1992, the government of the Republic of China (Taiwan) terminated the "military administration" of Matsu, allowing Lianjiang County (Matsu) to return to local autonomy, thus ending the 43-year period of military control [12]. Prior to 2017, there were no universities or colleges on the Matsu Islands. However, in September 2017, the Matsu Campus of the National Taiwan Ocean University (NTOU) was officially established in Banli Village, Beigan Township, opening a new era of higher education in the Matsu Islands [13].

Once relieved of its battlefield mission, the Matsu Islands changed its pattern of economic activity, transitioning from fulfilling the demands of the troop economy and supporting the needs of military personnel in Matsu, to fishery, island tourism, and preserving and promoting the local culture, which attracts visitors from both the main island of Taiwan and overseas [9]. The Matsu Islands are plentiful in interesting ecological features, including "Blue Tears" (the sparkling waters around Matsu) and the endangered Chinese Crested Tern (*Thalasseus bernsteini*). It also has a rich cultural heritage, as can be seen in its eastern-Min-style architecture (built by

Fig. 12.1 Location of Matsu Islands. Source: Tseng and Lin [9]

ancestors from the eastern part of Fujian), and a variety of religious-centered activities, such as the worship of Mazu (a Chinese Sea Goddess) [11].

However, the lack of human resources caused by Matsu's low birth rate and an aging population has created a critical situation that is impacting the economy and efforts aimed at cultural preservation. According to official statistics [14], the household population in the Matsu Islands currently stands at 13,983. Young people (those under the age of 15) and the elderly (those over 65) make up 25% of the resident population. Nevertheless, an average of 30,000 tourists visited Matsu in 2020 during the June to October high season.

The situation in Matsu provides an excellent opportunity for a Taiwanese university to partner with the community in the exercise of its USR responsibilities [9]. To take advantage of this opportunity and to make the pursuit of a liberal arts education more meaningful to their students, the authors took forty-four NTOU students enrolled in the liberal arts course, Creative Marketing Planning Practice, to the Matsu Islands to experience its ecological wonders and cultural heritage. The students were to analyze the needs of tourism development in Matsu, create a story to market Matsi Island tourism, and turn that story into a short film.

Today's college students are part of a generation of digital natives, brought up during the age of blossoming digital technology in which their use of computers, smart phones, and the Internet began at a very early age. They tend to acquire their information from the Internet and communicate with each other via social media such as Facebook, Instagram, and Twitter. Through this study, the participating students were encouraged to transform their passive role of information receivers to an active role as creators using digital technology.

Digital narrative is an emerging research method increasingly used to gather qualitative data [15]. However, very little research has taken the digital narrative approach to explore community revitalization. Previous studies have relied on literature review [16], observation [17], and questionnaires and interviews with stakeholders [18–20] to judge the efficacy of community revitalization efforts. Taking a different route, the authors adopted narrative inquiry as their primary research method and led students in NTOU's liberal arts program to explore ways to advance economic development in Matsu. Under the supervision of the authors, the students formed cross-disciplinary teams that worked in several targeted Matsu communities to take stock of community problems and needs and suggest effective solutions.

In pursuit of this objective, the participating students were asked to explore predominant images and imaginings of the Matsu Islands through the development of a digital narrative. The intent was to create a tourism video marketing strategy for Matsu while at the same time enhancing the ability of students to create effective digital narratives. The students were required to plan an itinerary to market Matsu using a particular theme that would attract travelers to the islands, particularly during the off-season.

12.2 Literature Review

Digital narrative, also known as digital storytelling, was first proposed by Joe Lambert and Dana Atchley in 1994 and used as a tool for community interaction, development, and empowerment [21]. In digital narrative, digital audio and visual content is used to create a short film that typically contains a reflective, emotional, and personal narrative [22–24]. The focus of a digital narrative is its intention or specific viewpoint [25]. The goal is "to stimulate reflection, deeper learning, and perhaps transformation" [26, p. 2]. Notably, the technical aspects of a digital narrative are not of major concern.

Lambert [27] proposed that digital narratives should include seven elements: point of view of the author, a dramatic question, emotional content, voice of narration, soundtrack to support the storyline, a concise length, and proper pacing of the story. The first element, point of the view, refers to the main point of the story and the perspective of the author. The second element, a dramatic question, is the key question that draws the viewer's attention and that will be answered by the end of the story. The third element, emotional content, refers to features that connect the story to the audience. The fourth element, voice of narration, is the way in which the storyteller uses his or her voice to tell the story in order to help the audience understand the context. The fifth element, the soundtrack, refers to the music or sounds used to support the storyline. The sixth element, concise length, requires the author of the narrative uses an appropriate length of content to tell the story without confusing or overloading the viewer. The seventh and final element, pacing, refers to the rhythm of the story.

Robin and McNeil [28] categorized digital narratives into three types: personal narratives, historical documentaries, and informative stories. Personal narratives are rooted in a significant event in the author's life and are often related to the memory of specific people and places, life adventures, achievements, challenges, or recovery. Digital historical documentaries use historical photographs or newspaper headlines to re-tell historical events. Informative or instructional digital stories are often used by instructors to present information to their students about course content and are widely used nowadays in flipped classrooms [28].

Past studies have shown that digital narratives have a positive impact on teaching and learning. De Jager and his colleagues (2017) noted that "digital narratives can promote reflection through telling a story, critical thinking, and help with digital literacy and writing skills" [21, p. 2552]. Robin and McNeil [28] agreed that the process of creating digital stories helps learners to organize and express their ideas, increase reading comprehension, and scaffold the development and formation of sociocultural identities and critical literacies.

In this study, the above seven elements [27] and three categories [28] of digital narratives were used to examine the participants' short films and to explore their perception of the Matsu Islands through digital storytelling. Accordingly, there are two research questions to be answered in this study:

RQ1: After the experiential learning during the field trip, what Matsu images do the students believe could be used to successfully promote Matsu's tourism?

RQ2: Based on Lambert's seven elements of digital storytelling, how effective were the digital narrative performances of the students?

12.3 Methodology

This research was integrated with the liberal arts curriculum at NTOU. Forty-four students from various departments participated in the study. The students were enrolled in Creative Marketing Planning Practice, a required course in their liberal arts education. In the first half of the semester, the instructor introduced the students to the Matsu Islands, the site of the research, from a historical, cultural, and natural perspective and imparted professional knowledge regarding creative business marketing, trip itinerary planning, and field research. In the second half of the semester, the students visited Beigan Township in the Matsu Islands (Fig. 12.2) for their experiential learning and field research.

In the research project conducted for this study, the participating students worked in teams, planned a trip itinerary, and created a ten-min short film featuring the

Fig. 12.2 Map of Beigan Township. Source: Tseng and Lin [9]

nature and culture found in Matsu in a way that would motivate travelers to visit during the off season. The students were also required make an oral presentation to explain their design concepts, which were then evaluated by domain experts and peers. The objectives, course content, instructional methods, and assessment of the course are described below:

Course Title: Creative Marketing Planning Practice

Course Objectives: The objectives of the course are twofold: First, it aims to fulfill NTOU's USR practice in Matsu. Learners need to complete a marketing plan, including characteristics of the field, manuals, a ten-minute film, the specific products chosen for promotion, and itinerary planning to help local communities solve some of their problems and to put into practice the university's social responsibilities. It also aims to enhance student abilities to create proper digital narratives and develop core competencies.

Course Content: Topics include an introduction to marketing, entrepreneurship concepts and planning, marketing planning practice, and short-film-making techniques. The weekly schedule of the course is listed in Table 12.1.

In the first 2 weeks, the instructor explains the course requirements and the research project, and introduces the research site. In Weeks 3 to 6, the instructor gives a comprehensive overview of the theories of marketing and tourism,

Table 12.1 Course weekly schedule

Week	Content	Focus
1	Course introduction and field introduction	Introduction to research site
2	Team building and Matsu field analysis	
3	Creative marketing planning (1): market environment, target market analysis/STP analysis	Theories of marketing & planning
4	Creative marketing planning (2): products, prices, channels and promotion strategies	
5	Tourism planning and design (1)	
6	Tourism planning and design (2)	
7	Fieldwork techniques (1)	Skill building 1
8	Fieldwork techniques (2)	
9	Fieldwork itinerary design + itinerary design planning report	
10	Keynote lecture: tour planning industry expert guidance and consultation	
11	Field survey	Field research & practice
12	Thematic tour design	
13	APP material organization and editing	
14	Experience event supporting design	
15	Creative marketing	
16	Short film making & editing techniques	Skill building 2
17	Marketing plan competition	Evaluation of learning outcome
18	Review & Revision	

Source: This study

particularly with respect to creative tourism marketing and planning. In Weeks 7 through 10, the instructor teaches fieldwork techniques and itinerary planning principles to build the required student skills for the project. A domain expert from the tourism sector will be invited to the class to share his/her expertise in creative tourism marketing and answer student questions about trip itinerary planning. In Week 11, the instructor will arrange a three-day field trip to Matsu so that the students can experience the local life and collect the materials for their short film project. In Weeks 12 to 16, the students work in groups of six or seven to finalize their ideas and create a short film and a proposal for the Matsu tourism marketing campaign. In the final two weeks, the instructor holds the Matsu marketing planning competition and invites domain experts as judges to evaluate the students' learning outcomes. The students then revise their film and proposal in accordance with the judges' feedback.

Instructional Methods: A variety of techniques are used to teach the course, including lectures, group discussion, forums with domain experts, field surveys, and a final project competition. The students acquire a range of knowledge and skills, in areas such as entrepreneurship planning, marketing planning, assessment of the inventory of local resource characteristics, principles of regional revitalization, and short film production, and present the results of their marketing enterprise planning project.

Learning Assessment: The learning progress of students is evaluated by attendance rate (20%), class participation (20%), a learning achievement report (40%), and a short film project (20%).

In this study, the short film project was closely scrutinized by the authors to assess the students' digital narrative skills. The authors developed a four-point rubric in accordance with Lambert's [7] seven elements of digital storytelling. In the applied rubric, a score of 1 indicates that the students did not have a specific element in their film; a score of 2 indicates that the students had the specific element in their film, but they needed to improve it; a score of 3 indicates that the students had the specific element in the short film and did a good job with it, but a minor improvement is needed to make the storytelling more effective. Finally, a score of 4 indicates that the students had included the specific element in their short film and did an excellent job with it.

12.4 Research Results and Discussion

To answer the two research questions, an careful analysis of the six short films produced by the groups, based on Lambert's [7] seven elements, was conducted. The results are summarized in the following sections.

12.4.1 Images and Imaginings Suited to Promoting Matsu's Tourism

The gist of each group's short film is described below, along with an illustrative example. Next, the locations used in the six short films are listed and the images of Matsu that the students perceived after their exploration of the Matsu Islands are discussed.

Group 1 Theme: A Romantic Trip to Matsu
The first group described a couple's romantic trip to Matsu. It began with a view from the airplane window as they burst through the clouds. Next, we see the couple riding a scooter to explore various sightseeing spots, including the Matsu distillery, the streets of Matsu, the only Starbucks in Matsu, the beach, and the Bishan Broadcasting Station (Fig. 12.3a). During the trip, the couple tried a variety of local dishes, such as red-yeast fried rice, fish noodles, mussels, golden dumplings with sweet potato, tofu pudding, aged liquor, and vermicelli made with aged liquor.

Group 2 Theme: Outing with Friends
The second group introduced Matsu by telling a story in which two friends reminisced about their trip in Matsu. It started with a view of the two friends sitting on the beach, watching the ocean. Next, the places they visited were shown, including

(a) Bishan Broadcasting Station.

(b) Banli Beach.

(c) The reindeer were lost because of strong winds.

(d) Jiguang buns.

(e) 327 Observatory.

(f) Treasure Map (Baigan Road Map).

Fig. 12.3 Example pages from the short films made by Groups 1–6. (**a**) Bishan Broadcasting Station, (**b**) Banli Beach, (**c**) The reindeer were lost because of strong winds, (**d**) Jiguang buns, (**e**) 327 Observatory, (**f**) Treasure Map (Baigan Road Map). Source: This study

a coffee shop, the 327 Observatory, a guesthouse, a restaurant, Qinbi village, Qinbi Mazu Temple, the Qinshan broadcasting station, Mt. Luo, and Clam Island (Fig. 12.3b).

Group 3 Theme: Santa Claus and His Reindeer

The third group told a story from the perspective of Santa Clause and his reindeer. As Santa Clause delivers his Christmas gifts to Matsu, his six reindeer are blown all over the Matsu Islands by strong winds. Santa Claus thus needed to find all his reindeer. He and his assistant, Xiao-Ming, found his first reindeer at the Temple of An-Ping Dragon King, a mythical figure similar to Poseidon in Greek Mythology. They then found the second reindeer at the Beigan Harbor Management Building, the third at the Beigan Visitor Center, the fourth at Biyuan Ecological Park, the fifth at the War and Peace Memorial Park Exhibition Center, and, finally, the sixth at the Fishery Exhibition Center (Fig. 12.3c).

Group 4 Theme: Searching for Three Representative Local Foods
The story of the fourth group began at the Beigan Airport. The protagonists needed to find three local dishes that represent Matsu in order to earn the blessing of the Goddess Mazu. The three representative local foods were vermicelli prepared with aged liquor, golden dumplings with sweet potato, and Jiguang buns. In the end, the protagonists completed their task. The Goddess Mazu granted them a wish, which they used to ask for world peace (Fig. 12.3d).

Group 5 Theme: The Trip Full of Memories
The fifth group focused on the memory of a couple's trip to Matsu. They recalled the exhilaration they felt when they boarded their first flight to Matsu. During the trip, they used their time to visit places that represented the culture of Matsu, including Banli Guesthouse, the Mazu Temple, the Mt. Luoshan Nature Trail, the beach, the Baigan Visitor Center, the War and Peace Memorial Park Exhibition Center, the Qinshan Broadcasting Station, Turtle Island, Qinbi Village, and the 327 Observatory (Fig. 12.3e).

Group 6 Theme: A Treasure-Hunting Trip
The sixth group used treasure hunting as the theme of their story. The protagonists attempted to find a treasure hidden somewhere in the Matsu Islands. During their search, they visited the War and Peace Memorial Park Exhibition Center, the Mt. Bishan Nature Trial in Baigan, Tangqi Trail, various restaurants, Qinbi Village, and the 327 Observatory. In the end, although the protagonists found no gold or jewelry, they realized that the process was, in fact, the treasure they sought, as it led them to see the invaluable scenes of Matsu (Fig. 12.3f).

According to the categorization of digital storytelling proposed by [8] Robin and McNeil, all six short films produced by the students properly belonged to the personal narratives categories. The students in three of the groups told their stories from a life experience point of view and linked their stories to the memory of a specific person, such as a girlfriend (Groups 1 and 5) or a close friend (Group 2). The other three groups used a life challenge (Groups 3 and 4) or an adventure (Group 6) to tell their stories. However, due to the age and limited life experience of the students, their personal narratives did not show profound reflection or indicate deep learning, which, according to Martin and his colleagues [26], are critical in digital narratives (2019).

12.4.2 Locations Chosen by Students

Table 12.2 shows the locations that the students chose as sightseeing spots representative of the Matsu Islands, listed according to the number of times the location was mentioned in the six films.

As can be seen from the table, the War and Peace Memorial Park Exhibition Center and the 327 Observatory were each mentioned a combined three times across the six films, while the Qinshan Broadcasting Station was mentioned twice. Because

Table 12.2 Frequencies shown in the short films

Frequency	Sightseeing spots	Local delicacies
3 times	1. War and Peace Memorial Park Exhibition Center 2. 327 Observatory 3. Banli Beach	None
2 times	1. Beigan Visitor Center 2. Qinbi village 3. Qinbi Mazu Temple 4. Qinshan Broadcasting Station 5. Mt. Loushan Nature Trial	1. fish noodles 2. golden dumplings with sweet potato 3. vermicelli made with the aged liquor
1 time	1. Matsu Distillery 2. Clam Island 3. Temple of An-Ping Dragon King 4. Beigan Harbor Management Building 5. Biyuan Ecological Park 6. Fishery Exhibition Center 7. Tuttle Island 8. Bishan Nature Trial 9. Tangchi Trial	1. red-yeast fried rice 2. mussels 3. tofu pudding 4. old liquor 5. Jiguang buns

Source: This study

all three of these locations are connected to the military, their more frequent mention would seem to imply that even though the Matsu islands were relieved of their battlefield missions in 1992, the military posts remain iconic images representing the history of Matsu. Beaches were also repeated images and served as a background for friendship or romance.

Another repeated image was that of liquor and related dishes. Because there are several distilleries in the Matsu Islands, local residents use aged liquor to supplement their dishes, including the famous vermicelli made with aged liquor. Seafood, such as mussels, and related products, such as fish noodles (noodles made of minced fish), also appeared frequently in the short films.

12.4.3 Evaluating the Students' Digital Narrative Performance

The authors used a four-point rubric based on Lambert (2010)'s [27] seven elements of digital storytelling to grade the six short films and assess the digital narrative skills of the students who produced the films. As shown in Table 12.3, the students did an excellent job on the elements of point of view, dramatic question, and soundtrack. Each group chose either the first- or the third-person point of view to tell their stories. Most also developed their stories with a dramatic question. For example, in order to receive the blessing of the Goddess Mazu, Group 4's dramatic question was where to find the three local dishes. Another example is Group 6's dramatic question asking where the treasure of the Matsu Islands was to be found.

Table 12.3 Statistics for Lambert's 7 elements

Elements	Group 1	Group 2	Group 3	Group 4	Group 5	Group 6
1. point of view	4	4	4	4	4	4
2. a dramatic question	3	3	4	4	3	4
3. emotional content	3	3	2	2	2	2
4. voice of narration	1	1	1	1	1	1
5. soundtrack	4	4	4	4	4	2
6. concise length	3	3	3	3	3	3
7. pacing	3	3	3	3	3	3

Source: This study

On the other hand, the students needed to improve their emotional content and the voice of the narration. Most groups chose not to add their voices to tell the stories but rather used captions to tell the audience what was happening. Because of this, it was not easy for the stories to connect with the audience's emotions.

Furthermore, even though the students belong to a generation of digital natives and have been exposed to countless clips of digital stories from sources such as YouTube, Instagram, and Netflix, their short films show that their digital narrative skills are in need of improvement in that their films showed little evidence of serious self-reflection. This agrees with the research findings of Janschitz et al. [29] and Kopp et al. [30], which suggest that university students are not necessarily able to transfer their personal digital competencies to their study situation and might not be as digitally competent as one might expect.

12.5 Conclusion

This study investigated student perceptions of the images and imaginings of the Matsu Islands through a digital narrative assignment, following their experiential learning in Matsu. From the students' perspective, the most prominent images of the Matsu Islands were battlefields, beaches, and liquor. In their digital narrative assignment, the students performed well in several aspects, including choosing a point of view and using a dramatic question to tell their stories. However, they needed to be encouraged to use their voices to tell their stories so that the audience can better relate to them and their work.

Importantly, the results of this study offer insights on tourism in the Matsu Islands that could be used to help shape tourism and cultural preservation policies there. The places, the dishes, and the activities mentioned in the short films likely reflect the interests of the young adult generation. Accordingly, the Traffic and Tourism Bureau of the Lienchiang County Government might consider brainstorming and planning trip itineraries to attract independent tourists, especially college students and similar-aged travelers from all over the world. According to the statistical data provided by the Traffic and Tourism Bureau of the Lienchiang County Government (2021), the average number of tourist visitors to the Matsu Islands in the high season is roughly three times that in the low season (28,500 vs. 8500).

Related to this point, it seems clear that the images of military posts, beaches, and liquor that were repeatedly shown in the student films are, in the eyes of college students, representative of Matsu culture. The Lienchiang County Government thus might make a special effort to preserve these points of interest to increase the number of tourists.

The study also has important implications regarding teaching practice: (1) During the community-based program, community and business leaders should be brought in to serve as Learning Mentors for the student teams. When faced with complex issues in the community, these Learning Mentors can help the student teams strengthen their team building skills, identify problems, propose solutions, and improve their teamwork; (2) A storytelling workshop needs to be arranged to increase the effectiveness of this type of course. Even though today's students have unlimited access to digital stories from sources such as YouTube, Disney Plus, and Netflix, this does not mean that they have the ability to create digital narratives without sufficient instruction. Both good and bad examples of digital stories can be analyzed by the class before making the digital narrative assignment. Such an exercise will give students a better understanding of what is required to produce a compelling narrative.

Acknowledgements The second author greatly appreciates the sponsorships provided from the MOE Teaching Research Program, Ministry of Education, Taiwan (Grant No. PSR1090395).

References

1. Chen, C.-Y. (2008). General education and the higher education of Taiwan. *Thought and Words Journal, 46*(2), 1–34. (In Chinese). https://doi.org/10.6431/TWJHSS.200806.0001
2. Chen, Y.-H. (2009). Reform of core course: Research of reform of general education at Harvard University. *Taiwan Journal of General Education*, 39–62. (In Chinese). https://doi.org/10.6360/TJGE.200912.0039
3. Niu, H.-C. (2019). Analyzing the efficacy of gamification approach of Kahoot quiz on student performance in general education. *General Education: Practice and Research, 26*, 49–98. (In Chinese). https://doi.org/10.7107/GEPR.201912_(26).0002
4. Cheng, W.-F. (2020). General education and literature: A case study of Shakespeare course in Chang Gung University. *Taiwan Journal of General Education, 26*, 9–34. (In Chinese). https://doi.org/10.6360/TJGE.202012_(26).0001
5. Li, P.-Y. (2013). Exploring student's learning effectiveness on core curriculum of General Education: A case study of National Central University. *Taiwan Journal of General Education, 11*, 67–93. (In Chinese). https://doi.org/10.6360/TJGE.201306_(11).0003
6. Wang, H.-R., & Huang, M.-L. (2021). Research on the application of flipped teaching model in Chinese "Reading and Writing" courses to improve reading motivation. *General Education: Practice and Research, 29*, 173–204. (In Chinese).
7. Chou, S.-M. (2021). The combination of borderless learning and reading and writing: Curriculum research of the cultural research of wuxia fiction. *General Education: Practice and Research, 30*, 27–63. (In Chinese).
8. Kuo, H.-J. (2022). The course "Western Literature and Medicine" as an example to demonstrate the concept of medical humanities reconsidered under the framework of liberal arts education. *General Education: Practice and Research, 32*, 75–114. (In Chinese).

9. Tseng, S.-W., & Lin, C.-Y. (2022). Transforming the street business model in a Matsu island village: The practice of university social responsibility in Taiwan. *International Journal of Social Sciences and Artistic Innovations, 2*(3), 6–14. https://doi.org/10.35745/ijssai2022v02.03.0002
10. Center for University Social Responsibility, Ministry of Education. (2017). *About the Project*. http://usr.moe.gov.tw/about-2.php/2023/01/12.
11. Matsu National Scenic Area Administration, Tourism Bureau. (2021). *About Matsu*. https://www.matsu-nsa.gov.tw/Articles.aspx?a=2866&l=1
12. Nangan Township Office, Lienchiang County. (2015). *Military administration*. https://www.matsu.gov.tw/chhtml/Detail/371040100A/2420?mcid=32904
13. National Taiwan Ocean University. (2017). *Introduction to campus*. https://matsu.ntou.edu.tw/p/412-1046-11164.php?Lang=zh-tw
14. Demographic statistics: 2023 February [Data file]. Civil Affairs Department, Lienchiang County Government.
15. Davey, N. G., & Benjaminsen, G. (2021). Telling tales: Digital storytelling as a tool for qualitative data interpretation and communication. *International Journal of Qualitative Methods, 20*, 1–10. https://doi.org/10.1177/16094069211022529
16. Liang, C. M. (2019). The exploration in Japanese placemaking policy and the act of ministry of education, culture, sports, science and technology. *Chung Cheng Educational Studies, 18*(2), 85–107. (In Chinese). https://doi.org/10.3966/168395522019121802003
17. Anderson, L. B. (2020). Exploring the role of communication in the aging in place experience: A quasi-ethnographic account of a local community. *Communication Monographs, 87-3*, 359–380. https://doi.org/10.1080/03637751.2020.1728562
18. Jung, J. Y., & Kwesell, A. (2021). The effects of perceived stigma and neighborhood storytelling networks on future outlook: Mixed-method research in Fukushima, Japan. *Journal of Applied Communication Research, 49*(3), 1–19. https://doi.org/10.1080/00909882.2021.1879391
19. Tsai, Y.-J., & Lai, T.-Y. (2020). *A study on the strategy of industrial revitalization in rural areas from the perspective of regional revitalization* [unpublished master's thesis]. National Chengchi University. (In Chinese).
20. Villanueva, G., Gonzalez, C., Son, M., Moreno, E., Liu, W., & Ball-Rokeach, S. (2017). Bringing local voices into community revitalization: Engaged communication research in Urban planning. *Journal of Applied Communication Research, 45*(5), 474–494. https://doi.org/10.1080/00909882.2017.1382711
21. De Jager, A., Fogarty, A., Tewson, A., Lenette, C., & Boydell, K. M. (2017). Digital storytelling in research: A systematic review. *The Qualitative Report, 22*(10), 2548–2582. https://doi.org/10.46743/2160-3715/2017.2970
22. Lambert, J., & Hessler, B. (2018). *Digital storytelling: Capturing lives, creating community* (5th ed.). Routledge. https://doi.org/10.4324/9781351266369
23. Yilmaz, R., Erdem, M. N., & Resuloglu, F. (2018). *Handbook of research on transmedia storytelling and narrative strategies*. IGI Global. https://doi.org/10.4018/978-1-5225-5357-1
24. Yilmaz, M. M., & Siğirtmaç, A. (2023). A material for education process and the Teacher: the use of digital storytelling in preschool science education. *Research in Science and Technological Education, 41*(1), 61–88. https://doi.org/10.1080/02635143.2020.1841148
25. Huang, H.-T. (2023). Examining the effect of digital storytelling on English speaking proficiency, willingness to communicate, and group cohension. *TESOL Quarterly, 57*(1), 242–269. https://doi.org/10.1002/tesq.3147
26. Martin, S. L., McLean, J., Brooks, C., & Wood, K. (2019). "I've been silenced for so long": Relational engagement and empowerment in a digital storytelling project with young women exposed to dating violence. *International Journal of Qualitative Methods, 18*, 1–12. https://doi.org/10.1177/1609406919825932
27. Lambert, J. (2010). *The digital storytelling cookbook*. Digital Diner Press. Retrieved from https://wrd.as.uky.edu/sites/default/files/cookbook.pdf
28. Robin, B. R., & McNeil, S. G. (2019). Digital storying. In R. Hobbs & P. Mihailidis (Eds.), *The international encyclopedia of media literacy* (pp. 1–8). Wiley-Blackwell.

29. Janschitz, G., & Penker, M. (2022). How digital are 'digital natives' actually? Developing an instrument to measure the degree of digitalisation of university students – the DDS-Index. *Bulletin of Sociological Methodology/Bulletin de Méthodologie Sociologique, 153*(1), 127–159. https://doi.org/10.1177/07591063211061760
30. Kopp, M., Gröblinger, O., & Adams, S. (2019). Five common assumptions that prevent digital transformation at higher education institutions. In *Inted2019 Proceedings* (pp. 1448–1457). IATED.

Editorial Afterword: Towards Community-Based Maritime Countries

This volume elucidates how maritime nations may adopt community-centered strategies to ensure a sustainable future. My involvement with University Social Responsibility (USR) programs and the Taiwan–Japan Alliance of Local Revitalization and Social Practice (TJ Alliance) has enabled me to guide students in fieldwork—particularly in Badouzi, a fishing village in Taiwan, and Kuroshio Town in Kochi Prefecture, Japan—and to facilitate scholarly exchanges among Taiwanese universities and institutions such as Kochi University and Ryukoku University. These collaborative endeavors have affirmed the principle that effective marine resource management and coastal community development must include local stakeholders, whose invaluable environmental and cultural knowledge forms the foundation of meaningful progress.

From Taiwan's fishing communities and Japan's Satoumi initiatives to Palau's ecotourism efforts, Japan's pioneering Blue Tech industry clusters, and endeavor for MPAs, each chapter underscores a crucial insight: sustainable development arises from empowering communities, rather than relying on top-down directives. Documented examples of collaboration—among universities, local governments, and fishing communities—offer compelling evidence that "people-centered" strategies can foster maritime resilience and vitality.

The case studies herein illustrate a harmonious integration of traditional knowledge and contemporary innovation. Whether through the digital preservation of cultural heritage, sustainable financing for marine protected areas, or USR initiatives, these examples demonstrate how long-standing relationships with the sea can be preserved while simultaneously creating new opportunities. They further emphasize the necessity of cross-sector cooperation and institutional innovation. Frameworks guided by local voices, including the Sustainable Livelihoods Framework and community-based ecotourism models, show how maritime development, when undertaken collaboratively, can benefit local economies, cultures, and environments in equal measure.

M. C. Huang et al. (eds.), *Innovative Social Practice and Community-Based Approach to the Ocean*, https://doi.org/10.1007/978-981-96-9104-3

A key thematic transformation emerges: coastal communities are no longer viewed as passive subjects of conservation or development, but rather as principal knowledge holders and decision-makers. This rebalancing of power undergirds sustainable marine management approaches aligned with the United Nations Sustainable Development Goals, concurrently producing tangible benefits for local populations.

It has been a privilege to collaborate with this book's distinguished editors. We would also like to express our sincere gratitude to Dr. Andrew J. Barnes for his indispensable contribution of the editorial review. We trust that our collective effort will galvanize academic researchers, policymakers, and practitioners toward deeper interdisciplinary engagement, ultimately progressing toward a more sustainable, equitable "blue future." Authentic maritime vitality, in the end, lies at the intersection of professional expertise and the voices of communities whose bond with the sea spans millennia. Attaining truly sustainable maritime societies requires integrating tradition and innovation through respectful community involvement and cooperative problem-solving, supported by civil society.

Ming-Hao Yang
College of Ocean Law and Policy
National Taiwan Ocean University

FSC www.fsc.org
MIX
Papier aus verantwortungsvollen Quellen
Paper from responsible sources
FSC® C105338

If you have any concerns about our products,
you can contact us on
ProductSafety@springernature.com

In case Publisher is established outside the EU,
the EU authorized representative is:
Springer Nature Customer Service Center GmbH
Europaplatz 3, 69115 Heidelberg, Germany

Printed by Libri Plureos GmbH
in Hamburg, Germany